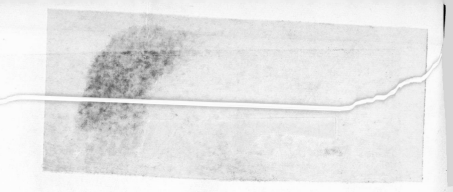

The Somers Mutiny Affair

THE U. S. BRIG-OF-WAR SOMERS.

EDITED BY

HARRISON HAYFORD
Associate Professor of English
Northwestern University

The

SOMERS

MUTINY

AFFAIR

Prentice-Hall, Inc.
Englewood Cliffs
New Jersey

1959

*This book is especially for Ralph H. Hayford,
my son, who has written good books of his own
about the sea and knows more about ships than
I ever will.*

Frontispiece: Currier lithograph of the Somers
*(see page 111). Courtesy of The Old Print Shop,
New York City.*

© 1959, by PRENTICE-HALL, INC.
Englewood Cliffs, N. J.

LIBRARY OF CONGRESS CATALOG CARD NUMBER: 59–14864

PRINTED IN THE UNITED STATES OF AMERICA

82260

Introduction

This is a book of documentary materials about the *Somers* mutiny affair. The *Somers* was a U. S. Naval brig sailing home late in 1842 from a training cruise to the coast of Africa, manned mostly by apprentice boys. The "mutiny" discovered aboard this ship has often (and erroneously) been called the only mutiny in our navy's whole history. Just as often, it is declared to have been no mutiny at all on the part of the men accused, but plain murder on the part of the officers who hanged them.

Mutiny, murder—or both—whatever it was that really happened at sea aboard the *Somers* constitutes the vital center of the case.

But what made an "affair" of it is what began to happen ashore as soon as the *Somers* cast anchor in New York harbor and the news broke that one of her midshipmen and two of her crew had been hanged for mutiny. From that day to this both the events of the cruise and what to make of them have been matters of the widest disagreement. Violent partisan feeling and honest differences of opinion have persisted concerning the character and guilt of the executed men, as well as the character, motives, legal justification, and especially the good judgment—even the sanity—of the officers who condemned them. First a naval court of inquiry and then a court martial took testimony from the officers and crew of the *Somers*. Newspapers and magazines aired all shades of opinion before, during, and sporadically for years after the inquiry and trial. Not only editors and general public, but naval officers, politicians, lawyers, and men of letters took sides, for the most mixed and contradictory reasons. Personal friendships and hatreds as well as political loyalties and rivalries were brought into play. It became one of the celebrated affairs of the century.

No more will be told of it here, for the method of this book is to let the reader follow the affair for himself just as it unfolded from the time the *Somers* reached home in December, 1842. The events on the cruise are revealed in the words and order in which they were made known at the time. Part One, "The News Breaks," sets forth some of the rumors, reports, and reactions of the first few days. Part Two, "The Court of Inquiry," presents the essential testimony given before that court. Part Three, "The Court Martial," continues with further testimony. And interspersed through all three of these parts are reactions of the press and of a number of eminent men who rallied to one side or the other during the three months of inquiry and trial. Part Four, "The Court of Opinion," follows public and private opinion as it developed during the months after the court martial. Finally, Part Five, "Into Memory," gives a sampling of later materials recorded from memory years afterward. Also included in this final part are brief selections from literary works by Herman Melville which drew upon his knowledge and feeling about the *Somers* case. These works show how the affair supplied matter upon which Melville's creative imagination worked. Readers will find it rewarding to read all of *White-Jacket* and *Billy Budd*.

Only a fraction of the voluminous records examined by the editor could be printed in this book; but it is a significant fraction. To the best of his judgment, all the essential facts from the testimony about what happened on the ship are given, as well as a fair representation of ensuing newspaper and personal comment. For a full understanding of the affair, of course, knowledge would be required about widening circles of contexts—biographical, naval, political, and social. The editor hopes many readers will be led on to explore some of these contexts. (He is himself doing so in preparing a book on Alexander Slidell Mackenzie and the *Somers* case.) Still, the story presented here in excerpts is sufficiently self-contained. The reader will find it a first-rate mystery. He must read carefully and critically, piecing together the story as he goes, suspecting every fact, discounting every opinion, weighing every motive. There are no ready-made conclusions: each reader must draw his own.

Though it is every reader's right to make up his own mind from the evidence, the editor has thought it his duty to supply notes of identification and elucidation along the way. A few relevant documents that fall outside the chronological limits of the book have been placed in an Appendix.

A word about documentation: selections are printed as they occur in their original sources, as to all essentials, but a finicky fidelity to inessential mechanical details has not been sought. Each item is introduced by a brief headnote citing the source from which it is taken. If it is from a book, the page-numbers are given, both in the headnote and in the text of the selection. In the text, each such original page-number appears in brackets *preceding* the first word on that page in the original source. If the source is a newspaper, only the date is given when (as was usual) the original pages were not numbered. If the source is an unpublished document, the present location of the original is cited in the headnote. By this system of headnoting and citation, the reader gains much of the effect of reading from the original sources themselves. (For the purposes of documented papers which he may wish to base upon this book, he may thus cite the original works and pages, or through these references he may easily locate desired passages in the original books.) In this method of documentation the book largely follows the style established in an earlier book, *Autobiog-*

raphy of Brook Farm, edited by Henry W. Sams, to whom acknowledgment is made for this as well as other assistance.

For the use of materials printed from manuscripts, acknowledgments are made in the appropriate headnotes. The footnoted information about the service records of naval officers is taken from Edward W. Callahan, ed., *A List of Officers of the Navy of the United States and of the Marine Corps from 1775 to 1900* (New York: L. R. Hamersly and Co., 1901), and supplemented by official naval records in the National Archives. The editor wishes here to express appreciation for generous assistance from staff-members of the libraries of Northwestern University, the University of Chicago, Harvard University, Yale University, the University of Washington, the Massachusetts Historical Society, also of the National Archives, the Boston Athenaeum, the Huntington Library, the New York Public Library, and the Newberry Library. For help in locating materials, grateful thanks are given to Merrell R. Davis, William H. Gilman, Hanson W. Baldwin, and, for matters relating to Chi Psi Fraternity, to H. Seger Slifer.

HARRISON HAYFORD

Contents

The Somers Mutiny Affair

Part One

THE
NEWS
BREAKS

December 17-28, 1842

Do not expect to find in Part One any accurate account of what happened on the *Somers*. Very little you can count on as reliable is told about the "mutiny" itself in this Part. Expect rather to see here what the "news" was, how the newspapers handled it, how it was taken by the public and by some of those closely touched. Do not be bothered by the repetitions, omissions, contradictions, rumors, and conjectures. See these all as parts of the picture of how the *Somers* story broke (perhaps of how any such story usually does break). Even so, as the affair develops in the first two weeks, you can already see patterns beginning to emerge, and discern some of the forces shaping them. After you have read the later Parts and have brought the story into focus, you will find it interesting to re-read this Part to see just how far off much of it is.

> From the diary of Philip Hone, New York, Saturday, December 17, 1842. Here reprinted from *The Diary of Philip Hone,* edited by Bayard Tuckerman (New York: Dodd, Mead & Co., 1889), II, ✓ ✓ ✓   163-164.*

December 17.   On our return to-day we found the city excited by the development of a dreadful story, of which there were some rumours when we went away. The United States brig "Somers," Captain Alexander Slidell McKenzie, arrived in this port on Wednesday night [Dec. 14] from a cruise on the African coast, and last from St. Thomas, from which latter port she had only eight days passage. During the whole of Thursday there was a strange mystery about this vessel. She lay in the bay; nobody, not even the near relations of the officers, was permitted to visit her; the brother of Lieutenant Gansevoort was forbidden to approach. The cause of all this is now explained. A dreadful mutiny had been formed when the brig left the coast of Africa, which was discovered soon after she sailed from St. Thomas. Of this conspiracy, Philip Spencer, a young man of twenty years of age, son of the Hon. John C. Spencer, Secretary of War, was the ringleader. The plan was to murder the captain and lieutenant, convert the brig into a pirate, and come to the American coast for the purpose of intercepting and robbing the packets, which were supposed to have large quantities of specie on board. The crew of the vessel consisted of about seventy-five young men from the [164] naval schools, who had been sent out to complete their education. The mutiny was disclosed by one of the conspirators, when measures were immediately taken for its suppression. Two-thirds of the crew were engaged in the plot; but Captain McKenzie appears to have acted with the utmost decision and bravery. The mutineers were confined under hatches, a court-martial was held, and young Spencer, with two of his confederates, were hung *at the yard- arm;* the rest of the mutineers put in irons, in which situation they were brought home, and have been transferred to the "North Carolina."

A messenger was sent to Washington, and nothing was allowed to transpire until the return of the mail from that place. The imminent danger of the captain and lieutenant, with so large a proportion of the crew in a state of insubordination, no doubt rendered this dreadful and summary exercise of power unavoidable, as an example and measure of safety. If

---

* Philip Hone (1781-1851) was a philanthropic New York merchant. A Whig in politics, he had served as alderman and mayor. His famous diary gives one of the best accounts of the times, from 1828 to 1851. His son, John Hone, married a daughter of Commodore Matthew C. Perry. Commodore Perry married Commander Mackenzie's sister. So Hone was the father-in-law of Mackenzie's niece.

it should so appear (as there seems to be no doubt), public opinion will support, and the government will approve, the conduct of Captain McKenzie. But if it should prove otherwise, he will have assumed an awful responsibility, and his reckoning with the distinguished individual, the father of the principal sufferer, will be fearful, indeed.

Captain Slidell McKenzie * is a brave, gallant young officer, son of my old friend Mr. John Slidell, of this city, brother of John and Thomas Slidell, of New Orleans, the latter of whom is husband to Fanny Callender. Young Spencer was a worthless fellow, who would have been cashiered for some misdemeanour on a former cruise but from feelings of delicacy for the respectable character and high station of his father, whose severe affliction is entitled to the deepest sympathy.

From the New York *Express,* December 17 [?], 1842. Reprinted
↗ ↗ ↗ here from the Chicago *Express,* December 29, 1842.

. . . The story we learn, is, that young Spencer offered his paper or roll of the conspirators to the master-at-arms to sign, who signed it, to quiet their suspicions, then immediately revealed the facts to the Commander. The moment the conspirators found out they were discovered, they met in a body, and went to the commander demanding possession of the ship, and young Spencer presented a pistol to his heart. All this was at night, and the chief part of the crew were below, when the officers on deck not knowing the extent of the conspiracy, immediately closed the hatches, and kept all confined who were below. The officers, after something of a struggle, as we understand, overpowered the conspirators, and regaining complete possession of the ship, instantly caused the ringleaders to be tried by Court Martial, and young Spencer, within ten minutes of the finding of the Court, was hung at the yard-arm, along with two of the men. . . .

Young Spencer is represented to us as a very dare-devil, from his childhood almost there are many stories told about his freaks, that occurred while he was at college at Geneva. A brother of his, our readers will recollect, has figured a great deal of late in the papers here, as a forger,

---

* Alexander Slidell Mackenzie (1803-1848) entered the navy as a midshipman at the age of twelve and through twenty-seven years' service had attained the rank of commander. (Born Slidell, he legally added his mother's name Mackenzie in 1837.) Of a literary turn, he had gained recognition for his travel books, *A Year in Spain* (1829), *The American in England* (1835), and *Spain Revisited* (1836). He had also written *Popular Essays on Naval Subjects* (1833), *The Life of Commodore Oliver Hazard Perry* (1840), and *The Life of John Paul Jones* (1841). Like his brother-in-law, Commodore M. C. Perry, he had long been concerned with the improvement of the naval service. At Perry's instance, the newly launched *Somers* had been detailed in 1842 as a training vessel, with Mackenzie in command of a crew of apprentices hand-picked by Perry and himself. This was her second cruise.

and in many parts of the South West, on pretty near the same points of view. . . .

✔ ✔ ✔   From the New York *Herald*, Sunday, December 18, 1842.*

. . . This is the first occurrence of the kind in our Navy. . . . The *Somers* is the fastest sailing vessel in the service. . . . These desperadoes might have . . . eluded detection and pursuit for years. . . . We can hardly find language to express our admiration of the conduct of Commander McKenzie. The public voice has already pronounced a verdict of unqualified and unanimous approbation. . . . By this one act, the Commander . . . has done more to sustain the supremacy of naval authority and to vindicate outraged law, than anything which has ever occurred in our Navy. . . . It is indeed fortunate that on such a man as Slidell McKenzie devolved the high responsibility of such a critical hour. . . . Had young Spencer been put in irons and brought home to meet his trial, he would in all probability have escaped. We have had of late such melancholy evidence of the facility with which criminals having wealthy and influential friends can evade the hands of justice . . . that we can hardly suppose this abandoned young man would have received the just demerit of his crime. . . .

✔ ✔ ✔   From the New York *Herald,* Tuesday morning, December 20, 1842, in a letter from its Washington correspondent dated Sunday night, December 18.

The news . . . reached this city yesterday but was not publicly known until the arrival of the cars from New York. . . . Everyone commended the conduct of Commodore McKenzie . . . , yet a deep and universal sympathy is felt for the Hon. Mr. Spencer. This gentleman, of course, is very deeply depressed about it, and his lady is almost broken hearted. She had just issued cards for a large party next Wednesday. . . . How much of the crime of this young man may be attributed to the miserable trash that the country is daily deluged with in the shape of romantic adventures of pirates, banditti, exploits of celebrated highwaymen, freebooters, etc.? . . . I think [James Fenimore] Cooper's "Red Rover" and "Water Witch" have done an incalculable amount of mischief. . . . I do

---

* This paper, edited by James Gordon Bennett, belonged to the sensational "penny press." Most New York papers had waged a "Moral War" against it in 1841, charging Bennett with indecency, blasphemy, blackmail, lying, and libel. Though Bennett claimed to be non-political, the paper was at this time generally considered a mouthpiece for President Tyler. See Oliver Carlson, *The Man Who Made News: James Gordon Bennett* (New York: Duell, Sloan and Pearce, 1942).

not think that "La Feu Follet," Cooper's last work, is free from the same powerful objection. . . .

It is supposed that young Spencer must have been crazy. . . .

↗ ↗ ↗ From the New York *Herald,* Monday morning, December 19, 1842.

. . . There now appears to be a division of opinion. . . . Yesterday and the day before facts have been . . . circulated . . . which throw a different light. . . . That one of the persons executed protested his innocence to the last moment . . . , that Spencer alone originated the mutiny . . . , that no one really and seriously joined him. . . . A great many members of the bar begin to object to the legality. . . . There was no doubt of the intention on the part of Spencer . . . ; that is admitted on all hands. . . . The boldness and decision with which a United States officer acted, can only be parallelled . . . in the early history of the Roman Republic. . . .

↗ ↗ ↗ From the New York *Herald,* Monday evening, December 19, 1842.

. . . There was no overt act. . . . The plot was merely *in embryo.* . . . In such circumstances a great difference of opinion exists as to the necessity and legality of McKenzie's conduct. . . . It also appears that there was no court martial. . . . The officers would seem to have acted under a panic. . . .

↗ ↗ ↗ Excerpt from a detailed account of the mutiny, in the New York *Courier and Enquirer,* Monday morning, December 19, 1842.*

. . . We had actually printed the material facts . . . on Friday, but

---

* Some question arose how the story was secured by this newspaper. The editor of the *Courier and Enquirer* was James Watson Webb (1802-1884). He was a friend and neighbor of Commander Mackenzie and of Commodore M. C. Perry, Mackenzie's brother-in-law, at the time commandant of the Brooklyn Navy Yard. The *Courier and Enquirer* was known as a "Wall Street" paper; it was Whig, conservative, but outspoken. Webb and Bennett (of the *Herald*) were constantly at each other's throats in the columns of their papers. Webb called the *Herald* a "dirty little paper," had joined the "Moral War" against it, and had even thrashed Bennett on the street. (Bennett had cheerfully made a story of it in his next edition.) Webb's paper was vociferously anti-administration. A few days before the *Somers* news broke, it had attacked both "His Accidency," as it loved to call President Tyler, and John C. Spencer, employing such epithets as "miserable trick," "veriest wretch," "unprincipled politician," "imbecile," "traitor," "disgraceful imbecile," and "greatest curse." One must wonder to what extent Webb's *Courier and Enquirer* and Bennett's *Herald* were affected by political considerations and by mutual dislike in their views of the *Somers* case.

suppressed them, on learning from the father-in-law of Captain Mackenzie, that although that officer had been on shore with his family, not a word had escaped him referring to any difficulties which had occurred during his cruise. . . . From respect for the *motives* of the Commandant in keeping his own counsels until the affair had been officially reported to the Navy Department, we suppressed [the story]. . . .

Now that the matter is before the public, we feel fully authorized to give the *facts* of this extraordinary proceeding. . . . Although our account is not *official,* and although it may not comport with Mr. Mackenzie's notions of naval *etiquette* to approve of such a detailed statement . . . , yet it may be relied upon as embracing most of the particulars of that gentleman's report to the secretary of the navy; and as we do not hold ourselves responsible to the distinguished naval officers . . . for what we may deem proper to make public under existing circumstances, we hope that they will agree with us, that the sooner the *truth* reaches the public the better it will be for all parties . . . , and in consequence not give themselves any unnecessary trouble to ascertain our source of information. . . .

[*A detailed summary of events is given, closely following Mackenzie's report (dated December 19) which was not made public until December 29. That report is reprinted in the present book, a few pages along.*]

. . . Sufficient is known already to establish beyond a question the necessity, imperative and immediate, however dreadful, of the course pursued by commander Mackenzie, than whom, a more humane, conscientious and gallant officer does not hold a commission in the navy of the United States. . . .

From the diary of Evert Duyckinck, Monday, December 19, 1842.*

Here reproduced from the Manuscript diary in the Duyckinck Collection of the New York Public Library, by permission.

A man, a respectable church-going, who-has-made-his-money-merchant and of course a man of most judicious sense [was] heard gravely to maintain that Spencer was never really hung till he was dead at sea but that he was cut down and smuggled ashore. . . .

A fact like the above shows not merely a certain amount of vileness in the person who utters such a saying but a general presumption of the relaxation of law and that a guilty person with influence will most likely escape. . . .

---

* Evert Duyckinck (1816-1878) was a New York editor and literary man.

From a letter of Benjamin F. Green to his mother, dated from
aboard the U. S. Ship *North Carolina* [New York Harbor], Monday,
December 19, 1842. Here reprinted from the New York *Weekly
Tribune,* January 7, 1843, which reprinted it from the Portland
(Maine) *American.* The *American's* item included the statement
that Green "is of a very respectable family in this city [Portland]."

On our passage . . . the most dreadful sight I ever saw was a Midshipman and two seamen, who were hanged for mutiny at the yard-arm.
Midshipman Spencer was about 22 years of age. Samuel Cromwell and
Elisha Small were the men; one was said to belong to Boston and the
other to New-York, but I think they were not Americans. Cromwell has
left a wife and children in Brooklyn. There have been twelve boys and
men sent on board the North Carolina, and I am one; but I hope you
will not be uneasy about it, for I knew nothing about it until it happened.
Mr. Gansevoort, our first lieutenant, told me there was nothing against
me more than suspicion.

From the New York *Herald,* Wednesday morning, December 21,
in a letter from its Washington correspondent dated Monday night,
December 19, 1842.

There is a difference of opinion and some doubt. . . . A majority
applaud. . . . The excellent mother of the wretched youth is quite beside
herself; she was in feeble health, and this shocking event has made her
quite delirious; two physicians are constantly in attendance, and her ultimate recovery is even doubtful. The father is perfectly inconsolable and
is confined to his room. . . . Young [Oliver Hazard] Perry * reached
here on Friday night with the news; and Judge Upshur [the Secretary of
the Navy] knew not how to break it to Mr. Spencer; at last he sent for
Mr. [Henry] Morris, the son-in-law and private secretary of the Secretary
at War and through him the sad intelligence was communicated. . . .

A notice and a communication signed "S" in the "official organ"
of the Administration, the *Madisonian* (Washington), Wednesday,
December 20, 1842. Here reprinted from *Niles' National Register,*
(Baltimore), LXXIII (December 24, 1842), 260-261.

In consideraton of the source whence the communication signed "S"
emanated, we placed it in the hands of the printers without reading it.
Although we give the writer an opportunity to be heard through our

---

* Mackenzie's nephew, son of Commodore M. C. Perry; he was the commander's
  clerk and an acting midshipman on the *Somers.* He carried Mackenzie's first dispatch
  to Washington.

columns, yet we desire to hold ourselves entirely uncommitted on the subject for the present.

COMMUNICATED

The friends of young Spencer, who was executed, together with two seamen, on the 1st inst. would have been content to abide the investigation which the laws of the country require in such cases, and would have trusted to that justice which our tribunals award to all entitled to the protection of the constitution and laws of the country. Various publications have however appeared in the New York papers, and been copied into a paper of extensive circulation at the seat of government, giving versions of the transaction, the materials for which, if not the versions themselves, were obviously furnished by some officers who had a hand in the bloody deed. This is evident from their containing some facts which could be known only to those officers—but so perverted, so exaggerated, and interspersed with so much surmise, and so much downright falsehood, as to evince the deep anxiety felt to make sure of the first impression on the public mind. An awful responsibility rests on those officers, and above all on their commander. Without the least desire to render that responsibility more hazardous than it now is, it is still deemed an act of simple and bare justice to the memory of *the slain,* to say that an examination of the papers transmitted by Com. Mackenzie shows these facts:

1st. That acting midshipman Spencer was put in double irons on the 26th of November, and the boatswain's mate Samuel Cromwell, and seaman Elisha Small, on the day following, on a charge of intended mutiny.

2d. That no disorder of a mutinous character appeared among the crew for the four succeeding days; that the vessel was going with good breezes and in good weather towards the island of St. Thomas, where she actually arrived and took in supplies on some day between the 1st and 5th of December.

3d. That on the 30th of November, the opinion of the officers was required by commander Mackenzie as to the disposition of the prisoners; that they appear to have examined thirteen seamen as witnesses to prove the alleged mutiny, (and who are therefore supposed innocent of any participation in it), which examination was had, so far as the papers show, in the absence of the prisoners, and without giving them any opportunity to cross-examine the witnesses or to make any explanation or defence, or to procure any testimony in their own behalf. These officers, without even the form of a court, without even the obligation of an oath, and upon this ex parte secret information, united in the opinion that the safety of the vessel required that the prisoners should be put to death! How far this recommendation was influenced by the acts or fears of Mr. Mackenzie, does not appear.

4th. That on the 1st of December, when every thing and person on board the vessel were perfectly quiet, after four days of entire security, the three persons were, by order of Mackenzie, hung at the yard arm at mid-day.

The allegation, in some of the papers, that it was proved to have been the intention of the mutineers to execute their project on arriving at St. Thomas, is wholly destitute of any evidence. And had it been their design, it was effectually frustrated so far as these prisoners were concerned, by their confinement. At St. Thomas, any of the crew might have been left, and the power of the officers of the vessel strengthened to any extent that was necessary.

The statement in the Intelligencer, copied apparently from the New York American, that Spencer violated an engagement formerly made to resign, seems to have been deemed necessary to prejudice the public mind against him, that those who slew him might have a more favorable hearing. It is untrue; he did resign, and the secretary of the navy, on the recommendation of his commanding officer, considering the nature and circumstances of the offence (inebriation) restored his warrant, with a strong admonition; and this was done without the solicitation of any of his friends. His age is represented in the same paper to have been over twenty. Had he lived, he would have been nineteen the 28th of January next.

As to the probability that such a mere boy—utterly unacquainted with navigation—brought up in the interior would seriously endeavor to seduce to mutiny an old seaman who had arrived at the rank of boatswain's mate, and who is represented to have been employed heretofore on board a slaver, or to have been a pirate—an impartial tribunal before which *both sides* will be heard, will determine.

The idea of the mutineers cruising off Sandy Hook to intercept the packets, seems to have been thrown in for the special benefit of the merchants of New York. The papers, such as they are, contain no such information.

The only account we have, given by Spencer himself, is, that *it was all a joke.* If it shall appear to have been the mere romance of a heedless boy, amusing himself, it is true, in a dangerous manner, but still devoid of such murderous designs as are imputed, and if the execution of him and two seamen (against one of whom at least, there is not yet a particle of evidence) should prove to have been the [261] result of unmanly fear, or of a despotic temper, and wholly unnecessary at the time to repress or prevent a mutiny—if all this can appear, it cannot be doubted that the laws will be vindicated. The laws of congress prescribing the navy regulations, forbid the taking of human life, even by the sentence of a court martial, before which all parties are heard, without the sanction of the president of the United States, or, if without the United States, of the commander of the fleet or squadron. This is believed to be the first instance in our history in which the law has been violated—the first in which prisoners—not of the enemy, but of our own citizens—have been put to death in cold blood.

These remarks are made, not to excite prejudice, but to repel the attempt to create it, and to enable the American people to see what mighty principles are involved in this unheard-of proceeding. Let justice be done; let it not be denied, because one of the victims was connected with a high functionary of government, nor because another is unknown, and has not a friend or relation on the face of the earth. And let not wanton opprobrium be heaped upon the memory of the dead, to justify the bloody deeds of the living.

S.

From the New York *Herald,* Wednesday morning, December 21, 1842, in a letter to the editor, James G. Bennett.

. . . Among the many reports concerning the unfortunate young Spencer, and the different causes assigned for his bloodthirsty conception, is his long and hopeless attachment to the young and lovely daughter of one of our most celebrated artists. It has been said that the young lady gilted [*sic*] him, and thus drove him to desperation. I apply to you for information about this *interesting* and romantic explanation . . .

A. B. C.

An entry in the diary of Philip Hone for Wednesday, December 21, 1842. Here reprinted from *The Diary of Philip Hone,* edited by Bayard Tuckerman (New York: Dodd, Mead & Co., 1889), II, 165-166.

December 21. A statement is published in the "Washington Madisonian," signed S., which will occasion some revulsion in the public mind in relation to the melancholy tragedy on board the brig "Somers." This statement . . . is evidently written by Mr. Spencer, the Secretary of War. It is one of those strong, forcible documents for which he is celebrated; fierce in style, rigid in argument, and certainly presents the subject of his son's execution in a light somewhat different from that in which it was received at first. If there exists any reasonable doubt of the absolute necessity for this awful exercise of power, Captain McKenzie may wish sincerely that he never had been born to meet such a responsibility. A more dangerous opponent than John C. Spencer could not be found in the United States; stern, uncompromising, obstinate in temper, determined and energetic in action, and with talents equal to any effort which his feelings may prompt, or his duty may call him to execute.* It is officially announced that the navy

---

* John Canfield Spencer (1788-1855) was an influential Whig politician from upstate New York. (His own father, Ambrose Spencer, who was still living, had been chief justice of the New York Supreme Court.) John C. Spencer's influence had secured

department is not in possession of information sufficient to form a statement for the public eye. This would appear unfavourable to Captain McKenzie. If his official report were not so clear as to leave "no hook on which to hang a doubt," the doubt, the hesitation alone would be fatal to him. If the cabinet should take part with the bereaved parent, who is one [166] of its prominent members, in denying the existence of the necessity for the execution of the ringleaders of the mutiny, and if the laws should not support the measure, Captain McKenzie is ruined past redemption.

An answer in the New York *American* (by the editor, Charles King) to the charge by "S" that officers of the *Somers* furnished reports to the papers in order to make the first impression on public opinion. As reprinted in the New York *Courier and Enquirer*, Thursday, December 22, 1842.

. . . This [charge] is wholly erroneous. So far from furnishing materials for, or prompting, any publication, the officers of the Somers were silent as those they are accused in this article of having *"slain."* The vessel was anchored off the Navy Yard, and all communication with her was strictly cut off—the Commander meaning and desiring that the first information should come back from Washington. . . . We [Charles King] happened to see and have a long conversation with Commander Mackenzie on the day of his arrival without hearing from him one syllable, or hint of any kind, of the dreadful occurrence on board the brig.

He made his report as in duty bound to Commodore Jacob Jones, Commander on this Station, and to Commodore [Matthew C.] Perry, Commander at the Navy Yard; and to no one else, not even to his nearest relatives, did he allude to the subject. He also transmitted his official report to the Navy Department.

The rumors . . . in this city on Friday, (the brig having arrived on Thursday) were derived, as is believed, from conversations held by Com. Jones. Yet, even after these rumors, Mr. Mackenzie remained silent; and Commodore Perry, to whom we addressed a note on Saturday morning,

---

his son Philip's appointment as acting midshipman in November, 1841. But his political position at the moment was peculiar; he was being reviled by most of the "respectable" Whig papers of the country for standing by President John Tyler. Elected vice-president in the "log-cabin" campaign of 1840, Tyler had "accidentally" become president by the death of William Henry Harrison a month after the inauguration. As president, he was not carrying out the policies the victorious Whigs had ardently expected of their man. Consequently, most of his inherited cabinet had resigned, and then Spencer had accepted appointment as Secretary of War. So along with Tyler he was being assailed as a traitor to the Whig party. To the Democrats he was a renegade, since he had left that party to go over to the Whigs only three or four years earlier. How much of the partisan animosity already directed at the father carried over into attitudes toward the case of the son?

urging the importance of having the facts accurately stated, replied that he was not at liberty to give any information. . . . We cannot conclude without again cautioning our readers against the seemingly calm and fair, but really deeply impassioned and insidious statement. The very choice of words . . . is made so as to imply everywhere, innocence or sportiveness on the part of the youth—guilt and cruelty on the part of the officers. . . .

From the New York *Weekly Tribune,* Thursday, December 22, ✓ ✓ ✓ 1842.*

. . . There are but very few expressions through the press . . . of censure upon Com. MACKENZIE . . . , and these few . . . rather spring from personal sympathy with the sufferers than a sound conviction of the injustice of their fate. . . . The Union of Tuesday, most improperly, it seems to us, said with a bitter and undeserved sneer, that *of course* "he would be acquitted and highly commended by a Naval Court Martial as this is *the aristocratic branch of the service.* . . ."

From a letter of Henry Morris (son-in-law of John C. Spencer) to Col. W. A. Stone, editor of the New York *Commercial Advertiser,* undated [c. December 22, 1842]. Reproduced here from the original ✓ ✓ ✓ letter in the New York Public Library, by permission.

You would much oblige Hon. J. C. Spencer by publishing in your paper the article in the inclosed Madisonian headed "The tragedy on board the Somers" as soon as you can conveniently. He asks this favor as an act of justice for the article that appeared in your paper a few days since on that melancholy subject.

✓ ✓ ✓ From the New York *Herald,* Friday morning, December 23, 1842.

The attempts made [by the *Courier and Enquirer* and the New York *American*] to prejudice this bloody affair have been most wicked, most atrocious, and most illegal. . . . If any persons connected with the navy, have been the means of furnishing and causing these statements to be made public, in advance of the legal inquiry, their conduct deserves the severest condemnation. . . . Much more censurable were the inflammatory appeals to the passions of the multitude on the imaginary deeds of blood, rapine, piracy, rape, and murder, which seem to have had no other existence than in the efforts of a misguided fancy, or the struggles of a guilty conscience trying to tear itself away from its own illegal deeds. . . .

---

* The *Tribune,* edited by Horace Greeley (1811-1872), was an independent Whig paper with national circulation.

From a letter of Gov. William H. Seward of New York [to his wife], Albany, December 23, 1842. Here reprinted from *William H. Seward: An Autobiography from 1801-1834. With a Memoir of His Life, and Selections from His Letters 1831-1846*, by Frederick W. Seward (New York: D. Appleton, 1877), pp. 640-641.

You have read all that has transpired concerning the awful calamity that has befallen the Spencers. Was ever a blow more appalling? I, of course, knew Philip only as friends know our children. I should as soon have expected a deer to ravage a sheepfold. There are all manner of reports from Washington concerning the manner in which the parents receive this last sad [641] blow, but I have no curiosity on the subject. I know that Nature has given no firmness to resist the immediate shock to the mother, but time may heal and obliterate the wound. The card which Mr. Spencer has published (or rather his communication) shows that his iron nerves were proof. Mr. [Thurlow] Weed is at Washington, but I have no information from him.*

Letter to the editors, *National Intelligencer* (Washington), December 24, 1842.*

The recent painful tragedy on board the . . . SOMERS, in which a son of the Secretary of War was so fatally concerned, having been made the occasion of unfounded and cruel accusations against another son of that distinguished citizen, I beg leave to submit a vindication of his character. . . .

The Secretary of War had three sons. The eldest [Ambrose] resided several years at Cleveland, Ohio, in the practise of the law. His second son, JOHN C. SPENCER, JR., is now in the Mediterranean, on board the U.S. ship [*Columbus*] commanded by his uncle Captain WILLIAM SPENCER.† This young gentleman, than whom one more exemplary estimable, and virtuous does not live, resided several years in Albany, where he was not only respected but beloved by all with whom he associated. And yet this youth, whose character is unblemished, and whose whole life has been blameless, is represented through the press as an inmate of the Sing Sing prison! . . .

W. [Thurlow Weed?]

---

* Thurlow Weed (1797-1882) was a Whig politician, editor of the Albany *Evening Journal,* and a close political associate of Seward. In his *Autobiography* (1883) he told of the above-mentioned journey to Washington; a passage on the *Somers* affair is reprinted in the present book under the date of its publication.
† On this cruise John C. Spencer, Jr., was acting as his Uncle William's clerk. He was appointed a purser in August, 1843; he died in service at sea in December, 1845. William A. Spencer, brother of John C. Spencer, was midshipman in 1809; lieutenant, 1814; commander, 1831; captain, March 17, 1841; assigned to command the *Columbus,* April 19, 1842; detached and permitted to return to the United States, February 27, 1843; on leave, June 7, 1843; resigned, December 9, 1843.

⟁ ⟁ ⟁ From the New York *Weekly Tribune,* December 24, 1842.

PHILIP SPENCER.—We copy the following particulars of the life and career of this unhappy young man, from the New-Haven *Palladium* [Dec. 19] . . . , by one who says he was once his "friend and messmate, and who continued and cherished the former term, until ingratitude marked by ferociousness of feeling and heartless depravity of character, burst asunder the chords of amity, which, in the beginning of his naval career, had every seeming of being lasting."

Philip Spencer was born in Canandaigua, New-York, and at the time of his awful death, was about 19 years of age—but in strength of mind, intelligence, literary attainments, and bold daring, was far, far beyond his years. Nothing in his history of much interest is the writer aware of, until his College career. He was sent to Union College, Schenectady, but did not graduate, as his conduct there became so notorious that he was expelled or had leave to absent himself. He returned to his friends where he remained some time. Being of a wandering turn of mind, and fond of anything bordering on the dangerous and marvelous, he eloped from his home and went to New-York; concealing his parentage, shipped for a whaler fitting out at Nantucket, and (along with many others of kindred feeling, but not of that daring, reckless spirit, fearless alike of life or death,) was sent to the latter place in a small schooner.

The ship that he was to embark in not being ready, he remained some time on the island. During this time, and previous to the gale of October, 1841, he volunteered to go out on the banks in a small vessel for what the whalemen denominate Black Fish, and in that gale came near being lost, as many were at the time; as it was, they got back to Nantucket quite a wreck. Here I told him that I was surprised that he should ever think of adopting that hazardous life, sought only by those whom friends and fortune had discarded, and whose last lingering star of hope had sank beneath the horizon, perhaps never to re-appear. He smiled at my astonishment at his deserting his happy, luxurious and delightful home; and now as I look back, as I often have since, I think of that smile of Spencer . . . that smile was not human! The wild rolling of his eyes told plainly enough, to any one at all discerning, that something was working in that heart that could not submit to the dull monotony of this peaceful, every day life.

His reply was that he "should like to harpoon a whale and see the blood spilt," that he "was not afraid of danger and liked an adventurous life." The ship being ready to receive her casks, he was compelled, with many others, to work from morning till late at night in getting them and her stores on board, being allowed only thirty minutes for their meals, which were of the coarsest kind, and only five hours rest at night in a miserable forecastle in close communion with the dregs of New-York streets. I told him I thought that this servile labor and hard living, would have satisfied his curiosity to see the world; but no—the excitement was to come. In confirmation of his assertions, he showed me his hands, and they, from their horny, hardened appearance, corroborated his statement of what he had undergone at Nantucket. Having disposed of his wardrobe and replaced them by the coarse and homely garb of the whaler, he was ready, as was also the ship, in two days, to sail for their cruising grounds in the South Seas.

In the interval of time from his disappearance from home to the time of our narrative, his friends had by diligent inquiries found his whereabouts, and knowing his uncontrollable disposition, and his determination at all hazards to go to sea, their influence and his father's position as one of the Cabinet at Washington, procured for him a midshipman's appointment, which was sent with all despatch to Nantucket, with a description of his person, &c. to the care of the owner of the ship. This and a letter from his father, was placed in his hands. This prospect of change from drudgery to a comparatively easy life, had not much effect on him as it would have had on most young men; but by the earnest persuasions of the owner and captain, after learning who he was, he was induced by them to give a volunteer $30 to take his place in the ship.

He came on to New-York and was there fitted out by his uncle, Captain [William A.] Spencer, of the Navy, and by him introduced on board of the guard-ship North Carolina. His sojourn on board of that ship (about four months) was passed, as is much of the time of some other young men in like circumstances, in occasional, and, I am sorry to say, frequent dissipation, principally at night, but not unfrequently in the face of day. Here he committed an aggravated and unprovoked assault upon his superior officer, which was investigated by the Commodore in the cabin of that ship, in the presence of the uncle, Capt. Spencer, and a commander of the navy. The written report made by the insulted officer to the Secretary of the Navy, though from the commandant of the station, was unheeded, supposed from family influence, and Spencer was ordered to the brig Somers.* The officer thus treated resigned from the service.†￼ The writer does not charge the excellent commander of the North Carolina with a knowledge of the facts of the dissipation among some of the young men on that ship; he believes it was entirely beyond his knowledge.

---

* Philip Spencer was appointed acting midshipman, November 20, 1841; ordered to the receiving ship *North Carolina* at New York, November 20, 1841; ordered to the *John Adams,* February 7, 1842, which sailed to the Brazil station; returned in the *Potomac* from Brazil, arriving July 31, 1842; ordered to the *Somers,* August 13, 1842; died aboard the *Somers,* December 1, 1842. See Appendix for documents relating to his naval service.

† The officer referred to was Passed Midshipman William Craney. See his account of this affair with Spencer, recorded by R. H. Dana, Jr., under the date April 25, 1843, below. It seems possible that he was the author of this sketch of Philip Spencer.

The horrid death of young Spencer must be most fearfully distressing to the feelings of his family, and the writer would not add another pang to their already broken hearts; but he trusts it may be a warning to many youths who wish to leave the happy fireside of their homes. . . .

TRITON.

From a poem reprinted in the New York *Weekly Tribune,* December 24, 1842.

The following, from the *American* of yesterday, bears the initials of H. T. Tuckerman, one of our most popular and gifted poets. It is a deserved tribute to the hero of a noble deed.

TO COM. ALEXANDER SLIDELL MACKENZIE

If, like the warrior whose immortal story,
    With kindred mind, thy pen so well hath traced,
Thou had'st brought home a victor's wreath of glory,
    A nation's praise thy coming would have graced. . . .*

How stern a conflict thy bold heart was rending
    When trait'rous shipmates all around thee pressed,
And honor's voice, with deep compassion blending,
    To voiceless anguish woke thy manly breast! . . .

A dearer tribute thou wert called to render,
    In yielding up another's forfeit life;
For brave men's hearts are not less firm than tender,
    And where Truth reigns is Feeling's keenest strife. . . .

But when oppressive grew thy nature's pleading,
    Unto the starry banner thou dids't turn,
With solemn trust thy mournful purpose feeding,
    To make the light of duty clearly burn!

When all was done—each word of sadness spoken,
    And loyal cheers again rose o'er the sea,
Calm was thy heart, in Duty's cause half-broken—
    Calm as the stars, and as the waters free!

H. T. T.

---

* The "warrior" in the first stanza was Oliver Hazard Perry (1785-1819), victor of the Battle of Lake Erie in the War of 1812. His brother, Matthew C. Perry, married Mackenzie's sister in 1814; and in 1815 Oliver Hazard Perry gave twelve-year-old Mackenzie (then named Slidell) an appointment as acting midshipman. Mackenzie sailed on a cruise to the Mediterranean under him in the frigate *Java* in 1816, and studied French and Spanish, swordsmanship, and dancing, in his cabin beneath his own eye. These facts Mackenzie mentions in his *Life of Commodore Oliver Hazard Perry* (1840), pp. 96, 140-141.

Taken from a letter of Peter Gansevoort to Lieut. Guert Ganse-
voort,* Albany, December 24, 1842, now in the Gansevoort-
Lansing Collection of the New York Public Library, by permission.
[The letter has also been reproduced by Jay Leyda in *The Melville
Log: A Documentary Life of Herman Melville* (New York: Har-
court Brace, 1951), I, 159.]

Since your return from the coast of Africa I have felt an intense interest
in the development of the solemn scenes in which you have participated
on board the brig Somers—

I avoid all comment, as nothing official has been made known & satisfy
myself with the remark, that I have at all times believed that your conduct throughout has been not only consistent with your manly course
through life, but marked by the exercise of those generous & chivalric
feelings which belong to true courage.

. . . But since the publication of S[pencer] at Washington I have
reflected with painful anxiety on the effect which the influence of a strong
power may exert over the proceedings in the nature of an Inquiry. . . .
You and your Commander will be placed upon the defensive under un-
paralleled circumstances. . . .

From a letter of John Lorimer Graham, postmaster of New York
City, to Silas M. Stilwell, United States Marshal in New York,
dated Washington, December 24, 1842. Here reproduced from the
original letter in the Manuscript Division of the New York Public
Library, by permission.

Sacredly confidential. . . . I speak from *high authority* when I say that
it will be particularly gratifying should our friend [Ogden] Hoffman [*U. S.
District Attorney, New York*] intimate that he would be pleased to have
some legal gentleman associated with him in the Court of Enquiry to sit
on the 28th inst. upon the *Somers Affair*—he should wish it on his own
account—it is a tremendous responsibility and in view of all the facts, I
should were I in his place, decline the appointment altogether—but should
he act, he ought to *share the responsibility*—

---

* Guert Gansevoort (1812-1868). His father had been sheriff of Albany; his grandfather was General Peter Gansevoort, a hero of the Revolution. He was a first-
cousin of Herman Melville. He entered the navy as midshipman in 1823, recommended by his Uncle Peter (the writer of the above letter, an Albany lawyer
influential in the ruling Democratic clique known as the "Albany Regency"), and
supported by a petition signed by such men as De Witt Clinton, William James,
and Chief Justice Ambrose Spencer (Philip's grandfather). He was promoted to
lieutenant in 1837; ordered to the Navy Yard, New York, January 7, 1842; attached
to the *Somers,* May 20, 1842; detached, March 8, 1843. He became commander,
1855; captain, 1862; retired, 1867.

Our friend Spencer is stricken down—he wishes impartial but stern justice done in this matter—it is a case that will agitate the nation—and the *facts* will disclose a case unparallelled in the history of civilized nations —You will at once perceive the importance of the proposed [?] Enquiry— it is the commencement of proceedings that will be watched with the most intense interest by the people of this Country.— Mr. S[pencer] has seen no one out of his own family, but myself.— I spent two hours with him today.—

I desire you will see Hoffman at once. Get him to write to the Secretary of the Navy, by return mail, that he desires the Secretary to associate Counsel with him—it is our wish that it should be done upon Mr. H's own request—it is unnecessary to say to him that *I* have made this suggestion to you. I shall depend upon your faithful attention to this matter, and to receive your reply by return mail— No time *should be lost——*

Our friends press me to urge upon you the exercise of your best judgment and skill, to prevail upon Mr. H. to adopt the suggestion I have made. In great haste, your friend, J.L.G.

[*A further note from Graham to Stilwell, of the same date as the above:*]

Since writing to you this afternoon yours of the 23d. inst. has come to hand— I had somewhat anticipated your views— Both you & myself will probably be designated to attend the Ct.— In the mean time say nothing about it— *I shall attend to it*— You will at once perceive the bearing of my note of to day, which do not fail to answer me promptly. In the greatest haste. . . .

> From a letter of Gov. William H. Seward to an unnamed correspondent [his wife?], dated Albany, December 25, 1842. Here reprinted from *William H. Seward: An Autobiography* . . . (New York: D. Appleton, 1877), p. 641.

✓ ✓ ✓

[Thurlow] Weed writes from Washington that Mrs. Spencer is heartbroken, and her husband scarcely less. That article in the *Madisonian* was his. Weed says that the papers sent to Washington do not show a necessity for the execution, and that the conduct of Mackenzie, as ascertained from these papers, appears to have been cowardly and murderous. This may all be, and yet the name and fame of Spencer be as irretrievable as his life. Mackenzie married a daughter of Morris Robinson, one of my Chautauqua associates, and brother-in-law of John Duer. . . .*

---

* Through his wife, Mackenzie had influential connections. Her father, Morris Robinson, was a well-known New York lawyer. Her mother's brothers, John and William A. Duer, were also both eminent lawyers. John Duer (1782-1858) had collaborated with John C. Spencer in revising the New York Statutes. William A. Duer (1780-1858) had been a New York Supreme Court Justice and was president of Columbia College, 1829-1842.

✓ ✓ ✓ From the Boston *Courier,* December 27, 1842.*

. . . We doubt exceedingly whether a "satisfactory opinion" will be the result of the inquiry; we mean, an opinion satisfactory to the people. We mean no imputation on the character of the gentlemen composing the Court; they are all honorable men, and will judge as impartially . . . as . . . any body of men of the same profession as the officer who committed the deed. . . . To expect an opinion unfavorable to Commander Mackenzie would be to expect of human nature a degree of impartiality contrary to all experience. . . .

✓ ✓ ✓ From the New York *Herald,* Tuesday morning, December 27, 1842.

. . . Subsequent information and examination convinced us that the first version of the story did not, by any means, present the exact state of the case. . . . While we have thus endeavored to steer clear of all partiality . . . , a considerable portion of the press has jumped into this affair with the spirit of partizanship. . . . We allude particularly to the conduct of the Wall St. press [*e.g.,* the *Courier and Enquirer*]. . . . This is, indeed . . . , a most important affair and bids fair to produce a terrible explosion among various distinguished families and *cliques* in this state. The excitement already reminds us of the factious disputes of the noble families that flourished in Florence, Venice, Mantua, and Genoa. . . .

From the New York *Courier and Enquirer,* Wednesday, December ✓ ✓ ✓ 28, 1842.

. . . One [newspaper, the *Herald*] which at first overloaded those officers with praise . . . , having been *doucered* [bribed] into a little natural depravity, or having come to the opinion that something may be made out of an excitement against Capt. Mackenzie . . . is too loathsome for a moment's serious notice. . . . A few infamous prints [have asserted] that these . . . officers have procured *ex parte* statements to appear in the *Courier and Enquirer.* . . . If rascality is ever appropriately punished . . . , the scoundrel [James Gordon Bennett] . . . will be whipped out of the country . . . by the indignant detestation . . . of every decent man, woman, and child. . . .

---

* This was a Whig paper, edited by Joseph T. Buckingham (1799-1861).

END
OF PART ONE
✓ ✓ ✓

Part Two

THE
COURT
OF
INQUIRY

December 28, 1842 to
January 28, 1843

In this part two stories unfold at the same time. One
is the continued story of the developing affair ashore. The other, in-
side this, is the story that gradually came out about what had happened on the cruise.

The main development in the shore-story is the naval court of inquiry. This was not a trial but an official investigation, ordered by

the Secretary of the Navy. No one stood accused. The court opened on December 28, in the cabin of the *North Carolina* drawn up at her winter berth at the Brooklyn Navy Yard. Here, day after day, testimony was taken. Almost everyone aboard told his version, except ten of the twelve men still under arrest—and of course the three who had been hanged.

Commander Mackenzie was not called to testify. Instead, his written report to the Secretary was read at the beginning. This detailed account, dated December 19, is the central document in the whole case, and as such it merits the closest study. Mackenzie's earliest report, dated December 5, at St. Thomas, is not given here since in substance it differs little from the later, published account. Perhaps the most interesting thing about the earlier report is the rhetorical strategy by which Mackenzie broke his bad news to the Secretary of the Navy. Comparing it with his later, amplified account, one is less struck by differences in their factual content than by obvious differences in the way the facts were presented. When Mackenzie wrote the report of December 19, after all, he was not breaking the news; he was filling out the story, and doing so in quite another context, one in which public opinion was already acclaiming him a hero. How much easier and better might Mackenzie have made out in the later court of public opinion, one wonders, had he not elaborated his first report as he did? Many of his stoutest defenders came to regret that document.

After Mackenzie's report was read, the Judge Advocate questioned all the officers and most of the men and boys. Commander Mackenzie was allowed to question them, too. Of all the testimony thus elicited, what seems most important is reprinted here, in the order in which it was given.

A word about the text of this testimony. No official transcript was published. It is reprinted here as reported (altogether objectively) by the New York *Tribune,* where it appeared first in the daily edition, then in the *Weekly Tribune* (whose dates are used here), and finally all together in a pamphlet. Other newspapers also carried reports, collation of some of which shows that the *Tribune* gave the testimony more or less *verbatim*, though sometimes running the answers to several questions together as one statement, and sometimes obviously summarizing. (The *Tribune* reporter sometimes put summarized matter within square brackets, which have been retained here. The present editor's insertions are italicized within square brackets.)

The events of the crucial days from November 25 to December 1 are told over and over by different witnesses, and from their various versions we must assemble our picture of what "really" went on. The reader must keep a mental (or written) calendar of days and fit on it a timetable of events. This can be done most easily from Mackenzie's report, with which the testimony of successive witnesses about each event can be matched. The salient events involved are relatively few. As to the facts about them, there is a certain amount of discrepancy in the testimony. As to their significance, there is more fundamental disagreement.

Major questions are these.

The guilt or innocence of the men hanged. Was Spencer, was Small, was Cromwell guilty, exactly as Mackenzie and his officers supposed? If guilty, was their hanging necessary, or might they safely have been brought home for trial? If not guilty, in Mackenzie's sense, then what *was* each of them actually up to?

Their character. What kind of men were they? What are we to make of the actions and motives of each of them, first in a literal way, and then, more subtly, in a psychological way? Was Philip Spencer a dangerous criminal, a juvenile delinquent, a psychiatric case, a foolish and badly misunderstood and mismanaged boy, or merely a high-spirited practical joker? Was Samuel Cromwell a seasoned and desperate villain ready for any extremes, or just a rough, short-tempered, profane sailorman? And Small?

As to Commander Mackenzie, why did he act as he did? Was he a brave and decisive officer who recognized real danger and acted to avert it? Or was he swept into a panic which he communicated to his officers and crew? Or was he a coward, a fool, a bully and sadist, or simply an incredible blunderer?

Was either Spencer or Mackenzie a hero? Was either (or were both) mad?

Questions, too, can be raised about lesser actors, about Lieutenant Gansevoort and about James Wales, the informant, for example.

Such questions indicate only the broad possibilities for labelling the actions and characters of the figures involved.

Again a caution. Though these basic questions arise at once, the answers to them do not—or at least should not be allowed to. Hold up your verdict until the evidence is all before you, and weighed. That is more than most contemporaries could, or would, do.

Already, before the court of inquiry opened, sides had been chosen, as we saw in Part One. Alignments that emerged there continue in this Part. Among the newspapers we still follow the forthrightly pro-Mackenzie *Courier and Enquirer* of James Watson Webb and the sinuously anti-Mackenzie *Herald* of James Gordon Bennett. Behind-scenes rallying of forces is indicated by enough documentation to show its nature: John C. Spencer employs every available means to bring to "justice" the officers who hanged his son; Mackenzie's professional friends move to avert civil reprisal upon him for the "justice" he had meted out in the course of his study. (Here motives are less in question than mechanisms employed.)

In the struggle to sway public opinion, two major champions are enlisted for Mackenzie, both of them legal and literary Bostonians: Charles Sumner and R. H. Dana, Jr. Sumner's major assistance comes later, in Part III. Dana's is rendered in this Part. (Here motives and mechanisms, too, are of interest. Both men, knights in righteous armor, might have been expected to champion justice. But why did they see it as lying on Mackenzie's side?)

On the other side appears an even more eminent literary man. James Fenimore Cooper begins to work up in private letters and conversations his powerful criticism of Mackenzie's course. Already involved in controversy with Mackenzie over another issue, Cooper will hold his fire for over a year. (His motives, too, are a study. He is rather anti-Mackenzie than pro-Spencer. Though trained as a naval officer, and proud of the navy, he does not stand in closed ranks with the officers in defense of the clan.)

From the New York *Weekly Tribune,* December 31, 1842, as reprinted in *Proceedings of the Court of Inquiry* . . . (New York: Greeley & McElrath, 1843), pp. [5]-6.

✓ ✓ ✓

WEDNESDAY, Dec. 28, 1842.

[5] The Court of Inquiry, appointed by the Secretary of the Navy to examine the facts connected with the recent alledged attempt at mutiny on board the U. S. Brig-of-War Somers, met to-day at 11 o'clock A. M

on board the U. S. receiving ship North-Carolina, at the Navy Yard. The Court consists of the following distinguished officers:

The President, Captain CHARLES STEWART, commander of the Home Squadron. . . .

The second member, Commodore A. J. DALLAS, commander of the Pensacola Navy Yard. . . .

The third, Commodore JACOB JONES, Port Admiral, commander of all the vessels afloat in this harbor. His flag ship is the North Carolina, on board of which the Court is held.

The Judge Advocate is Hon. OGDEN HOFFMAN, now U. S. Attorney for this Southern District of New-York. He was formerly attached to the Navy for some years, and was on board the United States with Decatur in his celebrated action about the middle of the last war, in which he captured the frigate Macedonian. . . .

Commander ALEXANDER SLIDELL MACKENZIE of the Somers, appeared in full uniform. He is a man of medium height, with a fine head covered rather thinly by light auburn hair, a high forehead, and of an amiable and pleasing rather than stern and commanding presence.

After administering the oath to the several members of the Court, the Judge Advocate read the warrant from Secretary UPSHUR, constituting the Court, and authorizing it to inquire into all the facts touching the alledged mutiny on board the Somers, and the conduct of Commander MACKENZIE in ordering the execution of Midshipman PHILIP SPENCER and of SAMUEL CROMWELL and ELIJAH SMALL, and *to report to the Department its opinion as to the right and propriety of those proceedings*. . . .

Com. Mackenzie . . . asked leave to be assisted . . . by Mr. John Hone, not as Counsel, but to take minutes of the proceedings. . . .

[6] The following are the names of the crew now in irons, of whom the first four were brought home in irons, and the others arrested immediately on the arrival of the Somers:

Names.	Age.	Born.	Rate.
Daniel McKinley,	20	Boston	Landsman
Benjamin F. Green,	19	Portland	Apprentice
Charles A. Wilson,	22	New York	Sail master's mate
Alexander McKee,	17	Ireland	Apprentice
Chas. J. Goldenham,	18	Boston	do
George W. Warner,	21	New-York	do
Charles Van Velzer,	18	do	do
Richard Hamilton,	17	Philadelphia	do
George Kneavels,	17	New-Haven	do
Edmund Gallia,	22	Malta	Old seaman
Eugene Sullivan,	17	Providence	Apprentice
Henry Wiltham,	23	New-York	Old seaman

. . . The following are the articles of the Naval law of the United States in reference to Mutiny on board of men-of-war:

ARTICLE 24—LAW OF 1789—*Mutiny and Sedition.*

Any officer, seaman, marine, or other person, who shall disobey the orders of his superior, or begin, excite, cause, or join in any mutiny or sedition in the ship to which he belongs, or in any ship or vessel in the service of the United States, on any pretence whatsoever, shall suffer death, or such other punishment as a court martial shall direct; and, farther, any person, in any ship or vessel belonging to the service aforesaid, who shall utter any words of sedition and mutiny, or endeavor to make any mutinous assembly, on any pretence whatsoever, shall suffer such punishment as a court martial shall inflict.

ARTICLE 13—LAW OF 1800.

If any person in the Navy shall make or attempt to make, any mutinous assembly, he shall, on conviction thereof by a court martial, suffer death; and if any person aforesaid shall utter any seditious and mutinous words, or shall conceive or connive at any mutinous or seditious practices, or shall treat with contempt his superior, being in the execution of his office, or, being witness to any mutiny or sedition, shall not do his utmost to suppress it, he shall be punished at the discretion of a court martial.

ARTICLE 14.

No officer or private in the Navy shall disobey the lawful orders of his superior officer, or strike him, or draw, or offer to draw, or raise, any weapon against him while in the execution of the duties of his office, on pain of death, or such other punishment as a court martial shall inflict.

⌁ ⌁ ⌁ From the New York *Herald,* Thursday morning, December 28, 1842, in its account of the first day of the Court of Inquiry.

. . . Captain Mackenzie, in full uniform . . . , is a man of fine intelligent and amiable countenance, and is apparently about forty years of age. He is tall, and thin, and his whole appearance is decidedly prepossessing. His manner was singularly composed and dignified; his entire demeanor indicative of calm but decided resolution. . . .

⌁ ⌁ ⌁ From a letter to the editor, Boston *Courier,* Wednesday, December 28, 1842.

"We regret," says the New-York American, "to see it stated that *the private letters of Mrs. Spencer to her son,* (admonishing him of the consequences of his waywardness) found in his trunk, were among the papers sent to the Navy Department." I regret it likewise, and moreover deem it a shameful violation of the sacred privacy of domestic confidence. . . . Something more than insinuation, has already met my eyes in print, respecting the want of proper management at home, as the cause of such ill conduct in the sons of that unhappy house. . . . Let those happy, prudent parents who are in such cases as this, so ready to "cast the first stone," see to it that their *own conduct* in reference to *their* children is immaculate. . . .

X. Y. Z

From two letters of Lieut. Charles H. Davis * to Charles Sumner, dated New York, December 28, 1842. Reproduced here from the original letters in the Sumner papers, in the Houghton Library ✓ ✓ ✓ of Harvard University, by permission.

I am very desirous of calling your attention to the late mutiny . . . , and of engaging your kind services in behalf of my most gallant, & excellent friend Mackenzie, who despite the correctness of his conduct, will have a great deal to contend against in the influence of young Spencer's friends. . . .

I am sure that it would be in the power of yourself, & [George S.] Hillard . . . to recur easily to any opinions or judgments bearing on this case,—and I make bold, since it is in behalf of a friend, to ask you both to lend your influence through the press to keep the public sentiment in Boston sound, and right upon this subject.

I, as well as your other friends have had occasion to admire the manner in which you have treated public questions of legal interest—a manner characterised by a liberal, comprehensive, and philosophical spirit, & by freedom from technical & professional narrowmindedness— If you would treat this subject in an article in the public prints it would be rendering to M. a most acceptable service—a service which he could not ask, but which I venture to request for him— He is not aware that I am writing this, and were the affair my own I should hesitate to address you— But my love for my friend is my motive, and my apology for writing. He is one who you will not regret having served—

He is not less amiable, than he is brave and honourable—

I venture to transmit to you a short piece which I wish to have inserted in some Boston newspaper— I have perused the documents relating to the mutiny, and have said only what I know to be correct— It is prepared in a great hurry, & I should be pleased to have either H[illard] or yourself make any alteration you please. . . . I have written in the editorial form. . . .

[*Another letter of the same date:*] Since writing you this morning I have seen Mackenzie who tells me that the Secretary of the Navy has requested him to suppress all allusion, in his report, to young Spencer's private letters—

In the piece I sent you this morning I cite those letters, the one from his father forwarding his appt. & at the same time charging him with

---

* Charles H. Davis (1807-1877) was, like his friend Sumner, a Bostonian and a Harvard man. Both rose to later eminence. Davis performed distinguished scientific and war service for the Navy, attaining the rank of rear admiral. Sumner (1811-1874) already known for his scholarly legal publications, was practising law in Boston and lecturing at the Cambridge Law School. In 1851 he succeeded Daniel Webster as U. S. Senator from Massachusetts and became most outspoken of the anti-slavery senators.

stealing from his parent $300, & another in which he confesses himself
"a liar, theif" [*sic*], & villain"— Will you please run your pen through
that sentence— Mackenzie will, in obedience to the Secretary's wishes,
and out of regard to the feelings of the parents withhold all communication
on this point unless it should be necessary—

Commodore Perry told me that Commodore Stewart, the Pres't of the
Court of enquiry asked him for precedents, and legal opinions in cases
similar to this mutiny—

If you can find time to forward to me at this place some legal references
which will bear upon the case you will confer a lasting favour.

The penny-press are engaged in hostility to M—but he is sustained by
the unqualified approbation of all the respectable papers—and of all
respectable individuals—

I am afraid you will charge me with giving you a great deal of trouble—
but my friend's necessities are urgent, & his friends must exert themselves
to secure him a fair hearing before the country, and an enlightened judgment from the Court. . . . Please direct to me to the care of Commodore
M. C. Perry—

> Letter from John C. Spencer to William H. Seward, no date as-
> signed, in *William H. Seward: An Autobiography*. (New York:
> D. Appleton, 1877), p. 646, from which it is here reprinted. Prob-
> ✓ ✓ ✓ able date late December, 1842 or early January, 1843.

I ought sooner to have acknowledged your kind and feeling note of
sympathy in the horrible calamity which has overtaken me and my family.
I now do so, with my grateful assurances of the consolation it has afforded;
but Mrs. S—and myself are well aware that we must look to a higher
than human source for that balm which only can heal the wounds of our
bleeding hearts.

> From a letter of John Lorimer Graham to Silas Stilwell, dated
> Washington, December 29, 1842. Here reproduced from the orig-
> inal letter in the Manuscript Division of the New York Public
> ✓ ✓ ✓ Library, by permission.

Private. . . . I have your letters communicating Mr. [Ogden] Hoffman's views—he has made a mistake—they have been received here with
surprise—as it was supposed he would have at once perceived the object
of the intimation—the kindest feelings were entertained towards him—
As it is, the affair will go in in its present shape, and a fearful responsibility

rests upon the ct. and especially upon Mr. H—. . . . Mr. S. has returned to his office and yesterday resumed his seat at a Cabinet meeting which is said to have been an affecting meeting.

It is altogether advisable that you should not attend the ct. of Enquiry. It is an *ex parte* proceeding—the laws of the Country will be vindicated through the Civil tribunals, where you will participate in having justice done to all concerned. . . .

Entry from the journal of Richard Henry Dana, Jr., Boston, December 29, 1842. Here reprinted from Charles Francis Adams, *Richard Henry Dana* (Boston: Houghton Mifflin, 1890), I, 49.

All the world is talking about the Somers mutiny and the execution of Spencer. The prevailing opinion (I have not met an exception) is that Mackenzie will justify himself. I have little doubt of it.

[*Richard H. Dana, Jr. (1815–1882), like Philip Spencer, James Fenimore Cooper, Herman Melville, and many another young man of good family, had gone to sea as a common sailor. Halfway through Harvard, his health led him to ship on a two-year voyage round Cape Horn to California (1834–1836). In 1840 he gained fame by his account of this voyage in* Two Years Before the Mast. *His explanation of his purpose in this book sheds a curious light on his attitude toward the Somers affair and the part he was soon to play in influencing public opinion:* ". . . *Since Mr. Cooper's* Pilot *and* Red Rover *there have been . . . many stories of sea-life written. . . .* [Almost] *all . . . by persons who have gained their experience as naval officers, or passengers, and of these there are very few which are intended to be taken as narratives of facts. . . . It must . . . be plain to every one that a naval officer, who goes to sea as a gentleman, 'with his gloves on,' as the phrase is, and who associates only with his fellow-officers, and hardly speaks to a sailor except through a boatswain's mate, must take a very different view . . . from that . . . taken by a common sailor. . . . There has been, of late years, a great deal of attention directed toward common seamen, and a strong sympathy awakened in their behalf. Yet I believe that, with* [a] *single exception . . . , there has not been a book . . . by one who has been one of them, and can know what their life really is. A voice from the forecastle has hardly yet been heard. . . ."* (*from the* Preface, *July, 1840). After his voyage, Dana returned to Harvard, was admitted to the bar in 1840, and specialized in admiralty law. In 1841 he published* The Seaman's Friend, *a manual telling sailors of their duties and rights. In the 1850's he became legal champion of fugitive slaves, when to do so took courage in Boston.*]

Commander Alexander Slidell Mackenzie's official report to the
Secretary of the Navy, dated December 19, 1842. The report was
first made public when read at the Court of Inquiry on December
29, 30, 1842. Since contemporary newspaper texts of the report
were incomplete and inaccurate (including that in the New York
Tribune whose report of the Court of Inquiry we are following),
a more accurate text is given. Here reprinted from *Proceedings of
the Naval Court Martial in the Case of Alexander Slidell Mackenzie*
✓ ✓ ✓ . . . (New York: Henry C. Langley, 1844), pp. 194-211.

"U. S. Brig Somers, }
"Dec. 19, 1842. {

[194] "Sir: Since my communication to you of the 14th inst., on which
day I arrived here with the vessel under my command, I have been engaged
in preparing a narrative of the cruise of the Somers, which should embrace
all the facts that might in any way illustrate the late mutiny on board her.
But I have been subjected to so many interruptions, from which it was the
less easy to escape, as they grew out of the sympathy and solicitude of real
friends, and the narrative grew so interminably as I advanced, that I have
deemed it due to the anxiety of the Navy Department, to receive a more
detailed statement of the facts of the mutiny, than I was at first able to
communicate—to break off at once from the elaborate narrative, in which
I was engaged, and confine myself to a statement of the principal occurrences. . . .

"On Saturday, the 26th of November, Lieutenant G. Gansevoort came
into the cabin, and informed me that a conspiracy existed on board of the
brig, to capture her, murder the commander, the officers, and most of the
crew, and convert her into a pirate, and that Acting-Midshipman Philip
Spencer was at the head of it. He stated that Mr. H. M. Heiskill, the purser,
had just informed him that Mr. J. W. Wales, his steward, had approached
him as if to converse on their joint duty, and revealed to him, for the
purpose of its being communicated to the commander the following information.

"The night previous, being that of the 25th of Nov., between the hours
of six and eight, he had been accosted by Mr. Spencer and invited by him
to get up on the booms, as he had something of importance to communicate.
When on the booms Mr. Spencer addressed him as follows: "Do you fear
death? do you fear a dead man? are you afraid to kill a man?" Mr. Wales
thus accosted, and having his curiosity excited, with admirable coolness
induced Mr. Spencer to go on, and took the oath of secrecy which was
administered to him. Mr. Spencer then informed him that he was leagued
with about twenty of the crew, to get possession of the vessel; murder the
commander and officers; choose, from among those of the crew who were
willing to join him, such as would be useful, and murder the rest; and
commence pirating. He mentioned all the details of his plan as you will

find it in the statement of Mr. Wales, and which was well suited to the attainment of his objects; involving much better notions of seamanship, than he was, himself, [195] capable of forming. As one of the inducements to her capture, he stated that a box, containing wine of a rare value, brought off with much care at Madeira, as a present from I. H. Burden, Esq., United States vice-consul at Funchal, to Commodore J. B. Nicholson, contained money or treasure to a large amount.

"It was his object to carry the vessel to the Isle of Pines, where one of his associates, who had been in the business before, had friends; to attack no vessels that he was not sure to capture; to destroy every vestige of the captured vessels, after having removed what was useful; to select such of the female passengers as were suitable, and after they had used them sufficiently to dispose of them. Mr. Spencer also stated that he had the written plan of his project in the back of his cravat, which he would show to Mr. Wales in the morning, after which they separated with terrible threats, on the part of Mr. Spencer, of instant death to Mr. Wales, from himself or his accomplices, should Mr. Wales utter one word of what passed.

"Such was the purport of the information laid before me by Lieutenant Gansevoort, and although he was evidently impressed with the reality of the project, yet, it seemed to me so monstrous, so improbable, that I could not forbear treating it with ridicule. I was under the impression that Mr. Spencer had been reading some piratical stories and had amused himself with Mr. Wales. Still I felt that this was joking on an improper theme, and determined to notice it hereafter. I also considered that duty required me to be on my guard, lest there should be a shadow of reality in this project, and I directed the first lieutenant to watch Mr. Spencer narrowly, without seeming to do so. In the course of the day Lieutenant Gansevoort informed me that Mr. Spencer had been in the wardroom examining a chart of the West Indies. He had asked the passed assistant surgeon some question about the Isle of Pines, and the latter had informed him that it was a place much frequented by pirates and dryly asked him if he had any acquaintances there. He passed the day rather sullenly in one corner of the steerage, as was his custom, engaged in examining a small piece of paper and writing on it with his pencil, and occasionally finding relaxation in working with a penknife at the tail of a devil-fish, one of the joints of which he had formed into a sliding ring for his cravat. Lieutenant Gansevoort also made an excuse of duty to follow him to the foretop, where he found him engaged in having some love-devices tattooed on his arm by Benjamin F. Green, ordinary seaman and apprentice; Lieutenant Gansevoort also learned that he had been endeavoring for some days to ascertain the rate of the chronometer by applying to Midshipman Rogers to whom it was unknown, and who referred him to the master. He had been seen in secret and nightly conferences with boatswain's mate, S. Cromwell, and seaman, Elisha Small. I also heard that he had given money to several of the crew, to Elisha Small on the 12th September, the day before our departure from New York, the same day on which, in reply to Commodore Perry's injunctions to reformation, he had made the most solemn promises of amendment; to Samuel Cromwell on the passage to Madeira; that he had been in the habit of distributing tobacco extensively among the apprentices, in defiance of the orders of the navy department, and my own, often reiterated; that he had corrupted the wardroom steward, caused him to steal brandy from the wardroom mess, which [196] he (Mr. Spencer) had drunk himself, occasionally getting drunk when removed from observation; and had also administered to several of the crew; that, finally, he was in the habit of amusing the crew by making music with his jaw, he had the faculty of throwing his jaw out of joint, and by the contact of the bones playing with accuracy and elegance a variety of airs. Servile in his intercourse with me, when among the crew he loaded me with blasphemous vituperations, and proclaimed that it would be a pleasing task to roll me off the roundhouse, overboard. He had sometime before drawn a brig with a black flag, and asked one of the midshipmen what he thought of it; he had repeatedly asserted in the early part of the cruise that the brig might easily be taken; he had quite recently examined the hand of Midshipman Rogers, told his fortune, and predicted for him a speedy and violent death.

"These various circumstances induced me to look back and recall all that I had heard of, or had observed in, Mr. Spencer. When he reported himself to me for duty at New York, about the 20th of August, I at once gave him my hand and welcomed him on board the Somers. I subsequently heard that he had quite recently been dismissed with disgrace from the Brazilian squadron, and compelled to resign, for drunkenness and scandalous conduct. This fact made me very desirous for his removal from the vessel, chiefly on account of the young men who were to mess with and be associated with him—the rather that two of them were connected with me by blood, and two by alliance, and the four intrusted to my especial care.* The circumstance of Mr. Spencer being a son of a high officer of the government, by enhancing his baseness in my estimation, made me more desirous to be rid of him; on this point, I beg that I may not be misunderstood—I revere authority, I recognise in the exercise of its higher functions in this free country, the evidence of genius, intelligence, and virtue; but I have no respect for a base son of an honored father—on the contrary, I consider that he, who by misconduct sullies the lustre of an honorable name, is more culpable than the unfriended individual whose disgrace falls

---

* The two connected by blood were the Perry boys—Oliver and Matthew Jr.—sons of Mackenzie's sister and her husband, Commodore Perry. The two connected by alliance were Adrian Deslondes, brother of Mackenzie's brother's wife, Mrs. John Slidell; and Henry Rodgers (of the distinguished naval family of Rodgers), to whom Mackenzie was affiliated through the Perrys.

only on himself. I wish, however, to have nothing to do with baseness in any shape—the navy is not the place for it. On these accounts, I readily sought the first opportunity of getting rid of Mr. Spencer. When we were on the eve of sailing, two midshipmen, who had been with me before, and in whom I had confidence, joined the vessel. This carried to seven the number to occupy a space capable of accommodating only five. I had heard that Mr. Spencer had expressed a willingness to be transferred from the Somers to the Grampus. I directed Lieutenant Gansevoort to say to him, that if he would apply to Commodore Perry to detach him (there was no time to communicate with the navy department), I would second the application. He made the application; I seconded it earnestly, urging that it should be granted on the score of the comfort of the young officers. The commodore declined detaching Mr. Spencer, but offered to detach Midshipman Henry Rogers, who had been last ordered. I could not consent to part with Midshipman Rogers, whom I knew to be a seaman, an officer, a gentleman, a young man of high attainment within his profession and beyond it.

"The Somers sailed with seven in her steerage; they could not all sit together round the table. The two oldest and most useful had no locker to put their clothes in, and have slept during the cruise on the steerage-deck, the camp-stools, the booms in the tops, or in the quarter-boats. They have submitted to these inconveniences without a murmur, and performed their duty to my utmost satisfaction.

"I recurred to this recollection; I endeavored to review the conduct of Mr. Spencer throughout the cruise. I had treated Mr. Spencer precisely like the other midshipmen. Perhaps I reproved him less [197] frequently than others for slight deviations from duty; I had little hope of essentially serving one who had been so great an enemy to himself.

"I had observed that he had very little intercourse with the officers, that he was exceedingly intimate with the crew; I had noticed the interchange of a passing joke, as individuals passed by him, a smile never seen but on such occasions, a strange flashing of the eye. These various recollections, added to what had been revealed to me, determined me to make sure at once of his person, though I had before meditated allowing Mr. Wales to have another interview with him that evening, for the purpose of ascertaining more of his plans, as had been agreed upon between them. If he was really in earnest, enough was already known. At evening quarters I ordered, through my clerk, O. H. Perry, doing the duty also of midshipman and aid, all the officers to lay aft on the quarter-deck, excepting the midshipmen stationed on the forecastle. The master was ordered to take the wheel, and those of the crew stationed abaft sent to the mainmast; I approached Mr. Spencer and said to him, 'I learn, Mr. Spencer, that you aspire to the command of the Somers?' With a deferential, but unmoved and gently smiling expression, he replied, 'Oh, no, sir.' 'Did you not tell Mr. Wales, sir, that you had a project to kill the commander, the officers, and a considerable portion of the crew, of this vessel, and convert her into a pirate?' 'I may have told him so, sir, but it was in joke.' 'You admit then that you told him so?' 'Yes, sir; but in joke.' 'This, sir, is joking on a forbidden subject—this joke may cost you your life. Be pleased to remove your neck handkerchief.' It was removed and opened, but nothing was found in it. I asked him what he had done with the papers containing an account of his project which he had told Mr. Wales was in the back of his neck handkerchief. 'It is a paper containing my day's work, and I have destroyed it.' 'It is a singular place to keep day's work in.' 'It is a convenient one,' he replied, with an air of deference and blandness. I said to him, 'You must have been aware that you could only have compassed your designs by passing over my dead body, and after that, the bodies of all the officers; you had given yourself, sir, a great deal to do; it will be necessary for me to confine you, sir.' I turned to Lieut. Gansevoort and said, 'Arrest Mr. Spencer, and put him in double irons.' Mr. Gansevoort stepped forward and took his sword. He was ordered to sit down on the stern-post, double ironed, and, as an additional security, hand-cuffed. I directed Lieut. Gansevoort to watch over his security, to order him to be put to instant death, if he was detected speaking to, or holding intelligence in any way with, any of the crew. He was himself made aware of the nature of these orders. I also directed Lieutenant Gansevoort to see that he had every comfort which his safe-keeping would admit of. In confiding this task to Lieutenant Gansevoort, his kindness and humanity gave me the assurance that it would be zealously attended to; and throughout the period of Mr. Spencer's confinement, Lieut. Gansevoort, while watching his person with an eagle eye, and ready at any movement to take his life, should he forfeit that condition of silence on which his safety depended, attended to all his wants, covered him with his own grego when squalls of rain were passing over, and ministered in every way to his comfort with the tenderness of a woman. Mr. Spencer being confined, the officers were remanded to their quarters, the crew and battery inspected, the ordinary reports made to the first lieutenant, and by him to me, and the retreat beaten. That night the officers of the watch were armed with cutlasses and pistols, and the rounds of both decks made frequently, to see that the crew were in their hammocks, and that there were no suspicious collections of individuals about the decks. On searching the locker of Mr. Spencer, a small razor-case was found, which he had recently drawn with a razor in it from the purser. Instead of the razor, the case was found to contain a small paper rolled in another; on the inner one were strange characters, which proved to be Greek, with which Mr. Spencer was familiar. It fortunately happened that there was another midshipman on board the Somers, who knew Greek, one whose Greek and everything else that he possessed was wholly his, devoted to his country. The Greek characters converted by Midship'n H. Rogers into our own, exhibited well-known names among the crew. The certain, the doubtful, those who were to be kept whether [198] they would or not, arranged in separate rows; those who were to do the work of murder in the various departments, to take the wheel, to open the arm-chest.

"The following day being Sunday, the crew were inspected at quarters at 10 o'clock. I took my station abaft, with the intention of particularly observing Cromwell and Small. The third or master's division, to which they both belonged, always mustered at morning quarters upon the after-part of the quarter-deck, in continuation of the lines formed by the crews of the guns. The persons of both were faultlessly clean; they were determined that their appearance in this respect should provoke no re-proof. Cromwell stood up to his full stature, his muscles braced, his battle-axe grasped resolutely, his cheek pale, but his eye fixed, as if in-differently, at the other side. He had a determined and dangerous air. Small made a very different figure. His appearance was ghastly, he shifted his weight from side to side, and his battle-axe passed from one hand to the other; his eye wandered irresolutely, but never toward mine. I at-tributed his conduct to fear. I have since been led to believe that the business upon which he had entered was repugnant to his nature, though the love of money and of rum had been too strong for his fidelity.

"After quarters the church was rigged. The crew mustered up with their prayerbooks, and took their seats without waiting for all hands to be called, and considerably before five bells, or half past ten, the usual time of divine service. The first lieutenant reported all ready, and asked me if he should call all hands to muster. I told him to wait for the ac-customed hour. Five bells was at length struck, and all hands called to muster. The crew were unusually attentive, and the responses more than commonly audible; the muster succeeded, and I examined very carefully the countenances of the crew, without discovering anything that gave me distrust. In the afternoon, the wind having moderated, skysails and royal-studdingsails were set. In going large, I had always been very particular to have no strain on the light braces leading forward, as the tendency of such a strain was to carry away the light yards and masts. While Ward M. Gagely, one of the best and most skillful of our apprentices, was yet on the main-royal-yard, after setting the main-skysail, a sudden jerk of the weather-main-royal-brace, given by Small and another whose name I have not discovered, carried the top-gallant-mast away in the sheare-hole, sending forward the royal-mast, with royal-skysail, royal studdingsail, main-top-gallant-staysail, and the head of the gaft-topsail. Gagely was on the royal-yard. I scarcely dared to look on the booms or in the larboard gangway, where he should have fallen. For a minute I was in intense agony; in the next I saw the shadow of the boy through the top-gallant-sail, rising rapidly toward the top-gallant-yard, which still remained at the mast-head. Presently he rose to view, descended on the afterside to the topmast-cap, and began to examine with coolness to see what was first to be done to clear the wreck. I did not dream at the time that the carrying away of this mast was the work of treachery; but I knew it was an occasion of this sort, the loss of a boy overboard, or an accident to a spar, creating confusion and interrupting the regularity of duty, which was likely to be taken advantage of by the conspirators, were they still bent on the prosecution of their enterprise. The greatest pains were therefore taken to prevent all confusion: the first lieutenant took the deck; everything connected with the wreck was sent down from aloft, the rigging unrove and coiled down, sails bent afresh to the yards, the spare top-gallant-mast got out and scraped and slushed, and the fid-hole cut, every one employed, and everything made to go on with undeviating regularity. To my astonishment, all those who were most conspicuously named in the programme of Mr. Spencer, no matter in what part of the vessel they might be stationed, mustered at the main-top-mast-head. Whether animated by some new-born zeal in the service of their country, or collected there for the purpose of conspiring, it was not easy to decide; the coincidence confirmed the existence of a dangerous conspiracy, suspended, yet perhaps not abandoned. The eye of Mr. Spencer travelled perpetually to the mast-head, and cast thither many of those strange and stealthy glances which I had heretofore noticed. The wreck being cleared, supper was piped before sending up the new mast; after supper the same persons mustered again at the mast-head, and the top-gallant-mast was fidded, the light yards [199] crossed and the sails set. By this time it was dark, and quarters had been unavoidably dispensed with; still I thought, under the circumstances, that it was scarcely safe to leave Cromwell at large during the night: the night was the season of danger. After consulting Lieutenant Gansevoort, I determined to arrest Cromwell; the moment he reached the deck, an officer was sent to leeward to guard the lee rigging, and the main-stays were also thought of, though not watched; as his voice was heard in the top descending the rigging, I met him at the foot of the jacob's-ladder surrounded by the officers, guided him aft on the quarter-deck and caused him to sit down; on questioning him as to a secret conversation he had held the night before with Mr. Spencer, he denied its being he: he said, "It was not me, sir, it was Small." Cromwell was the *tallest* man on board, and Small the *shortest*. Cromwell was immediately ironed; and Small then pointed out by an associate to increased suspicion, was also sent for, interrogated, and ironed. Increased vigilance was now enjoined upon all the officers; henceforward, all were perpetually armed; either myself or the first lieutenant was always on deck, and generally both of us were.

"On the morning of the following day, being Monday, the 28th November, two crimes of considerable magnitude appeared on the master-at-arms's report of prisoners. Charles Lambert, apprentice, had been guilty of theft, in stealing sinnit for a hat from Ward M. Gagely, and Henry Waltham, the wardroom steward, had stolen brandy from the wardroom mess, and given it to Mr. Spencer. These were vile offences: the present was not a time to bring the discipline of the vessel to a stand, and the prisoners were both punished to the extent of the law. Waltham, while in irons, had the night before told Daniel M'Kinley, who had access to the ward-room as cot-boy, where three bottles of wine could be found, his object being, no doubt, to furnish the means of excitement to the conspirators, to induce them to rise, release Waltham and get possession of the vessel. M'Kinley was down in the programme as certain, and as stationed at the arm-chest. He reported Waltham to the first lieutenant —an extraordinary denunciation under the circumstances, probably occasioned by his desire to relieve himself from suspicion. Waltham having thus, in contempt of discipline, committed a second offence while in confinement, was remanded into irons, to be subjected to a second punishment on the following day. The punishment being over, I thought this a fit opportunity to endeavor to make some impression on the crew. The number of them actually engaged in the conspiracy might not be great: that it was known to a majority of them, I had reason to believe. In general, they might be considered disaffected, and disposed on all occasions to hold back and resist the discipline of the ship; the mysterious agency that had been at work, since our departure from New York, to corrupt the crew, was now disclosed. I commenced by explaining to them the general nature of the project of Mr. Spencer, studiously avoiding to excite any suspicions that I was in the possession of the names of those who were implicated. I was willing, in fact, that the worst of them should repent and hide themselves among the well-disposed portion of the crew. I took care to inform them that the majority of them, whatever might be their inclination, were to share the fate of the officers. I endeavored to divert the minds of the slightly disaffected from the picture of successful vice which Mr. Spencer had presented to them. I alluded to the circumstance, that the most of the crew, unlike crews in general, leaving ties of kindred to render life dear to them, and expressed the hope that within three weeks we should be again among our friends. I thanked God that we had friends to follow us with solicitude and affection; for to have friends, and not to be unworthy of them, was the best guarantee that could be given for truth and fidelity.

"The effect of this upon the crew was various: it filled many with horror at the idea of what they had escaped from: it inspired others with terror at dangers awaiting them from their connexion with the conspiracy. The thoughts of returning to that home and those friends from whom it had been intended to have cut them off forever, caused many of them to weep. I now considered the crew tranquillized and the vessel safe. Having noticed Mr. Spencer's attempt to hold intelligence with the crew, I directed that all the prisoners should be turned with their faces aft. I also directed [200] that no tobacco should be furnished them after the supply they had on their persons when confined should be exhausted. They earnestly begged to be allowed tobacco. I told the first lieutenant to say that Mr. Spencer should have all his mess afforded (and his messmates in fact already took care of that), that the seamen should have their rations as it was allowed by the government, that everything should be supplied to them that was necessary to their health and comfort, but that tobacco was a stimulant, and wished them to tranquillize their minds and remain free from excitement. The day after Mr. Spencer's tobacco was stopped, his spirits gave way entirely. He remained the whole day with his face buried in the grego, and when it was for a moment raised, it was bathed in tears. He was touched by the gentle and untiring attentions of Lieutenant Gansevoort. He told him that he was in no state at that time to speak of anything—when he felt more composed he would tell him all—he would answer any questions that the commander might desire to put to him. On Tuesday, November 29th, immediately after quarters, all hands were again called to witness punishment, and Henry Waltham again punished to the extent of the law for offering the three bottles of wine to Daniel M'Kinley. I again spoke to the crew, urging them to conform to the discipline of the vessel: the orders were all known, and of easy observance. I mentioned that every punishment inflicted must be known to the secretary of the navy, and that the less punishment there was, the more creditable it would be to the commander and the crew. But the whole crew was far from being tranquillized: the most seriously implicated began once more to collect in knots: during the night, seditious words were heard through the vessel, and an insolent and menacing air assumed by many. Some of the petty officers had been sounded by the first lieutenant, and found to be true to their colors: they were under the impression that the vessel was yet far from safe—that there were still many at liberty who ought to be confined—that an outbreak, having for its object the rescue of the prisoners, was seriously contemplated. Various intelligence was from time to time obtained, of conferences among the disaffected: individuals not before supposed to be very deeply implicated, were now found in close association with those who were: several times during the night there were symptoms of an intention to strike some blow. Mr. Wales detected Charles A. Wilson attempting to draw out a handspike from under the launch, with an evident purpose of felling him, and when Wales cocked his pistol and approached, he could only offer some lame excuse for his presence there. I felt more anxious than I had yet done, and remained continually on deck. At 12 o'clock, when the watch was called and mustered, M'Kinley, Green, and others seriously implicated, missed their muster. That they should have been asleep at all that night, was not likely: that they should have missed their muster on that particular occasion, having never done so before, otherwise than intentionally, was impossible. Those who missed their muster had all some lame excuse: there was probably an agreement to meet around the officer of the deck, and commit some act of violence. I heard Green give as an excuse for missing his muster, that he was on deck, but could not get aft for want of room. I immediately went forward, rejected his excuse with some exclamation of impatience, and ordered him to take the look-out forward for four hours, directing the midshipman of the forecastle to watch him closely. The others who had missed their muster were similarly distributed. At 4 o'clock, others of the implicated also missed their muster. I could not contemplate this growth of disaffection without serious uneasiness. Where was this thing to end? Each new arrest of prisoners seemed to bring a fresh set of conspirators forward, to occupy the first place. With fine weather and bright nights, there was already a disposition to make an attack and rescue the prisoners. When bad weather should call off the attention of the officers—when the well-disposed portion of the crew should be occupied in shortening sail, and utter darkness should withdraw everything from view, how great the probability of a rescue. If the most deeply implicated were ironed, would all the dangerous be in custody? What sympathy might not be excited by the suffering of the prisoners? These grave considerations, the deep sense I had of the solemn obligation I was under to protect and defend the vessel which had been intrusted to me, and the lives of the officers and crew—the seas traversed by our peaceful merchantmen, and [201] the unarmed of all nations using the highways of the seas from the horrors which the conspirators had meditated, and above all to guard from violation the sanctity of the American flag displayed from the masthead of one of its cruisers—all impressed upon me the absolute necessity of adopting immediately some further measures for the security of the vessel. Hitherto I had consulted the first lieutenant only, and had been justified in everything I had done by finding his opinions identical with my own. In so grave a case, however, I was desirous of having the opinion of all the officers, and was particularly anxious that no shadow of doubt should remain as to the guilt of either of the prisoners, should their execution be deemed necessary. Under these circumstances, I addressed the following letter to all the officers on board excepting the acting-midshipmen. Though they had done men's duty in the late transaction, they were still boys: their opinion could add but little force to that of the other officers: it would have been hard, at their early age, to call upon them to say whether three of their fellow-creatures should live or die.

" 'U. S. BRIG SOMERS,
" 'Nov. 30, 1842.

" 'GENTLEMEN: The time has arrived when I am desirous of availing myself of your council in the responsible position in which, as commander of this vessel, I find myself placed. You are aware of the circumstances which have resulted in the confinement of Midshipman Philip Spencer, Boatswain's Mate Samuel Cromwell, and Seaman E. Small, as prisoners, and I purposely abstain from entering into any details of them, necessarily ignorant of the exact extent of disaffection among a crew which has so long and so systematically and assiduously been tampered with by *an officer*. Knowing that suspicions of the gravest nature attach to persons still at large, and whom the difficulty of taking care of the prisoners we already have, makes me more reluctant than I should otherwise be to apprehend, I have determined to address myself to you, and to ask your united council as to the best course to be now pursued, and I call upon you to take into deliberate and dispassionate consideration the present condition of the vessel, and the contingencies of every nature that the future may embrace, throughout the remainder of our cruise, and enlighten me with your opinion as to the best course to be pursued.

" 'I am, very respectfully, gentlemen, your most obedient,

" 'ALEX SLIDELL MACKENZIE,

" '*Commander.*

" 'To Lieutenant Guert Gansevoort, Passed-Assistant Surgeon R. W. Leacock, Purser H. M. Heiskill, Acting-Master M. C. Perry, Midshipman Henry Rogers, Midshipman Egbert Thompson, Midshipman Chas. W. Hayes.'

"After I had written the letter to the officers, but before I had sent it, 9 o'clock of Wednesday morning the 30th of November had arrived, and with it the customary morning quarters. Wilson having failed in his attempt to get up an outbreak in the night, and finding himself narrowly watched, and feeling indeed that he could be no longer left at large, had come forward with some lame and absurd confession, and the request that he should not be ironed. I immediately told him that, if he would make a real confession, he should not be molested, and that it was only an insult to offer me such a lame story as that which had been already reported to me by Lieutenant Gansevoort. Nothing more could be got from him, and at quarters he was ironed. In his sail-bag was found an African knife of an extraordinary shape—short, and gradually spreading in breadth, sharp on both sides; it was of no use for any honest purpose; it was fit only to kill; it had been secretly sharpened, by his own confession, the day before with a file to a perfect edge. He had begun also to sharpen his battle-axe with the same assistant; one part of it he had brought to an edge. The sharpening of battle-axes had never been allowed or practised on board of the Somers. M'Kinley, also down among the certain, and beyond a doubt correctly, was now arrested. Hitherto he had kept at large by his admirable steadiness and command of countenance. He is, in fact, the individual who, if the mutiny had been successful, would have made way with all his competitors and risen to the command.

"Remembering Green's demeanor during the past night, I sent for him, interrogated him, and ironed him. Alexander M'Kee, who was to have taken the wheel, and who [202] was entirely in the confidence of Cromwell, was also ironed. These individuals were made to sit down as they were taken; and when they were ironed, I walked deliberately round the battery, followed by the first lieutenant, and we made together a very careful inspection of the crew. Those who (though known to be very guilty) were considered to be the least dangerous, were called out and interrogated; care was taken not to awaken the suspicions of such as from courage and energy were really formidable, unless it were intended to arrest them. Our prisoners now amounted to seven, filling up the quarter-deck, and rendering it very difficult to keep them from communicating with each other, interfering essentially with the management of the vessel. The last prisoners taken were those to whom reference is made in my letter to the officers, written before, but not sent until after their captures. On the receipt of my letter, the officers immediately assembled in the wardroom and commenced the examination of witnesses; the witnesses were duly sworn, and the testimony accurately written down; in addition to the oath, each witness signed the evidence which he had given, after it had been read over to him. The officers passed the whole day in this occupation without interruption and without food. I remained in charge of the deck, with the three young midshipmen, on constant duty; the officers were excused from evening quarters. At nightfall, orders were sent to them to discontinue their deliberations and resume their watches, as the present safety of the vessel must be attended to.

"The risks and uncertainty of the preceding night had determined me that another such should not be passed. I drew up a watch-bill of all the officers, idlers included, dividing them into two watches, and assigning to each a separate station in different parts of the vessel. I took charge of the starboard watch myself, and assigned the larboard to the first lieutenant. This brought me with two watches on deck, but the first lieutenant had been as much on duty as myself; even this, however, was a great relief, as I obtained at intervals, during the midwatch, an hour or two of refreshing sleep.

"In the course of the morning of Thursday, the 1st of December, the first lieutenant presented to me the following letter, in answer to that which I had addressed the previous morning to the officers:—

> " 'U. S. BRIG SOMERS,
> " 'Dec. 1, 1842.

" 'SIR: In answer to your letter of yesterday, requesting our counsel as to the best course to be pursued with the prisoners, Acting-Midshipman Philip Spencer, Boatswain's Mate Samuel Cromwell, and Seaman Elisha Small, we would state, that the evidence which has come to our knowledge is of such a nature as, after as dispassionate and deliberate a consideration of the case as the exigencies of the time would admit, we have come to a cool, decided, and unanimous opinion, that they have been guilty of a full and determined intention to commit a mutiny on board of this vessel of a most atrocious nature; and that the revelation of circumstances having made it necessary to confine others with them, the uncertainty as to what extent they are leagued with others still at large, the impossibility of guarding against the contingencies which 'a day or an hour may bring forth,' we are convinced that it would be impossible to carry them to the United States, and that the safety of the public property, the lives of ourselves, and of those committed to our charge, require that (giving them sufficient time to prepare) they should be put to death, in a manner best calculated as an example to make a beneficial impression upon the disaffected. This opinion we give, bearing in mind our duty to our God, our country, and to the service.

" 'We are, sir, very respectfully, your obedient servants,

" 'GUERT GANSEVOORT, *Lieutenant,*

" 'R. W. LEECOCK, *Pas'd Ass. Surg'n,*

" 'H. M. HEISKILL, *Purser,*

" 'M. C. PERRY, *Act'g Master,*

" 'HENRY ROGERS, *Midshipman,*

" 'EGBERT THOMPSON, *Midshipman,*

" 'CHAS. W. HAYS, *Midshipman.*'

"I at once concurred in the justice of this opinion, and in the necessity of carrying its recommendation into immediate effect.* There were two others of the conspirators almost as guilty, so far as the intention was concerned, as the three ringleaders, who had been first confined, and to whose cases the attention of the officers had [203] been invited; but they could be kept in confinement without extreme danger to the ultimate safety of the vessel. The three chief conspirators alone were capable of navigating and sailing her. By their removal, the motive to a rescue, capture, and carrying out of the original design of piracy, was at once taken away. Their lives were justly forfeited to the country which they had betrayed, and the interests of that country, and the honor and security of its flag, required that the sacrifice, however painful, should be made. In the necessities of my position I found my law, and in them also I must trust to find my justification. I had for a day or two been disposed to arm the petty officers; on this subject alone the first lieutenant differed from me in opinion, influenced in some degree by the opinion of some of the petty officers themselves, who thought that, in the peculiar state of the vessel, the commander and officers could not tell whom to trust, and therefore had better trust no one. I had made up my own mind, reasoning more from the probabilities of the case than from my knowledge of their characters (which was necessarily less intimate than that of the first lieutenant), that they could be trusted, and determined to arm them. I directed the

* In his earliest report, of December 5, Mackenzie stated, "I had before made up my own mind on the subject, and determined if necessary to do without counsel what I knew to be necessary to my duty to the flag and vessel entrusted to my keeping." (*National Archives, Navy Branch.*)

first lieutenant to muster them on the quarter-deck, to issue to each a cutlass, pistol, and cartridge-box, and to report to me when they were armed. I then addressed them as follows: 'My lads, you are to look at me, to obey my orders, and to see my orders obeyed. Go forward.'

"I gave orders to make immediate preparations for hanging the three principal criminals at the main-yard arms; all hands were now called to witness punishment. The after-guard and idlers of both watches, were mustered on the quarter-deck at the whip intended for Mr. Spencer; the forecastle men and foretopmen at that of Cromwell, to whose corruption they had been chiefly exposed; the maintopmen of both watches at that intended for Small, who for a month or more had held the situation of captain of the maintop. The officers were stationed about the decks according to the watch-bill I had made out the night before, and the petty officers were similarly distributed, with orders to cut down whoever should let go the whip with even one hand, or fail to haul on it when ordered. The ensign and pendant being bent on and ready for hoisting, I now put on my full uniform and proceeded to execute the most painful duty that has ever devolved on an American commander—that of an announcing to the criminals their fate. I informed Mr. Spencer that when he had been about to take my life, and dishonor me as an officer when in the execution of my rightful duty, without cause of offence to him, on speculation; it had been his intentions to remove me suddenly from the world in the darkness of night, in my sleep, without a moment to utter one murmur of affection to my wife and children, one prayer for their welfare. His life was now forfeited to his country, and the necessities of the case, growing out of his corruption of the crew, compelled me to take it. I would not, however, imitate his intended example, as to the manner of claiming the sacrifice. If there yet remained to him one feeling true to nature, it should be gratified. If he had any word to send to his parents, it should be recorded and faithfully delivered. Ten minutes should be granted him for this purpose, and Midshipman E. Thompson was called to note the time, and inform me when the ten minutes had elapsed.

This intimation overcame him entirely. He sank, with tears, upon his knees and said he was not fit to die. I repeated to him his own catechism, and begged him at least to let the officer set, to the men he had corrupted and seduced, the example of dying with decorum.

This immediately restored him to entire self-possession; and, while he was engaged in prayer, I went and made in succession the same communication to Cromwell, and Small. Cromwell fell upon his knees completely unmanned, protested his innocence, and invoked the name of his wife. Mr. Spencer said to me, "As these are the last words I have to say, I trust they will be believed, Cromwell is innocent." The evidence had been conclusive, yet I was staggered. I sent for Lieutenant Gansevoort and consulted him, he said there was not a shadow of doubt. I told him to consult the petty officers. He was condemned by acclamation by the petty officers. He was the one man of whom they had real apprehensions; the accomplice at first, and afterward [204] the urger on of Mr. Spencer, who had trained him to the act by which he intended to benefit.

I returned to Mr. Spencer; I explained to him how Cromwell had made use of him; I told him that remarks had been made about the two not very flattering to him, and which he might not care to hear; which showed the relative share ascribed to each of them in the contemplated transaction. He expressed great anxiety to hear what was said. One had told the first lieutenant "In my opinion, sir, you have the damned fool on the larboard arm-chest, and the damned villain on the starboard;" another had remarked that after the vessel should have been captured by Mr. Spencer, Cromwell might allow him to live, provided he made himself useful; he would probably make him his secretary. I remarked, "I do not think this would have suited your temper." This effectually aroused him, his countenance assumed a demonaical expression; he said no more of the innocence of Cromwell; subsequent circumstances too surely confirm his admission of his guilt. He might, perhaps, have wished to save him in fulfilment of some mutual oath. He more probably hoped he might yet get possession of the vessel and carry out the scheme of murder and outrage matured between them. It was on Cromwell that he had apparently trusted in fulfilment of some agreement for a rescue, and eloquently pleaded to Lieutenant Gansevoort, when Cromwell was ironed for his release, as altogether ignorant of his designs and innocent. He had endeavored to make of the E. Andrews appearing on the list of the certain, an alias for Small, though his name, as Small, also appeared in the list among those to effect the murder in the cabin, by falsely asserting that Small was a feigned name, when we had evidence in a letter addressed by Small's mother to him, that Small was her name as well as his. Small alone, whom we had set down as the poltroon of the three, and on that account had, at first determined not to iron, received the announcement of his fate with composure. When asked if he had any preparation to make, any message to send, he said, 'I have nobody to care for me but my poor old mother, and I would rather that she should not know how I have died.'

"I returned to Mr. Spencer and asked him if he had no message to send to his friends; he answered, 'None that they would wish to receive.' When urged still farther to send some words of consolation in so great an affliction, he said, 'Tell them I die wishing them every blessing and happiness; I deserve death for this and many other crimes—there are few crimes that I have not committed; I feel sincerely penitent, and my only fear of death is that my repentance may be too late.' I asked him if there was any one whom he had injured to whom he could yet make reparation—any one who was suffering obloquy for crimes which he had committed; he made no answer, but soon after continued, 'I have wronged many persons, but chiefly my parents;' he said, 'this will kill my poor mother.' I was not before aware that he had a mother; when recovered from the pain of this announcement, I asked him if it would not have been still more dreadful had he succeeded in his attempt, murdered the officers and the greater part of the crew of the vessel, and run that career of crime which with so much satisfaction he had marked out for himself; he replied, after a pause, 'I do not know what would have become of me had I succeeded.' I told him that Cromwell would soon have made way with him, and M'Kinley probably have cleared the whole of them from his path. 'I fear,' said he, 'this may injure my father.' I told him it was almost too late to think of that—that had he succeeded in his wishes, it would have injured his father much more—that had it been possible to have taken him home, as I intended to do, it was not in nature that his father should not have interfered to save him—that for those who have friends or money in America there was no punishment for the worst of crimes *—that though this had nothing to do with my determination, which had been forced upon me in spite of every effort which I had made to avert it, I on this account the less regretted the dilemma in which I was placed; it would injure his father a great deal more, if he got home alive, should he be condemned and yet escape; the best and only service he could do his father was to die. 'I will tell you frankly,' he said, 'what I intended to do had I got home—I [205] should have attempted to escape; I had the same project on board the John Adams and Potomac—it seemed to be a mania with me.' 'Do you not think,' I asked, 'that this is a mania which should be discouraged in the navy?' 'I do, most certainly.' Afterward he said to me, 'But have you not formed an exaggerated estimate of the extent of this conspiracy?' I told him 'No,' that his systematic efforts to corrupt the crew and prepare them for the indulgence of every evil passion; since the day before our departure from New York, had been but too successful. I knew that the conspiracy was still extensive—I did not know how extensive. I recapitulated to him the arts which he had used; he was startled by my telling him that he had made the wardroom steward steal brandy and had given it to the crew; he said, 'I did not make him steal it;' I told him it was brought at his request—that he knew where it came from—it was, if possible, more criminal to seduce another to commit crime than to commit crime one's self; he admitted the justice of this view. He turned again to say to me, 'But are you not going too far—are you not fast? does the law entirely justify you?' I replied that he had not consulted me in making his arrangements—that his opinion could not be an unprejudiced one—that I had consulted all his brother officers, his messmates included, except the boys, and I placed before him their opinion. He stated that it was just, that he deserved death; he asked me what was the manner of death; I explained it to him; he objected to it and asked to be shot; I told him that I could not make any distinction between him and those whom he had corrupted;

---

* Perhaps this was an extreme and erroneous opinion, which I do not attempt to justify; I am only faithfully recording what passed on the occasion.

he admitted that this also was just; he objected to the shortness of the time for preparation, and asked for an hour; no answer was made to this request, but he was not hurried, and more than the hour he asked for was allowed to elapse. He requested that his face might be covered; this was readily granted, and he was asked what it should be covered with; he did not care; a handkerchief was sought for in his locker, none but a black one found, and this brought for the purpose.

I now ordered that the other criminals should be consulted as to their wishes in this particular; they joined in the request, and frocks were taken from their bags to cover their heads. Mr. Spencer asked to have his irons removed; this could not be granted: he asked for a bible and prayer-book; they were brought, and others ordered to be furnished to his accomplices. 'I am a believer,' he said—'do you think that repentance at this late hour can be accepted?' I called to his recollection the case of the penitent thief who was pardoned by our Savior upon the cross. He then read in the Bible, kneeled down and read in the prayer-book; he again asked if I thought that his repentance could be accepted—that the time was so short, and he did not know if he really was changed. I told him that GOD, who was all-merciful as well as all-wise, could not only understand the difficulties of his situation, but extend to him such a measure of mercy as his necessities might require. He said, 'I beg your forgiveness for what I have meditated against you.' I gave him my hand, and assured him of my sincere forgiveness; I asked him if I had ever done anything to him to make him seek my life, or whether the hatred he had conceived for me, and of which I had only recently become aware, was fostered for the purpose of giving himself some plea of justification. He said, 'It was only a fancy—perhaps there might have been something in your manner which offended me.' He read over what I had written down: I had stated hurriedly in the third person, 'He excused himself by saying that he had entertained the same idea in the John Adams and Potomac.' He asked that that might be corrected—'I did not offer it as an excuse, I only stated it as a fact.' More than an hour had now elapsed during the continuance of this scene; the petty officers had been assigned according to rank, to conduct the several prisoners to the gangway; at the break of the quarter-deck is a narrow passage between the trunk and pumpwell—Mr. Spencer and Cromwell met exactly on either side. I directed Cromwell to stop, to allow Mr. Spencer to pass first; at this moment Mr. Spencer himself paused and asked to be allowed to see Mr. Wales; he was called, and Cromwell now passed on, almost touching Mr. Spencer. Not one word was now said by Mr. Spencer of the innocence of Cromwell: no appeal was made by Cromwell to Mr. Spencer to attest his innocence. When Mr. Wales came up, Mr. Spencer extending [206] his hand to him, said, 'Mr. Wales, I earnestly hope you will forgive me for tampering with your fidelity.' Mr. Spencer was wholly unmoved, Mr. Wales almost overcome with emotion; he replied, 'I do forgive you from the bottom of my heart, and I hope that

God may forgive you also. 'Farewell,' exclaimed Mr. Spencer, and Mr. Wales, weeping and causing others to weep, responded 'Farewell.' Mr. Spencer now passed on; about this time he asked for Midshipman Rogers; the message was carried to Mr. Rogers, but he had no orders to leave his station: I was only afterward aware of the request. At the gangway Mr. Spencer met Small with the same calm manner, but with a nearer approach to emotion; he placed himself in front of Small, extended his hand and said, 'Small, forgive me for leading you into this trouble.' Small drew back with horror—'No, by God! Mr. Spencer, I can't forgive you.' On a repetition of the request, Small exclaimed in a searching voice, 'Ah! Mr. Spencer, that is a hard thing for you to ask me; we shall soon be before the face of God, and there we shall know all about it.' 'You must forgive me, Small—I can not die without your forgiveness.' I went to Small and urged him to be more generous—that this was no time for resentment. He relented at once, held out his hand to take the still-extended hand of Mr. Spencer, and said with frankness and emotion, 'I do forgive you, Mr. Spencer; may God Almighty forgive you, also!' Small now asked my forgiveness; he was the one, of the three, who was most entitled to compassion; I took his hand, and expressed my complete forgiveness in the strongest terms that I was able; I asked him what I had ever said or done to him to make him seek my life, conscious of no injustice or provocation of any sort: I felt that it was yet necessary to my comfort to receive the assurance from his own lips. If any wrong had been done him—if any word of harshness, in the impatience or excitement of duty, had escaped me, I was ready myself to ask also for forgiveness. I had hardly asked the question before he exclaimed, 'What have you done to me, Captain Mackenzie? what have you done to me, sir?—nothing, but treat me like a man.' I told him, in justification of the course which I was pursuing, that I had high responsibilities to fulfil—that there were duties that I owed to the government which had intrusted me with this vessel—to the officers placed under my command—to those boys whom it was intended either to put to death, or reserve for a fate more deplorable: there was yet a higher duty to the flag of my country. He was touched by this: 'You are right, sir; you are doing your duty, and I honor you for it; God bless that flag and prosper it! Now, brother topmates,' he said, turning to those who held the whip, 'give me a quick and easy death.' He was placed on the hammocks forward of the gangway, with his face inboard. Mr. Spencer was similarly placed abaft the gangway, and Cromwell also on the other side.

"Mr. Spencer, about this time, sent for Lieut. Gansevoort, and told him that he might have heard that his courage had been doubted, he wished him to bear testimony that he died like a brave man. He then asked me what was to be the signal of the execution. I told him that being desirous to hoist the colors at the moment of execution, at once to give solemnity to the act and to indicate that by it the colors of the Somers were fixed to the mast head, I had intended to beat the call as for hoisting the colors, then roll off, and at the third roll fire a gun. He asked to be allowed himself to give the word to fire the gun; I acceded to the request, and the drum and fife were dismissed. He asked if the gun was under him; I told him it was next but one to him. He begged that no interval might elapse between giving the word, and firing the gun. I asked if they were firing with the lock and wafer, which had always proved quick and sure, but was told that they had a tube and priming, and were prepared to fire with a match; some delay would have been necessary to have opened the arm-chest, and get out a wafer, I ordered a supply of live coal to be passed aft from the galley, and fresh ones perpetually supplied; then assured him there would be no delay. Time still wearing away in this manner, Small requested leave to address the crew. Mr. Spencer having leave to give the word, was asked if he would consent to the delay. He assented, and Small's face being uncovered, he spoke as follows—'Shipmates and topmates, take warning by my example; I never was a pirate, I never killed a man; it's for saying that I would do it, that I am [207] about to depart this life; see what a word will do. It was going in a Guinea-man that brought me to this; beware of a Guinea-man.' He turned to Mr. Spencer, and said to him, 'I am now ready to die, Mr. Spencer, are you?'

"Cromwell's last words were, 'Tell my wife I die an innocent man; tell Lieut. Morris, I die an innocent man.' But it had been the game of this man to appear innocent, to urge Mr. Spencer on, to furnish him with professional ideas, to bring about a catastrophe, of which Mr. Spencer was to take all the risk, and from which he, Cromwell, was to derive all the benefit. He had taken a great many precautions to appear innocent, but he had not taken enough. I now placed myself on the trunk, in a situation from which my eye could take in everything. I waited for some time, but no word was given. At length Browning saluted me, and said, 'Mr. Spencer says he can not give the word; he wishes the commander to give the word himself.' The word was accordingly given, and the execution took place. The crew were now ordered aft, and I addressed them from the trunk on which I was standing. I called their attention first, to the fate of the unfortunate young man, whose ill-regulated ambition, directed to the most infamous end, had been the exciting cause of the tragedy they had just witnessed. I spoke of his honored parents, of his distinguished father, whose talents and character had raised him to one of the highest stations in the land, to be one of the six appointed counsellors of the representation of our national sovereignty. I spoke of the distinguished social position to which this young man had been born, of the advantages of every sort, that attended the outset of his career; and of the professional honors to which a long, steady, and faithful perseverance in the course of duty, might ultimately have raised him. After a few months' service at sea most wretchedly employed, so far as the acquisition of professional knowledge was concerned, he had aspired to supplant me in command, which I had only reached after nearly thirty years of faithful servitude, and for what object I had already explained to them. I told them that their future fortunes were within their own control; they had advantages of every sort, and in an eminent degree, for the attainment of professional knowledge. The situations of warrant officers, and of masters in the navy, were open to them. They might rise to command in the merchant service—to respectability, competence, and to fortune. But they must advance regularly, and step by step; every step, to be sure, must be guided by truth, honor, and fidelity. I called their attention to Cromwell's case; he must have received an excellent education; his handwriting was even elegant; but he had also fallen through brutish sensuality, and the greedy thirst for gold. The first fifteen dollars given to him by Mr. Spencer, had bought him; and the hope of plunder held out to him by Mr. Spencer, who, to completely win him, had converted a box of old wine into treasure, had secured the purchase. There was an anecdote told by Collins in his mess, which, with Cromwell's commentary, had reached my ears. I caused Collins to stand up on the pumpwell, and relate it to the boys. Collins had been in an Indiaman, on board of which the supercargo, a Mr. Thorndyke, had brought a keg of doubloons. Collins stowed it in the run, and was alone intrusted with the secret of its being on board. He said not a word about it, until it went ashore. Cromwell, on hearing this, laughed at Collins, and said, had the case been his he would have run away with the keg. The story, and what had passed before their eyes, contained all the moral that it was necessary to enforce. I told the boys, in conclusion, that they had only to choose between the morality of Cromwell and that of Collins—Cromwell at the yard-arm, and Collins piping with his call. Small had also been born for better things. He had enjoyed the benefits of education, was a navigator, had been an officer in a merchantman, but he could not resist the brandy which had been proffered to him, nor the prospect of dishonorable gain; he had, however, at least died invoking blessings on the flag of his country. The crew were now piped down from witnessing punishment, and all hands called to cheer the ship. I gave the order, 'Stand by, to give three hearty cheers for the flag of our country;' never were three heartier cheers given. In that electric moment, I do not doubt that the patriotism of even the worst of the conspirators, for an instant, broke forth. I felt that I once more was completely commander of the vessel that was intrusted to me, [208] equal to do with her whatever the honor of my country might require. The crew were now piped down, and piped to dinner. I noticed with pain, that many of the boys, as they looked at the yard-arm, indulged in laughter and derision. I still earnestly desired that Mr. Spencer should be buried as officers usually are, in a coffin. I ordered one to be forthwith made from a portion of the birth-deck; but Lieut. Gansevoort having offered to relinquish two mess-chests, used instead of a ward-room stores-room, they were soon converted into a substantial coffin.

"When the hour usually given to the crew's dinner was over, the watch was set and the bodies lowered from the yard-arms and received by the messmates of the deceased, to be decently laid out for burial, the midshipmen assisting in person. When all was ready, the first lieutenant invited me to accompany him, to see that these duties had been duly performed. Mr. Spencer was laid out on the starboard arm-chest, dressed in complete uniform, except the sword, which he had forfeited the right to wear. Further forward, the two seamen were also laid out with neatness. I noticed with pain that the taste of one of the sailors had led him to bind the hands of Cromwell with a riband, having on it, in gold letters, the name of that chivalrous Somers who had died a self-devoted victim in the cause of his country. But that particular badge had been dishonored by the treason of its wearer, and it was suffered to remain. Traces of a sabre-cut were visible on his forehead, and on the removal of his hair, four or five more were discovered, indicating that he had been where wounds had been given and received. Cromwell, by his own admission, had been in a slaver, and had been an inmate of the Moro Castle at Havana. It was the general impression of the honest part of the crew, that he had already been a pirate. He only could answer to the description of the individual alluded to by Mr. Spencer as having been 'already in the business.'

"At this moment a sudden squall sprung up, making it necessary to reduce sail; it was attended by heavy rain, and tarpaulins were hastily thrown over the corpses. The squall over, the sailors were sewed up in their hammocks—the body of Mr. Spencer was placed in the coffin. The three corpses, arranged according to rank, Mr. Spencer aft, were placed along the deck. All hands were now called to bury the dead, the procession was formed according to rank; reversed of the colors which had continued to fly, the ensign was lowered to half-mast. Before the corpses had been placed on the lee, hammock-sails were ready for lowering overboard. The night had already set in; all the battle-lanterns, and the other lanterns in the vessel, were lighted and distributed among the crew. Collected, with their prayer-books, on the booms, in the gangways, and lee-quarter-boat, the service was then read, the responses audibly and devoutly made by the officers and crew, and the bodies consigned to the deep. This office was closed with that prayer, so appropriate to our situations, appointed to be read in our ships-of-war—'Preserve us from the dangers of the sea and from the violence of enemies, that we may be a safeguard unto the United States of America, and a security for such as pass on the seas upon their lawful occasions; that the inhabitants of our land may in peace and quietness serve thee, our God: and that we may return in safety to enjoy the blessings of the land with the fruit of our labor, and with a thankful remembrance of thy mercies, to praise and glorify thy holy name, through Jesus Christ, our Lord.' In reading this, and recollecting the uses to which the Somers had been destined, as I now find, before she quitted the

United States, I could not but humbly hope that divine sanction would not be wanting to the deed of that day.

"As the last transaction connected with this subject, I may mention that on the following Sunday, being the 4th December, after the laws for the government of the navy had been read, according to our invariable custom in the Somers, on the first Sunday of the month, I took occasion to draw from the past history and example of the criminals whose execution they had so recently beheld, all the useful lessons that they afforded, to win back to the paths of duty and virtue the youthful crew which they had been so instrumental in leading astray. I showed how the leader in the projected mutiny had turned aside from the example of his honored parents, and trampled on the wise counsels and solemn warnings which had been lavished on him. In the Bible of poor Small, I had found a letter [209] to him from his aged mother, filled with affectionate endearment and pious counsel. She expressed the joy with which she had learned from him that he was so happy on board the Somers (at that time Mr. Spencer had not joined her), that no grog was served on board of her. Within the folds of this sacred volume, he had preserved a copy of verses, taken from the 'Sailor's Magazine,' enforcing the value of the Bible to seamen. I read these verses to the crew. Small had evidently valued his Bible, but he could not resist temptation. I urged upon the youthful sailors to cherish their Bibles with a more entire love than Small had done—to value their prayer-books also; they would find in them a prayer for every necessity, however great—a medicine for every ailment of the mind. I endeavored to call to their recollection the terror with which the three malefactors had found themselves suddenly called to enter the presence of an offended God. No one who had witnessed that scene, could for a moment believe even in the existence of such a feeling as *honest* atheism—a disbelief in the existence of a God. They should also remember that Mr. Spencer, in his last moments, had said that he had wronged many people, but chiefly his parents. From these two circumstances they might draw two useful lessons—a lesson of filial piety, and a piety toward God: with these two principles for their guide, they could never go astray. In conclusion I told them that they had shown that they could give cheers for their country—they should now give cheers for their God, for they would do this when they sang praises to his name (the colors were now hoisted); and, above the American ensign, the only banner to which it may give place, the banner of the cross. The hundredth Psalm was now sung by all the officers and crew, after which the usual service followed. When it was over, I could not avoid contrasting the spectacle presented on that day by the Somers, with what it would have been had she been in pirate's hands.

"But on this subject I forbear to enlarge; I would not have described this scene at all, so different from the ordinary topics of an official communication, but for the unwonted circumstances in which we were placed, and the marked effect which it produced on the ship's company—even on those deeply guilty members of it who sat manacled behind me, and that it was considered to have done much toward restoring the allegiance of the crew.

"In closing this report, a pleasing yet solemn duty devolves upon me, which I feel unable adequately to fulfil—to do justice to the noble conduct of every one of the officers of the Somers, from the first lieutenant to the commander's clerk, who has also, since her equipment, performed the duty of midshipman. Throughout the whole duration of the difficulties in which we have been involved, their conduct has been courageous, determined, calmly self-possessed—animated and upheld always by a lofty and chivalrous patriotism, perpetually armed by day and by night, waking and sleeping, with pistols often cocked for hours together. The single accidental explosion which took place was from a very delicate weapon, a repeating pistol, in the hand of the first lieutenant, when I was arresting Cromwell in the night. I can not forbear to speak particularly of Lieut. Gansevoort. Next to me in rank on board the Somers, he was my equal in every exertion to protect and defend her. The perfect harmony of our opinions, and of our views of what should be done, on each new development of the dangers that menaced the integrity of command, gave us a unity of action that added materially to our strength. Never since the existence of our navy has a commanding officer been more ably and zealously seconded by his first lieutenant. Where all, without exception, have behaved admirably, it might seem invidious to particularize; yet I can not refrain from calling your attention to the noble conduct of Purser H. W. Heiskill, and of Passed Assistant-Surgeon R. W. Leecock, for the services which they so freely yielded beyond the sphere of their regular duties. Both moreover were in delicate health. Assistant-Surgeon Leecock was, indeed, in no condition to go to sea when he joined the Somers. He had recently returned in the Dolphin from the coast of Africa, where his constitution had been completely shattered by a fever contracted in the river Muny. He came however to his duty, determined and apparently likely to die at his post. He has partially recovered, but is still in delicate health. Both he and Mr. Heiskill cheerfully obeyed my orders to go perpetually armed, to keep a regular watch, to guard the prisoners; the worst weather [210] could not drive them from their posts, or draw from them a murmur.

"I respectfully request that the thanks of the navy department may be presented to all the officers of the Somers, for their exertions in the critical situation in which she has been placed. It is true that they have but performed their duty, but they have performed it with fidelity and zeal.

"If it shall be proved that, when solemnly called upon by me, they gave an erroneous opinion, that opinion involved no official responsibility —the opinion was theirs; the opinion also, the act which followed it, and the responsibility, were mine; and I fully meet that responsibility, trusting to the consciousness of rectitude within my own bosom, which has never for one moment forsaken me or wavered.

"I respectfully submit, that Mr. J. W. Wales, by his coolness, his presence of mind, and his fidelity, has rendered to the American navy a memorable service. I had a trifling difficulty with him, not discreditable to his character, on the previous cruise to Porto Rico. On that account he was sought out and tampered with; but he was honest, patriotic, humane; he resisted temptation, was faithful to his flag, and was instrumental in saving it from dishonor. A pursership in the navy, or a handsome pecuniary reward, would after all be an inconsiderable recompense, compared with the magnitude of his services. Of the conduct of Sergeant Michael H. Garty, I will only say it was worthy of the noble corps to which he has the honor to belong; confined to his hammock by a malady which threatened to be dangerous, at the moment when the conspiracy was discovered, he rose upon his feet a well man. Throughout the whole period, from the day of Mr. Spencer's arrest to the day after our arrival, and until the removal of the mutineers, his conduct was calm, steady, and soldierlike. But when his duty was done, and health was no longer indispensable to its performance, his malady returned upon him, and he is still in his hammock. In view of this fine conduct, I respectfully recommend that Sergeant Garty be promoted to a second lieutenancy in the marine corps. Should I pass without dishonor through the ordeal which probably awaits me, and attain in due time to the command of a vessel entitled to a marine officer, I ask no better fortune than to have the services of Sergeant Garty in that capacity.

"I further respectfully recommend that Boatswain's-Mates, Oliver H. Browning and William Collins, and Captain-of-the-Forecastle Charles Stewart, may be appointed boatswains in the navy; that Gunner's-Mates Henry King and Andrew Anderson, and Quartermaster Charles Rogers, be appointed gunners, and Thomas Dickerson a carpenter, in the navy. I believe that nearly all of them would make excellent forward officers. I know that all of them, without exception, would find on the navy register associates inferior to themselves; if promoted and found unworthy, they will quietly fall back into the stations from which they were advanced. It would be remembered in the navy, that in the only mutiny which has been regularly organized in it, the stern law of necessity had, in the opinion of the commanding officer, compelled him to hang the ringleaders at the yard-arm; that the petty officers, who had been found faithful to their colors, had been promoted, it will not be recorded whether they subsequently failed by sobriety and good conduct to sustain themselves in the honorable elevation to which their fidelity had raised them.

"If I shall be deemed by the navy department to have any merit in preserving the Somers from those treasonable toils, by which she had been surrounded, since before her departure from the United States, I respectfully request that it may accrue, without reservation, to the benefit of Nephew O. H. Perry, now clerk on board the Somers, and that his name may be placed on the register, in the number left vacant by the treason of Mr. Spencer.*

"I think, under the peculiar circumstances of the case, an act of Congress, if necessary, might be obtained to authorize the appointment; throughout the whole period of his service on board the Somers, he has performed zealously, and with ability, the duty of midshipman, and since the discovery of the mutiny, with an energy and courage not unworthy of his name. I pledge my self to his entire worthiness. If he were not worthy, the navy is the last profession in whose lists I would wish to see his name enrolled.

"For myself, I only ask that in whatever proceedings it may be necessary to institute against me, as I have considered before all [211] things the honor of my country and the sanctity of its flag, my own honor may also meet with the consideration. I ask only that I may not be deprived of my command until proved to be unworthy of it.

"I have the honor to be, very respectfully your most obedient,

"ALEX. SLIDELL MACKENZIE,
"*Commander U. S. N.*

"Hon. A. P. UPSHUR,
  "*Secretary of the Navy,*
    "*Washington.*"

An entry in the diary of Philip Hone for December 29, 1842. Here reprinted from *The Diary of Philip Hone,* edited by Bayard Tuckerman (New York: Dodd, Mead & Co., 1889), II, 166-168.

[166] *December 29.*—Great interest is excited by the proceedings of the court of inquiry. . . . The first testimony was the production of the report . . . by Captain McKenzie . . . ; and well would it have been for him if it had never seen the light. "Oh that mine enemy should write a book!" was the vindictive exclamation of some such person as the Secretary of War. I have learned by experience and observation, that nine-tenths of all the scrapes men get into are occasioned by writing or saying *too much.* Here is a document ten times longer than was necessary, written without consultation with any judicious friend, who, from not being immediately interested in the event, would have been better able to look at the consequences, full of public details of trifling circumstances and irrelevant conversation, and interspersed with sage reflections. . . .

---

* Midshipman's appointments had been strictly limited by Congress in 1842 because for years too many had been made. No appointment was available even for a lad bearing the heroic name Oliver Hazard Perry; he was aboard officially only as his Uncle Alexander Mackenzie's clerk, but in fact, by his uncle's altogether extraofficial action, he was serving as acting midshipman while awaiting an appointment.

[167] Not only the character of Captain McKenzie, but that of the flag under which he sails and of the nation which he serves, is deeply concerned in his making out a complete justification. There is no middle ground in this business; it was altogether right, or altogether wrong. And here, instead of a concise, manly statement of his proceeding on the discovery of the mutiny, the necessity which, in his judgment, existed for his summary exercise of power, and his regret that he had been called upon to adopt measures so painful to his feelings, we have a long rigmarole story about private letters discovered on the person of young Spencer, orders to blow out the brains of "refractory men," religious ceremonies, cheers for the American flag, and conversations with the accused, in one of which he said to Spencer that "he hung him, because if he took him to the United States he would escape punishment, for everybody got clear who had money and friends,"—a national reproach, which, even allowing it to be true, came with a bad grace from an officer of the American navy.

He makes an apology, it is true, for this indiscreet expression. But, in the name of all that is wonderful, why should he stigmatize himself by relating such a conversation in a document which will be carried on the wings of the wind to the most distant part of the earth? The truth is, there is much to be seen, in this statement, of the pride of authorship. Captain McKenzie, when he was Alexander Slidell, wrote a clever book called "A Year in Spain," which gave him some reputation as an author, and he disdained to take advice in regard either to the matter or the manner of the narrative. Even in this particular it is a failure; it will add nothing to his literary renown.

The oral testimony of his officers thus far is greatly in his favour, [168] and I trust he will stand justified before God and his country, notwithstanding his ill-judged report. . . .

From the New York *Weekly Tribune,* January 7, 1843, as reprinted in *Proceedings of the Court of Inquiry* . . . (New York: Greeley & ✓ ✓ ✓   McElrath, 1843), pp. 15-21.

[FRIDAY, Dec. 30, 1842.]

[15] . . . JAMES W. WALES, sworn by the President, testified as follows: I was Purser's Steward on board the Somers in her late cruise.* I was informed on the night of the 25th of November last of an intended mutiny

---

* According to his testimony and various news items, Wales was a native of Newport, R. I.; had been a compositor on the Providence *Journal,* a book-keeper for the New Bedford *Mercury* and in New York City; and had been in naval service about three years. "The Purser [has] under his charge all the financial affairs of a man-of-war. . . . The Purser's steward . . . is the right-hand man and confidential deputy and clerk of the Purser, who intrusts to him all his accounts with the crew. . . ." Herman Melville, *White-Jacket,* Ch. 48.

on board that vessel. I was standing forward by the bitts when Mr. Spencer came forward, and, after some few remarks relative to the weather, requested me to get on top of the booms,* telling me at the same time that he had something *very important* to communicate to me. I accordingly got on top of the booms with him and he commenced the conversation by asking me if I 'was afraid of death?' I was then alone with him. "Was I afraid of death—and did I fear a dead man and dare I kill a person," were the questions he asked me. I was very much surprised at these remarks and looked up to see if he was in earnest; I found that he was very serious and very much in earnest in what he said. I replied that I was not particularly anxious to die quite yet, that I had no cause to fear a dead person and that did a man sufficiently abuse or insult me, I thought I could muster sufficient courage to kill him if necessary. Mr. Spencer replied, "I don't doubt your courage at all; I know it." "But," said he, "can you keep a secret? and will you keep one?" "If so," he added, "take the oath." He then dictated an oath, of which I cannot recollect the whole; but the purport of it was that I should never make known to any person the conversation which was about to take place between us. I took the oath as directed by Mr. Spencer. The oath was merely administered by word of mouth, no Bible being used. He then went on to state that he was leagued with about *twenty* of the brig's company, to take her, murder all her officers and commence pirating. The plan and stations of the men, he said, he had all arranged in secret writing, done up in his neck handkerchief. He requested me to feel of his neck-handkerchief. I did so and there was a rumpling which showed that there was paper in the back part of it. He went on to state to me the plan he should pursue. The affray would commence some night when he had the mid-watch.— Some of his men would get into a fight on the forecastle. He (Spencer) was to bring them up to the mast and call Mr. Rogers, the officer of the deck, to pretend to settle the difficulty.— As soon as Mr. Rogers had got to the gangway they were immediately to seize and throw him overboard. They would then have the vessel in their own possession. The keys of the arm-chest, he said, he could lay his hands on at any moment. The arm chest was to be opened and the arms distributed to his men. He was then to station his men at the hatches to prevent any one from coming up on deck, and he should proceed to the cabin and murder the Commander with the least noise possible. He should then proceed with some of his men to the ward room; and then murder the ward-room and steerage officers. He stated that the officers had no arms in the ward room with the exception of the First Lieutenant, and all the arms that he had there was an old cutlass, which he should secure before the affray commenced.

This accomplished, he said he should go on deck, have the two after guns slewed around so as to command, from a raking position, the deck.

---

* *Booms:* extra spars piled on the deck.

He would then cause all the crew to be called on deck, and select a number from them such as would suit his purposes; the remainder he should cause to be thrown overboard. (The words "suit his purposes" were the very ones he used.) This done, he should commence clearing the deck, beginning by throwing overboard the launch and all the spare spars and rigging of the vessel, as they only tended to lumber up the deck; that should they stand in need of any spare spars or rigging, they could take them from vessels that they would capture.

This done, the brig was to proceed to Cape San Antonio, or to the Isle of Pines; and there take on board *one who was familiar with their intended business, and who was ready and willing to join them.* The name of this person was not mentioned. This done, they were to commence cruising for prizes; that whenever they took a vessel, after taking from her that which would be of use to them, they were to murder all on board and scuttle the vessel, so as to leave no traces of her. Should there be any females on board of the vessels they would take, they would have them removed to the brig for the use of the officers and men—using them as long as they saw fit, and then making way with them.

Spencer then called up ELISHA SMALL, seaman [16] on board. He came and stood by the railing, but did not get up on the booms. (This was before I made any reply to what he said—because I *could not* reply.) He commenced talking to him in Spanish, but I could not tell what they were talking about, as I did not understand the language. Small looked surprised, however, at what he told him. I saw Small's face very plainly. Spencer then remarked to Small, in English, "O, you need not be under any apprehension of fear on his (witness's) account, as I have sounded him pretty well and find he is one of us." Small seemed pleased, and remarked that he "was very glad to hear it." Small was then called away to execute some order. Before going Spencer told him that he (Spencer) should have the mid-watch that night, and wished to have some farther conversation with him (Small) relative to their plans; and desired Small to 'see that foretop-man' meantime. (He did not name him.)

Small then left. Spencer made overtures to me, saying that if I would join them he would give me the post of third officer in command. He then went on to state that the Commander had a large amount of money on board. This, he said, with what the Purser had would make a pretty little sum to commence with. He then asked me what I thought of the project. I thought it prudent to dissemble as much as possible in order to gain further information, and told him that I was favorably disposed towards it. My duty then called me away. Spencer remarked that we would have another interview on the morrow, when he would show me the plan he had drawn up. He followed me to the gangway saying that if I lisped a syllable of what he had communicated to me I should be murdered; that if he did not do it himself those connected with him would; that go where I might my life would not be worth a straw. I said "No, I would not make any mention of it." This conversation lasted upwards of an hour—nearly two hours. It was contrary to the rules of the ship to sit on the booms at all; we were on the centre out of sight. I recollect no other part of the conversation which occurred there. I took the first opportunity that I could to make the matter known to Commander Mackenzie. It was about 9 o'clock at night when I left Mr. Spencer, and he went below to turn in. It was very light—moonlight I think, though I will not be sure. I proceeded as far aft as the cabin, intending to communicate the intelligence to Commander Mackenzie, but I observed that Small was watching me closely. Seeing this I turned back and thought I would try to get into the wardroom, but there I was again put off; for Spencer put up his head, and wanted to know "what the devil I was about, cruising around there," or something to that amount. Spencer's hammock was hung right over the ward-room door, and to reach the door I had to pass by it. I made no reply but pretended to be getting into the Purser's store-room. I then went on the first deck again. About one hour after I went again to the steerage and found Spencer still awake. I had returned there with the intention of getting into the ward-room. I saw that the lights were out and that the ward-room gentlemen had retired.

I then let the matter rest till morning, but did not go to sleep, though I tried. In the morning, as soon as I could get in, before breakfast, (about 7 o'clock I should think,) I communicated the matter to Purser Heiskell, and then went on deck and told the First Lieutenant that the Purser wished to see him immediately in the ward-room. I merely gave the Purser to understand that there was a mutiny on foot, and wished him to get it to the Commander as soon as possible. I condensed Spencer's statement, and went up to the First Lieutenant of my own accord, for fear the Purser would neglect it. I was watched as closely as possible by Small, Cromwell, Wilson, McKinley and Spencer, and therefore kept out of the way of the officers as much as possible. These men I frequently noticed clubbing together, and I believe they knew I was playing them false. I had no farther interview with Spencer, though I endeavored to do so. He was continually engaged with the forecastle-man—Benj. F. Green—on the foretop, so that I could not see him. Spencer was arrested on the evening of the 26th November. . . .

[*the arrest*]

After this I observed dissatisfaction among the men. When an order was given it had to be repeated several times, and even then they obeyed it sullenly, as if they did not care a farthing whether the order was executed or not. Cromwell, whose hammock was slung next to mine, was called by some officer to go on deck, and went muttering—but I could not understand what he said. The same evening I observed Wilson, McKinley and three or four others collected on the forecastle talking together: and when the officers went toward them they would separate and go to other parts of the ship. I heard nothing at all of their conversations. Nothing else occurred that night, to my knowledge.

[17] The next day I noticed nothing suspicious in the conduct of the men, except that they were surly about doing their duty. This surliness was general among the men. I think that on that day Cromwell and Small were put in irons, though I will not be sure.

After these three were in irons I saw that the crew was disorderly. In the morning, while holy-stoning the deck, I being officer over the prisoners, I observed signs passed between Spencer, Wilson and McKinley; they put their hands to their chins and Cromwell, who was lying on the arm chest, rose up. I told him my orders were to shoot him down, and I should do so if he did not lie still. He lay down. I then went back with my pistol cocked, to the launch, where Wilson was poking about, and found that he had a number of the holy-stones out and that he was taking out a hand-spike. I told him that if I saw him making any farther signs I would blow his brains out. He said nothing, did not put the hand-spike back but went to draw some water. I put the handspike back myself. I expressed my fears to Commander Mackenzie and the First Lieutenant, telling them that I thought it dangerous to leave the holy-stones about, as they might be easily used. I went to the Commander to tell him this. While Spencer was in irons, near the battle-axe rack, I observed him trying how he could work one—moving the axe up and down. Cromwell and Small were at this time confined. After I told this to the First Lieutenant he told it to the Commander and the battle axes were removed to the arm-chest. That morning Wilson, McKinley, McKee and Green missed their muster and congregated round the stern of the launch. The next day, at morning quarters, they came forward and made some acknowledgement; they were then put in irons; it was then 9 o'clock. After they were put in irons I could see that the men and boys were still surly; they went to work, when orders were given, with evident dissatisfaction. I heard nothing said among them, however. This dissatisfaction kept on till the execution, when the whole feeling changed. Those who before had been slow to execute an order were, after that, the first to run to obey it.— After the arrest of Spencer and previous to the execution this dissatisfaction was evidently on the increase, so much so as to be perceptible from day to day. More than half the crew, I should think, exhibited it.

I was present at the time of the execution. I did not hear any conversation between Commander Mackenzie and Spencer and Cromwell, though I heard him ask Small to forgive Spencer. Small sat on the gangway. Spencer said "Small, I hope you will forgive me;" Small replied, "Mr. Spencer how can you ask me that when you have brought me to this?" Commander Mackenzie said to Small "Don't go out of the world with any hard feelings at your heart—forgive him." Small replied "Since you request it, sir, I forgive him." Small then bade Lieut. Gansevoort farewell. Commander Mackenzie said "Small, what have you against me that you will not shake hands with me and bid me good bye?" Small said, "Nothing, sir, only I did not think that you would shake hands with a poor fellow like me and bid him good bye." He reached out his hand, shook that of Commander Mackenzie very cordially, and bade him farewell. I heard Small say, looking up to the flag, "God bless that flag!" He was then addressing his shipmates, having asked permission to do so of the Commander which had readily been granted him. I cannot recollect the words of his address though I heard him warn them from his fate; and heard him say that his sentence was right and just, and that it was right that he should die. He then looked up and said "God bless that flag!" and asked Mr. Spencer if he was ready to die—saying "*I* am." Spencer made no reply at all. He had permission to give the order to fire the signal gun, but waited some time, not being able to do so.

Previous to this Commander Mackenzie told me that Spencer wished to speak with me. I went up to him, and he said to me, "Mr. Wales I sincerely hope that you will forgive me for tampering with your fidelity."— Commander Mackenzie was standing by his side—I replied that I did, and hoped that God would forgive him. He then shook my hand and said farewell. I had no other conversation with either of them.

While we were at Mesurado, going ashore in the boat, on the 11th of November, Spencer was officer of the boat, and I was with him. I believe Mr. Rogers was also in the boat, though I am not sure. The Commander had told Spencer before he got into the boat that he was not in uniform.— He was just going into the boat as this was said. He muttered some reply, but I could not hear what it was. After we had got some 20 or 30 yards from the Brig the Captain hailed us and asked if we had the American ensign in the boat. Spencer replied that he had not got it, and added, (not, however, so the Captain could hear) that he'd "be G—d d—d if he was going back after it either, for the d—d old humbug. Go to h—ll." He continued cursing all the way to shore—though I cannot call to mind the particular expressions that he used. I think McKinley was in the boat, and Golding also—though I am not sure. This was the second cutter. This was all that took place at that time. Spencer's remarks seemed to please the crew.

About two weeks before the revelation of the mutiny was made, while bound from Mesurado to St. Thomas, Mr. Spencer having the watch on deck, (though I do not recollect the day or the place of the vessel,) Mr. Rogers sung out to let go some brace. Spencer was talking with Cromwell, (who was boatswain's mate of the watch,) and some others of the crew. None of them paid any attention to the order. Mr. Rogers called out again and again. They paid no attention. Mr. Rogers then came forward and gave the order himself. (I was forward standing by the Jacob's ladder. They were as near Mr. Rogers as I was and could hear as well.) Capt. Mackenzie, who was on deck, noticed it, and sent for Spencer to come aft. I did not hear the conversation between them, but when Spencer came forward he was muttering curses against the Commander. I asked him: "Spencer, what's the matter?" Said he, "the Commander says that I don't pay attention to my duty, and urges me to pay better attention hereafter. G—d d—n him, I'd like some of these dark nights to catch him on top of that roundhouse, and plunge him overboard. It would be a pleasing task for me, and (he muttered between his teeth,) G—d d—n him, *I'll do it yet.*" I made no reply. He went forward and began [18] talking with some of the men—four or five. I went below. I did not repeat this language to any of the officers. I have had frequent conversations with Spencer on general subjects, but no others which would throw light on the matter. I did not know at the time that there were mutinous expressions. Other officers were near and must have heard his words.

Spencer had a picture in the ward-room at one time. Once the Purser called the trysail the mainsail, and they had quite a dispute about it.— Spencer brought out a picture of a brig, with a *black flag* flying at the peak. He made no remarks at that time or any other to me about the picture or the color of the flag.

At Madeira, when we were getting under weigh, Cromwell spoke against Commander Mackenzie. Capt. M. asked why some rigging had not been attended to. Cromwell was stationed forward and Capt. M. went aft. Cromwell then said he "did not care a d—n about the rigging: Captain Mackenzie was desirous of getting too much work out of the crew; that there was no necessity of getting under weigh that night at all," at the same time wishing the "Commander and the Brig farther in h—ll than they were out." This he said loud enough to be heard by all forward. Several of the officers were forward at the time, but in the hurry of getting under weigh, paid no attention to it.— Shortly after we left New-York, Cromwell, while giving some money to the Sergeant of Marines to take care of, told me that Spencer had given him $15; he mentioned no purpose, though he said something about its being a "pretty good present." Spencer also drew some $15 or $20 worth of tobacco and cigars during the cruise, which he distributed to the crew—the tobacco rather to the boys than the men. He gave Cromwell a bunch or two of cigars at one time, and also to Small. I saw him give money to Small at Santa Cruz, while going ashore. I saw two silver pieces, though I could not see how much there was. I have seen Spencer give Green and Van Velcher a pound of tobacco at a time, and to others smaller amounts. I recollect no other conversation or facts that would throw any light upon the mutiny.

Cross-Examination.

The President informed Commander MACKENZIE that he had the privilege of cross-examining the witness, by questions in writing, to be approved by the Court. He handed the following questions:

Q. Did you ever hear Cromwell speak of his wife?

A. I have. Two or three days after we were out we had a heavy gale. Cromwell came down and began to speak about friends at home. He spoke of his wife in a very light manner for a man who has just been married, at least. [The words he used indicated that he cared nothing for her chastity while he was gone.]

The Judge Advocate objected to the question, and asked why Com. Mackenzie wished to ask it.

Com. Mackenzie said it was merely to counteract any feeling of sympathy that might be sought to be drawn from his wife and family.

The Judge Advocate said that purpose was already sufficiently answered.

Q. Was it not on the occasion of your interview with Spencer on the booms, that he complained of Com. Mackenzie's treatment?

A. He did say something about it then, though I do not remember what. He said, I believe, that Capt. M. was proud of his command.

Q. Did Mr. Spencer state that the pistols alluded to in his conversation on the booms were loaded?

A. He did, and also a musket.

Q. Did you hear Mr. Spencer make any remark about dead men telling no tales?

A. I did. He said that his motto was "dead men tell no tales." He alluded to this in connection with what he said of scuttling vessels that he might capture.

Q. Was any thing said about 'small fry' and 'eating biscuit' in that conversation?

A. Yes, sir. He said that they would eat considerable, and that he would make them walk the plank; they would be useless on board. He meant the small boys—the smaller apprentices. There were some very small on board.

Q. What effect, if any, did Mr. Spencer's remark about throwing Com. Mackenzie overboard have upon the crew?

A. It rather pleased them. I saw smiles upon the faces of several of them; Cromwell and Small were among them. . . .

SATURDAY, Dec. 31, 1842.

[19] . . . J. W. Wales was recalled . . . He said he omitted to mention yesterday the difference in Cromwell's treatment of the boys. When the vessel first sailed from New-York he was very tyrannical toward the apprentices, having no conversation with them, and keeping aloof from them altogether; and when called upon to inflict punishment he would strike with all his might, as though it was pleasing to him to whip them. He whipped them hard, the same as though they were men instead of boys. I have frequently heard Commander Mackenzie censure him for

whipping them so hard, and he has often ordered him to stop. Just previous to our arrival at Madeira I noticed a sudden change in his manner toward the boys: he then 'made free' with them, and let them talk and play with him and pull him about. I have heard Mr. Spencer remark to the crew that Com. Mackenzie gave orders to the crew merely to see them work—that there was no necessity for taking in sail and making sail. And when he gave the tobacco, of which I spoke yesterday, to the men and boys, he would say that if Capt. Mackenzie would not let them have it *he* could accommodate them.

Cross-examination.—Commander Mackenzie desired to ask the following questions, and was allowed:

Q.—Did you ever hear Commander Mackenzie reprove Cromwell for cursing the boys?

A.—Yes, sir; I have known him several times send for him aft and reprove him in my presence.

Q.—Did you ever see Spencer give money to others than Cromwell and Small; and if so to whom?

A.—I have seen him at several times throw money upon the deck—a shilling or so—and tell the boys to scramble for it. I can't specify to whom he gave it. Though I do not know that it would be of any interest to the Court, I will mention that Small and Cromwell have frequently told me of their having been in slavers.

The Court requested Mr. Wales to confine himself to what he knew, not to what he had heard.

The Judge Advocate said he certainly considered this evidence.

Q. Did you before you replied to Mr. Spencer's catechism in the interview you had with him pause to see whether he was in earnest or not?

A. I did, sir, for some time and found him very serious indeed. Witness was allowed then to state that Cromwell and Small had frequently told him of having been in slavers. Cromwell said he had been taken in a slaver, carried to Havana and confined in the Moro Castle. He was there for some time and was finally liberated by a woman who had considerable influence with the Governor of the Island. He did not specify what kind of a vessel he was taken by.

Q. Will you from recollection repeat the oath administered to you by Spencer?

A. I can only remember that he said I was never to reveal any thing that he should tell me— "So help me God." He invoked the name of God.

Q. What was the state of the crew as to good conduct and subordination between New-York and Madeira when outward bound, and what was it afterwards?

A. Between New-York and Madeira it was very good indeed; but after we left Madeira for Santa Cruz it could be seen that dissatisfaction was arising, and it continued to increase during the whole interval up to the execution of the men. I noticed a change instantly after that. Those who had been the most surly immediately turned about.

Q. Was there any motive, so far as you know, for this discontent, arising from the treatment of the crew?

A. I think not. The treatment, after leaving Madeira, was the same as it had been before.— The same rules and regulations were enforced and the same duties were performed.

Q. Did you ever see the paper purporting to be the list of persons engaged in Spencer's plans?

A. I saw it the night it was taken out of his locker. Previous to seeing the list, I had noticed that most of those who were found to be on the list were disorderly and disobedient before the mutiny broke out; and I had brought up one or two of them for it. At that time the Master-at Arms was sick, and I attended to his duties and had charge of the berth-deck.

Q. How soon after your interview with Mr. Spencer did you understand the mutiny was to take effect?

A. I understood that it was to be very shortly;—before our arrival at St. Thomas.

Q. Did Cromwell tell you at what time he had been in a slaver?

A. He did not, but only that he had been in one and had been taken.

The testimony was then read over and Mr. Wales was dismissed.

Lieut. GUERT GANSEVOORT called and sworn:

I was First Lieutenant on board the brig Somers. There were on board the following officers—twelve in number, viz: Commander MACKENZIE, First Lieut. Gansevoort, Dr. Lincock, Purser Heiskell, Acting Master Perry, Midshipmen Rogers, Thompson, Hayes, De Long, Tillotson, Spencer, and Mr. Oliver Perry who did Midshipman's duty.

We sailed from New-York on the 13th of Sept. and arrived at Madeira —I do not clearly remember at what date, but about the 5th of October I believe. I first heard of the mutiny on the 26th of November and Mr. Spencer was ironed on the evening of the same day—at about sundown. Cromwell and Small were arrested on the next day—the 27th. I believe, they were all executed on the 1st of December. *We arrived at St. Thomas, on the 5th of December—I think, though I am not positive.* [Commander Mackenzie said this was a mistake, and the Judge Advocate said he only wished for general dates.] In the morning at about 10 o'clock I met Mr. Wales at the fore-hatch. I was told by him that the Purser wished to see me. I went down to the ward-room and found Mr. Heiskell. He asked me if I was aware that a plot existed on board to take the vessel out of the hands of her officers and murder them all? I told him that I was not aware of any thing of the kind. He then gave to me the information that Mr. Wales had given him. . . . [20] I was anxious to make it known to the Commander, and did not stay to hear all he had to say. I immediately entered the cabin and mentioned the circumstances. He received it with great coolness—said that the vessel was in good discipline, and expressed his doubts as to the truth of the report. I asked him if I should see Mr. Wales myself and get the information from him. He said no— he did not wish me to do so, or to say any thing about it. He assigned no reason at this time for this, but ordered me to keep a strict look out upon Mr. Spencer and the crew generally, which I did. About dinner time I missed Mr. Spencer from the deck. This was about 2 o'clock. I discovered that he was in the fore top, and immediately went up to see what he was about. He was sitting on the lee side of the top, with his chin resting on his breast—apparently in deep thought. He did not observe me till I had got into the top and was standing erect. He raised his head, and as soon as he discovered me got up and evinced some confusion. He asked me some questions about the rigging, and about the foremast head, which I answered in my usual manner. . . . I observed to him that, as I came through the steerage, I saw dinner was ready, and asked him if he didn't dine. He said he didn't care about it just then. I came on deck and left him in the top. I should think it was about an hour after that I discovered Green in the top with him. He appeared to be engaged in pricking India ink in Spencer's arm. The crew were employed in slinging clean hammocks. I hailed the top and ordered Green to come out. Mr. Spencer put his head over the top-rail, and from his manner I thought he wished Green to remain, though he asked no question. I repeated the order, and then ordered Spencer to send Green and other men that might be in the top on deck. Green came down immediately but no others.— Spencer remained in the top. I had not ordered him to come out. I saw no others in the top. I ordered Green to sling his hammock. He answered that he had done so already. I was engaged in mustering the men for the purpose of having the hammocks stowed. When I got abreast of the Jacob's ladder on the starboard side forward, I observed Mr. Spencer sitting on the ladder. I turned my eye towards him and immediately caught his eye, which he kept staring upon me for more than a minute, *with the most infernal expression I have ever seen upon a human face. It satisfied me at once of the man's guilt.* As soon as the hammocks were stowed, I reported the circumstances to the commander, and told him that I thought something should be done, in order to secure him. He replied that we would keep a sharp look out—that he did not wish to do anything hastily: and that by evening quarters he would decide what it was best to do. I think it was just before the drum beat to quarters, that he asked me what I would do if I were in his situation as Commander of the vessel. I told him that I would bring that young man aft (alluding to Mr. Spencer) and iron him and keep him on the quarter deck. He told me that that was the course which he intended to pursue; and that he was very glad to find that I agreed with him.

[*The arrest.*]

The next day in the morning I had a conversation with some of the men—whom I suppose to be true: the Carpenter's mate Dickerson, and the Gunner's mate, King; though I am not positive that it was not the evening of Spencer's arrest. I think the Carpenter's mate said "that big fellow forward is more dangerous than the rest; he ought to be confined." I asked him whom he meant—and he said Cromwell, the Boatswain's mate. I think King was then present. I cannot recollect all the conversations I had for I was constantly passing about the ship. I am positive that Dickerson and King, in that and all other conversations I had with them, up to Cromwell's arrest, impressed me with the belief that it was necessary to have him confined; and after that they appeared to be relieved. [21] They said that they believed him to be dangerous and desired that he might be ironed.

The carpenter told me that once when he had made for me a single stick, he told Cromwell that he was going to put it in the Boatswain's store room. Cromwell said he should not. Dickerson said it belonged to me (witness). Cromwell answered that he "didn't care a d—n," (or something of that sort), and that it shouldn't go there. He put it there, however, and it was allowed to remain. As he was coming up the ladder, Cromwell said, *"I'll pay you for this before long,"* or words to that effect.

In the afternoon of that day (the 27th) while sitting in the ward-room I heard the officer of the deck, Mr. Hayes or Mr. Thompson, sing out "Belay," "Belay," several times; and I think I heard the Commander repeat the order. I looked up the hatch and found main royal mast was gone. I went on deck immediately, and the Commander ordered me to take charge of the deck. In looking aloft I saw Cromwell, Small, Wilson, I think Golding, and some others, whom I had previously suspected of being engaged in the plot collected about the mast-head and in the cross trees. I think the commander observed it also. They did not appear to be very active in clearing away the wreck. Cromwell, who was generally very noisy and blustering on occasions of that sort, now said very little; I do not recollect hearing his voice. The men seemed to have gone aloft more for conversation than for work. I think I had before mentioned the suspicions of the men in reference to Cromwell. A short time after the Commander said he thought it necessary to confine Cromwell. I told him that I agreed with him, and that I believed him to be a dangerous person. My mind had been carried back to many things that had occurred before this thing was known, which I never could account for till the disclosure of this plot; such as Cromwell's absent manner. [This, however, it was thought best to omit for the present.] I was about to hail the top and order him to come down; but the commander told me to wait till he did come down, and then tell him that the Commander wished to see him.

As soon as he came upon the Jacob's ladder I cocked my pistol and pointed it at him, and when he got on deck I told him the Captain wished to see him. When he came to the Captain he was ordered to sit down. The Commander told him, in effect, that there were many suspicions about him, and that he considered it necessary to confine him . . . in the same way with Mr. Spencer, and [take him] home, where he would be tried . . . and acquitted if he was innocent; if guilty he would be punished. He replied, "Yes, sir; but I don't know any thing about this; I assure you that I don't know any thing about it." Something else passed, which I do not at this time recollect. The Commander then said something to me about Small, and asked if I did not think it best to confine him. I told him I thought it was, and he then told me to order him aft. Nearly the same conversation then passed as with Cromwell. The Commander told him he would be confined as the others were, brought home and tried. Small did not deny having had conversation with Spencer. The Captain said to him, "Spencer has talked with you about the plot," in which Small acquiesced and said Yes sir. He did not deny it and made no objection to being confined. The night Spencer was confined I think Small admitted he had talked to him about the mutiny. Small was then confined in irons. All the officers were armed when Cromwell first came down from the rigging; and were stationed about the mast on different parts of the deck ready for action in case of any attack. They wore their arms afterward until their arrival here.

On the 28th or 29th, I think Wilson, McKinley, McKee and Green were confined. Wilson had had a knife in a bag, which he bought on the coast of Africa, and King told me that the night before he had kept it concealed about the guns. I came up and found King and Dickinson talking together. King said to me *"Has Wilson drawn two or three knives from the store-room lately?"* I told him none that I knew of. He said, "I heard that he had several knives in his sail-bag, and I think it would be a good plan to over-haul it; he has had his bag there at the after part of that gun where Mr. Spencer is, nearly all day, and a knife hid away in the rigging," which he thought he *intended to put into the hands of Mr. Spencer.* I over-hauled the sail-bag, and found no other knife than an African dirk, very sharp, and having the appearance of having been lately sharpened. This is the knife. [It was produced; the blade was about six inches long and an inch and a half wide near the haft—sharp on both sides and pointed. It had a sheath and a bone handle.] It had the appearance of having been recently sharpened. I was told that there was another knife in the possession of Warner. That was sharp only only on one side and curved on the back. I had seen it before. I ordered it brought to me and placed both in the arm-chest for safe keeping.

I think it was at the same time that I said to Dickenson, (King having left,) "What do you think of these fellows?" alluding to Spencer, Cromwell and Small. His reply was, that in his opinion "the d--d fool was on the larboard, and the d--d scoundrel (or rascal) on the starboard arm-chest." Small and Cromwell were both on the starboard side, and I said to him, "You mean Cromwell," being pretty well satisfied of the same thing in my own mind. He said, "Yes, sir, *he is the most dangerous man on board the ship.*" I recollect nothing else that happened.

I had several conversations with King, Dickenson, I think Browning, and Anderson, Captain of the forecastle; and they all thought Cromwell the *most dangerous man concerned in the plot.*—I had several conversations with them every day; and used to ask them what they saw about the vessel. They told me what they had seen—that before the affair they had seen Cromwell talking frequently with Spencer; that they were very intimate, &c. King told me that he thought there was a collection of arms in the store-room. I overhauled it but found none. I then collected all the monkey-tails, holy-stones, marling-spikes, and such things as might be used against us. They were locked up in the store-room and otherwise secured. I did not know then that any other of the crew were implicated; but I think it was King who told me that he thought all the older boys were. . . .

⁄ ⁄ ⁄ From the New York *Herald,* Saturday morning, December 31, 1842.

[Commander Mackenzie's narrative is] a singular mixture of folly, silliness, and blasphemy. . . . One fact is now certain, the identity of this narrative with the article in the "Courier and Enquirer" [December 19] is perfect and complete. . . .

> Entry from the diary of Evert Duyckinck, New York, December 31, 1842. Here reproduced from the original diary in the Duyckinck
> ⁄ ⁄ ⁄ Collection of the New York Public Library, by permission.

. . . Today is published the statement of Mackenzie himself. . . . A thrilling narrative full of character and a paper that will not be forgotten in the history of the country. . . .

> Letter from Mary A. Gansevoort [mother of Lieut. Guert Gansevoort] to her brother-in-law Peter, dated New York, January 2, 1843. Reproduced here by permission from holograph letter in the Gansevoort-Lansing Collection of the New York Public Library. [See excerpts from this letter published by Jay Leyda in *The Melville Log: A Documentary Life of Herman Melville* (New York:
> ⁄ ⁄ ⁄ Harcourt Brace, 1951), I, 159, 161.]

Guert dined with us yesterday; & just before he left; he said, "I intended to have written to Uncle Peter, before I returned to the Brig;

for it is impossible for me to do any thing of the kind there; & turning to me, begged that I would do so for him—knowing that he is constantly occupied; I cheerfully, said I would do it—He then said, "Tell my uncle, I thank him for his letter—for the good opinion he here expresses, ever to have entertained of me; which God grant I may never give him cause to change, that when a man is troubled he sets a high value on the approbation of his friends—Tell him, that nothing that S. [John C. Spencer] can say, can make the least change in my feelings, as regard the treatment & execution of those mutineers. I *feel,* that we did our duty; & the consciousness of having *done my duty;* shall ever sustain me— It was not only the public property, the Flag of my country; & my own life that was in the utmost jeopardy; but the lives of the crew, (*those that were true*); but of those apprentices, those *children,* entrusted to the care of the Officers; for whose safety we were responsible,—to God, to their country, & to their *parents;* to many of whom, before we sailed; I had pledged myself, to extend parental care & advice—Tell him, that nothing was done in "fear or haste"—& I believe it was *approved* of God; & I have faith to trust, it will be by my fellow man." Tell my Uncle, I thank him, for the offer of his counsel; & sincerely wish that *distance,* did not prevent my benefitting by it—I have no doubt it would be useful to me—if the river had have been open, I should have run up; & paid a short call on him & my Grandparents; before the Court set—at present, I can only leave the ship for a few hours at the time. I hope to see him however before many weeks at his own house; relate to him all the circumstances of the melancholly affair; which I shall do, in perfect confidence of his approval; & *conviction* of the *necessity."*

He then sends his love, & many kisses to those sweet little children; after whom he enquired with great affection, on his first visit to us; which was made almost by stealth at 9 ocl[oc]k in the eve[nin]g. He was then in such a situation from fatigue & exposure; that I scarcely knew him— he had a violent cold; coughing constantly; very hoarse his limbs so contracted; that he walked like an infirm man of seventy; his eyes were red & swollen, & his whole face very much bloated—his back & sides were so sore, from the strap & weight of the huge & heavy ships Pistols; that he could not raise himself erect—Having imprisoned so many of the crew; they were short of hands & he, poor fellow, did more than double duty— the eve[nin]g of which I speak, his first visit to us; he had not had even his coat off in four days. Mr. Upshure wrote to Mr. Mackensie, for Guert to proceed to Washinton [*sic*]—He was here, & had just sent a note to Mackensie, saying that he was really sick, & that I had prevailed on him to remain, & have medical attendance; which he would do—unless he expressed a wish for him to return to the yard—Before his messenger got to Mackensie—*his* dispatch to Guert, arrived here—one, a very friendly & confidential letter; inquiring about his health—the other an official Order nothing could stop him; he went; was sick one night at

Phila. but got there safe—had three interviews with the Secretary [Up-shur]—*very satisfactory to Guert*—but this to *your ear only*. Commander Mackensie & Guert seem well pleased with the Officers composing the Court—God grant, that all *is,* & *was* right. . . .

Paragraph from a column in the National Intelligencer (Washington), January 5, 1843, "From our New York Correspondent," dated January 2.

The gaiety of the holydays, however, is but an ellipse in the discussion of the exciting subject of *the Mutiny*. . . . It is the one table-talk—the theme of the boys at the corners, of the hackmen in the street, of servants and masters, of the grave and the gay, the busy and the idle. The case is every where argued and tried, and the precedent will at least be well understood hereafter. With the publication of the first half of Capt. MACKENZIE'S statement, public opinion was turned ominously against him, but the remainder, given on the following day with WALES'S testimony, seemed again to justify him. . . .

From the New York Weekly Tribune, January 14, 1843, as reprinted in Proceedings of the Court of Inquiry . . . (New York: Greeley & McElrath, 1843), pp. 22-25.

TUESDAY, Jan. 3, 1843.

[22] . . . LIEUT. GANSEVOORT then proceeded with his testimony as follows:

On the morning of the 1st, the day on which the men were executed, Commander Mackenzie ordered me to arm all the petty officers whom I thought to be true to the flag. He had expressed a wish that they should be armed before, but not having myself full confidence in them, I had until now discouraged it. On that morning I obeyed the order . . . ; there were seven of them. The Commander . . . gave them their orders . . . that if they saw an attempt made to rescue the prisoners, to blow out the brains of both the prisoners and those making the attempt; if they saw the prisoners forward of the mainmast and in communication with the crew, they were to destroy them; they were to keep a watchful eye upon the crew, and if they saw any mutinous attempt they were to use their arms upon them. He then ordered them forward. I forgot to mention that a letter was addressed by Commander Mackenzie to the officers and sent the day before, the 30th, ordering us to give him our opinion as to the guilt of Spencer, Cromwell and Small and as to the best course to be pursued. We collected in the ward-room where we spent the day in examining witnesses. It was at about 6 o'clock, I think, that the Commander ordered me to break up the Council, as he considered the vessel in danger and wished to show a force about the decks. In examining the witnesses I administered an oath of which I have a copy, and took down the testimony. . . . After hearing them read three of those who could write signed the depositions—those who could not, made their marks. The original minutes are in the hands of Mr. Heiskell, the copies are in the possession of Com. Mackenzie. [The papers alluded to were then sent for.] Commander Mackenzie intimated that the danger he apprehended was from the crew, not from the elements.

The investigation was continued on the next morning at about 9 o'clock, I believe. On the previous day we examined eight or nine of the crew I believe. Most of them were petty officers: some from among the apprentices whom I suspected to be concerned in the plot. The Commander was exceedingly anxious to know the result of the investigation, which occupied not a great while the next day. I was not present during the whole of it, it being necessary for me to be on deck. . . . As soon as the Council came to a decision, I repeated the result to the commander, telling him that I would hand it to him in writing as soon as it was published. I told him what opinion we had come to, and that it was unanimous. He expressed a wish that the letter we were drawing up should be put immediately into his hands. There was considerable delay from mistakes made in copying. When it was done I handed it to him. He read it and showed it to Midshipman Spencer. . . . I went forward to my duty and left the Commander in conversation with Mr. Spencer. I was not near enough to hear the reply which Mr. Spencer made to Com. Mackenzie's remarks. When I saw them again Mr. Spencer had a Bible in his hand and the Commander was seated near him with a paper upon which he appeared to be writing. I did not hear the conversation then. The Commander had detailed the different men who were to take the men under the main yard, on which they were to be executed. He told me that the two of the highest rank were to [23] take Mr. Spencer. Just before he had ordered me to take the men there; then I applied to him for permission to take leave of Mr. Spencer. He gave me permission. I went up to Mr. Spencer, who took my hand in both of his, and begged me very earnestly to forgive him for the many injuries he had done me. He said he did not object to the sentence—he thought it was right and that his punishment was just. He said that he deserved death but did not like the way which the Commander had chosen to put him to death; or words to that effect; and added that he should have been glad to have a longer time to prepare. They were then taken to the gangway; Mr. Spencer and Small in the starboard gangway and Cromwell in the larboard. While I was standing in the gangway near Small he asked me if I would bid him good-bye, and if I would forgive him. He told me that he was guilty and deserved his punishment. I think the Commander said to him "Small, what have *I* done to you that you won't bid me good-bye?" Small replied "I did not know that you would bid a poor *bugger* like me good-bye sir." I think the Commander asked him if he had ever treated him badly or something to that effect and told him that he was sorry he had to take the course he did but that the honor of the flag and the safety of the crew required it—or something to that amount. To which Small replied *"Yes, sir, and I honor you for it; God bless that flag!"*

Mr. Spencer then asked Small if he wouldn't forgive him. Small replied "Ah Mr. Spencer that's a hard thing for me to do. For you brought me to this." The Commander said "Forgive him Small; don't go out of the world with any hard feelings in your heart." I did not hear Small's reply, but went over to the other side of the deck.

Cromwell was sitting on the hammock cloths with the whip around his neck. I bade him good-bye. He asked me to forgive him, and seized my hand, grasping it very violently. He said that he was innocent, and hoped that we'd find it out before six months; or words to that effect. I then went over into the starboard gangway again, and Mr. Spencer called to me. Mr. Spencer said, as near as I can recollect—"You may have heard that I am a coward, and *you* may think that I'm not a brave man. You can judge for yourself whether I die like a coward or a brave man." At this time I was sitting in the gangway. I stepped down the ladder, and Small asked permission to address the crew. The Commander gave permission, and he said:

"Mess-mates and Ship-mates!—I am no pirate. I never murdered any body, but I only said *I would*. Now see what words will do. Take warning by me." He said that his punishment was a just one; that he did not object to it; it was all right. He said something else, which, though I heard his voice, I did not understand. Mr. Spencer had asked permission to give the order to fire the gun. The Commander gave him permission to do so. I heard Small tell Spencer after his speech, that he was all ready. Mr. Spencer afterwards told Browning, the Boatswain's mate, who was holding him in the gangway that he had not power to give the order, and wished the Commander to give it. The Commander immediately gave the order, 'fire,' or 'stand by—fire'—I forget which. I sung out 'whip,' and the men were run up the main yard; the whips were belayed, and the order given to pipe down and pipe to dinner. Previous to the men going to dinner the Commander asked how I thought it would do to give three cheers; I told him I thought it would do well, as it would be easy perhaps to tell from that among those who were left who were wrong and who were right.—When the men assembled aft he told them to give three cheers for the American flag, which they did, and hearty ones they were.

They then went to dinner, and after the prisoners had hung about an hour the Commander ordered me to deliver them over to their respective messmates and have them decently laid out. After they were laid out, the Commander and myself walked round and inspected them. They were afterwards sewed up in hammocks, and Mr. Spencer laid in a coffin which had been made from two mess-chests. They were buried by candle light—on the second dog watch—at about 7 I should think, when it was so dark that you could not read print. It had been squally in the afternoon, and we had covered the bodies over with tarpaulin.

I omitted a conversation I had with Small—on the 30th, I think—in the morning. I said to him—"Small, you see we have taken more prisoners." This was after McKinley and Green were ironed. I asked—"Do you know of any others that are at large from whom we may apprehend danger?" He said that was a "hard thing for him to say." I then asked him if Cromwell was not engaged with Mr. Spencer in this plot. He replied—"That's a hard thing for me to say, Sir:" and added that they were intimate together, and he had seen Spencer give Cromwell more money than *he'd* like to give him or lend him, either. I said to him—"That's not the thing: I want a plain answer to a plain question. Is not Cromwell deeply engaged with Mr. Spencer in this plot of Spencer's to take the vessel out of the hands of the officers?" He replied—"If any body aboard of the brig is, *he* is, Sir." I said I thought so—and remained a few moments by his side. He made no farther communication about it. At this time, Wilson, McKinley, McKee and Green, besides Spencer, Cromwell and Small were in confinement.

I also omitted a conversation I had with Mr. Spencer some time after he was confined, two or three days after, I think. He told me that he wished to have a conversation with me. I told him that I was ready to hear it. He said his mind was not then in a proper state to talk about it. I asked him if he would send for me when he was disposed to hold any conversation. He said he would. The next morning I went to him at about 10 o'clock, and asked him if he was ready to converse with me. He commenced by saying that he had formed this plot on board of every vessel he had been in—both in the John Adams and in the Potomac. He said he knew that it would get him into difficulty—that he had tried to break himself of it—but it was impossible: *it was a mania with him.* I think he wished me to mention it to the Commander. I did so—though I think not immediately. I am not positive how soon after.

Judge Advocate.—Was there any change in the conduct of the crew after the execution from what it had been before?

Ans. There was, sir. I think orders were obeyed with more alacrity; and there was less [24] sullenness than there had been before in the manner of some of the men.

Judge Adv. What were those things to which you said your mind was carried back when you spoke of Cromwell's arrest?

Ans. I alluded to things which had occurred as far back as Madeira when no one but myself, Mr. Spencer, Cromwell and Wales were on board.—There was a good deal of work to be done—getting in water, provisions, &c. Cromwell was grumbling about the amount of duty required. I heard him say that "it was d—d hard usage:" he said that to the crew. He did not appear to drive on the duty and assist in carrying out my orders as he had done them before. He would repeat my orders and then stand on the forecastle without making any attmpt to see them executed: he would do nothing more than repeat what I said to him.

At another time, between Madeira and Mesurado, I observed an absent manner in him. He was sitting near the forecastle; I called to him three or four times, to order him to pipe the bags down. He got up very lazily, with a pipe in his mouth. His manner was disrespectful, and he merely ordered the bags piped down, letting his own bag remain on deck. He would often go into the most violent fits of rage from some small matter, and at times used most outrageous and blasphemous language toward the boys. I recollect one night while hauling down the head sails, the lacings got jammed in the stays. He said "G—d d—n the jib and stay and the d—d fool that invented it," or something like that. I reproved him severely for this; he knew that the Commander had caused it to be so fitted, as I had told him of it before. When I reproved him for this and other offences, his manner was sullen. Such instances were continually occurring —all of which it is impossible for me to recollect. A change of manner on board ship is very easily observed, and I had observed it in this case, but could not trace it to any cause until I was told that there was a mutiny on board, and then my mind turned back to many instances which had occurred. . . .

Judge Adv.—Had you observed any change in the general conduct of the crew—and at what time did it take place?

Ans.—Before we reached Madeira their conduct was very good, but after leaving there the crew were very slack; and I had frequently to drive them to their work. They would frequently disobey small orders, such as putting clothes away, &c., and this continued to increase up to the day of execution. Before, if I told them to put away an article of clothing they would do it readily; after that they paid no attention to it.

Judge Adv.—At the time of the execution how far were you from St. Thomas?

Ans.—I am not positive but think that it was five or six hundred miles.

Judge Adv.—Have you mentioned all the conversations you had with King and Dickerson?

Ans.—No, sir; but all I can recollect.

Judge Adv.—*After their arrest what circumstances led you to think a rescue was intended?*

Ans.—The men whose names were in the paper found in Spencer's locker, were McKinly, McKee, Green, Goldeman and Sullivan, and some others I do not recollect. I had seen looks passing between Mr. Spencer and McKee, McKinly. Mr. Wales reported to me one morning that Mr. Spencer was exercising his hands upon a battle-axe, as if for the purpose of using it. I immediately went upon deck and saw him have hold of the axe, moving it up and down, apparently to see what use he could make of it with his irons on; Wilson's having concealed the knife I have mentioned was also a suspicious circumstance. Mr. Wales, I think, mentioned Wilson's having been about the launch, and McKinly's having his hand upon a hand-spike as if they were looking about for some weapon. His manner was so threatening as to induce Mr. Wales to cock his pistol and keep it upon him.

Judge Adv.—Was the conduct of the rest of the crew after the arrest of Spencer, Cromwell and Small, improved or otherwise?

A. Otherwise, decidedly; and from them I drew my conclusion that a rescue was intended. They continually hovered about the mainmast, collecting in knots and talking together on the forecastle and in gangways, and often separating on my appearance, and never talking so that I could hear. So far as I could judge it *was and is my firm belief that an attack and a rescue were intended.*

[25]   *Cross-examined.*—Capt. MACKENZIE proposed to Mr. Gansevoort the following questions: . . .

Q. From what you observed and knew of the spirit and feelings of the crew and of the progress of the mutiny up to the time of the execution of the ringleaders, did you then, or do you now believe that the Somers could, or could not have been safely brought into port unless the ringleaders were executed?

A. I did believe that she could not have been otherwise brought into port, and I do believe so now. I think she never could have reached port in the hands of her Officers, if the execution had not taken place. I thought so then; I think so now. . . .

Q. Did you see in the Commander or any of the officers of the Somers, during the difficulties, any traces of unmanly fear, of a despotic temper, or any qualities unbecoming an American officer?

A. I saw nothing of the kind. The conduct of the Commander throughout the whole was of the most unexceptionable character, and I consider the country fortunate in having had such a Commander, a man of so much decision, at such a time and under such circumstances of responsibility and danger as then existed. Too much praise cannot be awarded to all the officers. . . .

From a letter of Charles Sumner to Lt. Charles H. Davis, Boston, January 3, 1843. Here reprinted from Edward L. Pierce, *Memoir and Letters of Charles Sumner* (London: Lowe, Marston, Searle, ✓ ✓ ✓   and Rivington, 1878), II, 225.

I have had a long conversation with Judge [Joseph] Story about the execution on board the "Somers." Perhaps his judgment would be of higher authority than that of any civilian in the country; and I know it will gratify you very much, and perhaps your friend. The Judge had not the least doubt that Mackenzie was justified in the alternative he took. He thought the circumstances would form a complete defence for a homicide on shore, in the view of an enlightened civil tribune; *a fortiori,* they would at sea, on shipboard, and under the stern laws of war. . . . The law does not compel a person to stand still till he actually sees the blow descending which is to take his life. He may anticipate it; and his justification will be found in the circumstances which created a reasonable ground of fear for his life. I may add that Judge [William] Prescott, one of the first authorities on a topic of legal interest, thinks Mackenzie's course entirely justifiable. . . . If you care to mention Judge Story's opinion to Mackenzie, I can have no objections, but, considering his position, it is more proper to regard it as confidential.*

✓ ✓ ✓   From the New York *Herald,* Wednesday morning, January 4, 1843.

As yet we have expressed no opinion on the conduct of MacKenzie. . . . In relation to [his] narrative . . . , the bad taste in its style— the trivial incidents and horrid execution—the ambitious effort at fine writing—and the awful catastrophe at the yard arm—and the strange jumble of pious ideas, insignificant circumstances, patriotic sentiments, and over-charged figures of speech . . . create a feeling . . . of horror in the mind. . . . It does not seem to be written by a human being, with the ordinary feelings of nature. . . .

> From a letter from James Fenimore Cooper to his wife, dated Albany, January 4, 1843. Here reprinted, by permission, from *Correspondence of James Fenimore-Cooper,* edited by his grandson, James Fenimore Cooper (New Haven: Yale University Press,
> ✓ ✓ ✓   1922), II, 487-488.

. . . Mackenzie's affairs look bad enough. The report he sent to Washington is considered to be the work of a man scarcely *compos mentis.* I never read a more miserable thing in my life—he has actually got in one of the prayers he read to his crew. To crown all he admits he told Spencer that he would not be hanged if he got in, on account of his father's influence, and he actually recommends his nephew to fill his vacancy. In a word, such a medley of [488] folly, conceit, illegality, feebleness and fanaticism was never before assembled in a public document. . . .

---

* Joseph Story (1779-1845) was an associate justice of the U. S. Supreme Court from 1811 to 1845. He was one of the most eminent of American jurists. Judge William Prescott (1762-1844) was the son of Col. William Prescott, who commanded at Bunker Hill, and the father of W. H. Prescott the historian.

Tell Paul [Fenimore Cooper] * I saw Professor Webster yesterday, and he gave him a good character. He gave poor Phil [Spencer] as bad a one as possible. . . .

[James Fenimore Cooper (1789-1851) was to play a leading part in forming later public opinion about the Somers *affair. He knew ships and the sea firsthand, was the country's leading sea-writer, and was not unacquainted with either Mackenzie or John C. Spencer. Like Philip Spencer, he had come from a good upstate New York family, had got into disciplinary trouble in college (he was expelled from Yale for some prank), had gone to sea (1806) in a merchant vessel, and had then become a midshipman in the navy (1808-1811). But unlike Spencer, and like Dana and Melville, he had gone on to a distinguished career. Resigning from the navy when he married (1811), he had achieved great popularity during the 1820's with his novels of American history, of Indians and the frontier, and of the sea. But after some years in Europe (1826-1833) he had written several books vigorously criticizing the American social and political scene. These, and a quarrel with his hometown neighbors, involved him in several libel suits against Whig editors: Thurlow Weed, Horace Greeley, James Watson Webb (who had called him "a base minded caitiff who has traduced his country for filthy lucre . . . , a* slanderer . . . , *a traitor to national pride . . . , the viper so long nourished in our bosom . . ."), and others. The very newspaper columns that carried reports of the* Somers *affair were resounding with the latest salvos between Cooper and the editors.*

A branch of this warfare had already involved Cooper, in his role of naval historian, with both Alexander Slidell Mackenzie and John C. Spencer. In his History of the Navy of the United States of America *(1839), his account of the Battle of Lake Erie had led Perry clansmen to attack the book in the press. William A. Duer, president of Columbia, who was Mrs. Mackenzie's uncle, had done a personally abusive piece, while Mackenzie himself had reviewed it more mildly in the* North American Review *(October 1839). Concerning this review Cooper complained to his wife (October 19, 1839): "Mackenzie is superficial and jesuitical. He does not meet the question fairly, cavils at the plainest significance, and shows anything but honesty or talent. . . . This review alone satisfies me as to the man's character. He wants candor and a sense of right."* (Correspondence, II, 404.) *Next Mackenzie wrote a* Life of Oliver Hazard Perry *(1840) to correct Cooper's errors, and then he and Cooper exchanged broadsides about the Battle of Lake Erie in William Cullen Bryant's New York* Evening Post *(March 20, April 7, 1841).*

Meanwhile, too, Cooper had run afoul of John C. Spencer. As State

---

* Paul Fenimore Cooper, the novelist's son, attended Geneva College, now Hobart, during the same years as did Philip Spencer. He wrote a later reminiscence of Spencer (see excerpt reprinted from *Purple and Gold*, under date April, 1885).

Superintendent of Schools, Spencer had declined endorsing Cooper's Naval History *for inclusion in Harpers' District School Library, saying it was "controversial." But, as Cooper wrote to a naval friend, in November, 1841, "the d—d scoundrel had put in Mackenzie's life of Perry, which is* all *controversy." To Cooper's mind this illustrated Spencer's character as a politician, and he described him as "one precious fellow. . . . If he does not 'breed a riot' I shall be mistaken." (Correspondence, II, 454-455.). But it was Philip, not John C. Spencer who bred the riot—or was it Alexander Slidell Mackenzie?]*

From the New York *Weekly Tribune,* January 14, 1843, as reprinted in *Proceedings of the Court of Inquiry* . . . (New York: Greeley & McElrath, 1843), pp. 25-28.

WEDNESDAY, Jan. 4, 1843.

[25] . . . M. C. PERRY was then called, and sworn. He testified as follows:

I was on board the Somers on her late cruise, in the capacity of Acting Master.* The discipline on board, after leaving Madeira, was good until reaching Porto Praya—after which time, until the execution of Midshipman Spencer, it was not so good. The elder portion of the crew were surly and morose in their manner. Orders had to be repeated several times before they were obeyed. There was a marked difference in their manner—though it is not easy to describe it. It daily grew worse until the execution. I first heard of the intended mutiny immediately after evening quarters on the 26th of November. . . .

[26] [*The arrest.*]

The next day in the afternoon the main top gallant mast was carried away at the upper part of the sheave-hole of the top gallant yard rope. Mr. Spencer alone was then in confinement. I was in the ward room and merely saw the mast carried away through the sky-light. I went forward and let go the main weather top gallant brace. I noticed that Wilson, Cromwell and Small were aloft, and I thought then that it was very singular that Wilson should be there, as he was no sailor and was then doing nothing. I soon went below again. I do not know how the mast was carried away. . . .

On the 28th Mr. Gansevoort asked me if I thought it safe to take any more prisoners, and whether, if necessary to do so, Spencer, Cromwell and Small ought first to be disposed of. I came to the conclusion that the officers could not take care of any more than the first three, and if they

---

* M. C. Perry, Jr., was midshipman, 1835; passed midshipman, 1841; master, 1847; lieutenant, 1848; retired list, 1862; captain, 1867; died, 1873. As acting master on the *Somers,* he was navigator and kept the log.

had to take any more prisoners the safety of the vessel required that the first three should be put to death. . . .

About 9 of the 1st I took charge of the deck, and remained there till the other officers had made up their opinion, when I was relieved, went below, and coincided in their opinion, which was the same that I had expressed before. I went on deck and took charge of the forecastle. I heard the Commander tell Cromwell that he allowed him ten minutes to live, and that he should then hang him to the main yard-arm. Cromwell said "I am innocent—Lord of the Universe look down upon me!" I went forward to my station. . . .

[*The execution.*]

Previous to the arrest of Spencer, I heard Mr. Rogers report Green disobedient several times. There was a great falling off in the discipline previous to the arrest: parties of the crew mustered together in different parts of the ship. Mr. Spencer's familiarity with those suspected and his keeping aloof from his messmates were also noticed. Mr. Spencer did not mess with me. I had heard him make no declaration concerning the intended mutiny. I knew of his giving Small tobacco. This familiarity was chiefly with Cromwell, Green, Warner, and Small, and others whom I do not remember. He was continually laughing and joking with them in a manner not usual with officers. This had attracted my notice before the arrest. . . .

The evidence before the council, Green's familiarity with Spencer, Wilson's being so much about the mainmast, and his disposition to speak to the prisoners, led to their confinement, as did also the fact that their names were upon Spencer's paper, with those of McKinley and McKee. I had seen no acts of insubordination in McKinley and McKee.

After the prisoners were confined, I was led to believe that a rescue was intended by the facts that those whose names were upon Spencer's paper were continually about the main-mast in sight of [27] the prisoners, and collected in knots about the vessel; that they did not obey their orders with the same alacrity as previous to the arrest of Mr. Spencer; and by the general disposition of those found upon the paper. The carrying away of the mast also added to my suspicion. When I had charge of the deck, moreover, in the first watch of the 29th, *the boom tackle was carried away, and in a moment a great many persons appeared to rush aft.* I immediately told the boy at the wheel to get hold of the weather-sheet. I picked out two or three of the best and most trusty seamen to stay, and ordered the rest to go forward. *They did not seem disposed to go.* They did not move. I repeated the order and I walked forward. The commander coming on deck at the time, they left the quarter deck. It was then quite dark. I saw the indescribable manner to which I have before alluded. *I should think fifteen or eighteen men rushed aft,* though there was no necessity for more than three or four. Of those who rushed aft some men I considered trusty. The order I gave was "Some of you, come aft."

When the men were collected in knots, they never permitted me to hear what they were saying, though sometimes they would speak up loudly upon some other subject. Their manner on such occasions was very unusual. Four was the largest number I ever saw together. These were the circumstances that led me to believe a rescue would be attempted. . . .

QUESTIONS BY COMMANDER MACKENZIE . . .

Ques. Do you know of any place on board the Somers where three prisoners could be kept in safety beyond the reach of rescue from the crew?

Ans. I do not, sir.

Ques. At the time of the execution did you, or do you now believe, that the Somers could have been brought into port if the execution had not taken place?

Ans. I did not then think so, and I have been confirmed in the opinion since. I think now that *she could not have been brought into any port* if the execution had not taken place.

Ques. Do you believe that after the arrest and before the execution the Somers was in a condition to go into action with a prospect of sustaining the honor of the American flag?

Ans. I do not think she was, on account of the crew. . . .

Mr. Perry's examination was here closed.

H. M. HEISKELL was then called.*—I was Purser on board the Somers, and first heard of the intended mutiny on the morning of the 26th November, from Mr. Wales, who came into the ward-room and said to me, in a low tone, that Spencer had on the evening previous revealed to him the plan of the mutiny.

[*Tells his part in relaying Wales' report.*]

Three or four weeks before this I saw Spencer tear up a piece of paper in the ward-room, upon which were written secret characters—though what they were I could not tell. From remarks made then I think by Mr. Spencer himself, I knew they were secret characters, though I could not see them. The paper was about as large as half a sheet of letter paper and there were a number of lines upon it. About ten days before the plot was discovered, Mr. Spencer and myself were standing by the forward hatch, when he commenced speaking about piratical vessels; and remarked that if he were onboard of one he would cruise on the Spanish Main and would make it a rule never to chase a vessel if there was [28] another in sight, and (I believe) never to attack one unless he were certain of overpowering her. I think he added that he would not carry any spare spars or sails, but supply himself from the vessels that he might take, and that he would destroy all traces of the vessels taken. When he wished to retire

---

* Horace M. Heiskell: purser, September, 1841; pay director, 1871; retired list, 1875; died, 1891. The purser is the ship's financial officer and has no watch duties.

from that line of life he said he would mislead his men when on shore by going in a contrary direction from the one he would tell them he intended to pursue. He remarked that it required money to get a vessel. I do not remember what led to this conversation.

Eight or nine days before the mutiny was disclosed, the Doctor, Mr. Spencer and myself were in the ward-room—the two first sitting at the table, I reclining on the berth. On the table was a chart of the West India Islands. Mr. Spencer began speaking to the Doctor about the Isle of Pines, and commenced searching for it on the chart. The Doctor told him that it was a place frequented by pirates, and asked if he had any acquaintance there. He made no reply. I once saw in the ward-room a picture of a schooner, of which I think the masts raked very much, though I do not remember that she had a flag. I had no conversation with Spencer, Cromwell or Small before or subsequent to the arrest; nor with any other of the crew, touching the alleged mutiny. . . .

I heard no declarations of Small, Spencer, or Cromwell at the time of the execution, as I stood too far off. The evidence taken before the Council of officers induced me, with Mr. Wales's statement, to unite with the opinion they gave to the Commander. The witnesses, mingling with the crew, had every opportunity to judge of their feelings and dispositions. . . .

QUESTIONS BY COMMANDER MACKENZIE.

Ques. How much tobacco, segars and soap did Mr. Spencer draw from you during the cruise?

Ans. (On reference to his book.) From Sept. 12 to Nov. 26 he drew 725 segars, 11 pounds of tobacco and four bars of soap. This was a very unusual quantity—much more than any other officer drew, except of soap. . . .

Ques. As a gentleman unacquainted with the naval service, and fresh from private life, did you ever see any treatment of the crew not in perfect accordance with your sense of justice, and humane and kind as the proprieties of life required?

Ans. I never did.

Ques. Did you believe and do you now believe that the Somers could have been brought into port if the execution had not taken place?

Ans. I thought then and still think that there was *great danger every moment that those persons were on board.*

Ques. Did you observe in the commander or other officers an indication of unusual fear, a despotic temper, or of any qualities unbecoming an American officer?

Ans. No, sir. . . .

Entry from the journal of Richard Henry Dana, Jr., New York, January 4, 1843. Here reprinted from Charles Francis Adams, ✦ ✦ ✦ *Richard Henry Dana* (Boston: Houghton Mifflin, 1890), II, 49.

. . . Called on C. W. Hoffman at the Custom House, where he has an office. Talked over the Somers mutiny and Captain Mackenzie. He sympathizes with Mackenzie very much, and has a horrid idea of Spencer's father, the Secretary of War, whom he thinks capable of feeing [*paying*] the papers to attack Mackenzie.

Saw Mr. Ogden Hoffman, who invited me to go on board the North Carolina, and attend the court martial. . . . [*The rest of the entry, recording his visit to the "court-martial," as he loosely calls the court of inquiry, is incorporated, in other words, in his published letter on the subject, dated Jan. 11, which is reprinted below. Dana's entry for January 4 continues with passages not printed in Adams' biography. They are here reproduced from the original manuscript journal in the collections of Massachusetts Historical Society, by permission.*]

[108] . . . Called upon . . . Theodore Sedgwick Jr. . . . [109] Dined at Mrs. [Robert] Sedgwick's. . . . Nothing talked of but the Somers Mutiny. All are well disposed toward Mackenzie.

Mrs. Mackenzie (wife of the commander) called upon Mrs. S. & I was introduced to her. She is a sensible & rather handsome woman. She spoke of her husband's case, & said that as soon as she saw him upon his arrival she perceived, that he looked dreadfully, & asked him at once "what is the matter?" He turned her off by saying that he had had no sleep, & that they had experienced bad weather &c &c. He did not mention it to them, until all the papers had been sent to Washington.

Item in the *National Intelligencer* (Washington), January 5, 1843, ✦ ✦ ✦ reprinted from the Philadelphia *United States Gazette*.

PHILIP SPENCER.—We do an act of simple justice and humanity, in relieving the memory of this unfortunate youth from some of the unnecessary calumnies which have been heaped upon it.

The assertions, which we have several times seen made, that he was convicted of infamous crimes, such as having stolen a watch, and others of like character while on the Brazilian station, and that his retention was an outrage upon the navy which would not have been tolerated in any one with less powerful connexions, are entirely unfounded. The facts of the case, as we have them from one likely to be well informed, are the following:

In a state of inebriety, Spencer grossly insulted an English Midshipman, which fact, coming to the knowledge of Commodore MORRIS, induced him to order a court martial. Spencer addressed to the Commodore a very penitential letter, deprecating the disgrace of a trial, and pleading a first offence. The Commodore did not feel at liberty to grant his request. Captain STORER, Spencer's immediate commander, addressed a letter to Commodore Morris in his favor, and proposing that Spencer should go home and place himself at the disposal of the Department. This was acceded to, and Spencer sent home. Upon examination at the Department, it appeared in truth to have been his first offence. In accordance with the uniform custom of the Department with a first offence, unless it be one totally incompatible with the character of an honorable man, he was permitted to retain his warrant, receiving at the same time a severe admonition, with notice that in case of a second offence, this would be remembered against him to prevent a pardon.*

The theft of a watch attributed to young Spencer was the act of another midshipman, who was, in consequence, dismissed from the service.

PHILIP SPENCER received just precisely that consideration, and no other, which every one in similar circumstances had met with; for, if every one guilty of a single indiscretion should have been banished the navy, many of its brightest ornaments spared to add lustre to its glory never would have had the opportunity. . . .

> Entry from the journal of Richard Henry Dana, Jr., January 5, 1843. Here reprinted from Charles Francis Adams, *Richard Henry Dana* (Boston: Houghton Mifflin, 1890), I, 50.

. . . Passing the Navy Yard, I saw a man pointing out the Independence, sixty guns, as the Somers. I took an opportunity afterwards to ask him what vessel that was in the stream. He answered, the Somers, which gave me an opportunity to point out the Somers to him as the little brig lying in by the wharf. He could hardly believe it was so small. I made a point upon that in favor of Mackenzie.

> From the New York *Weekly Tribune*, January 14, 1843, as reprinted in *Proceedings of the Court of Inquiry* . . . (New York: Greeley & McElrath, 1843), pp. 29-32.

THURSDAY, Jan. 5, 1843.

[29] . . . DR. LEECOCK: † I was on board the Somers as Passed Assistant Surgeon during her late cruise. I first heard of the intended

---

* See documents concerning this episode, in Appendix. See also the reminiscence of it by Robert C. Rogers, below, under the date July, 1890.

† Richard W. Leacock was assistant surgeon, 1837; passed assistant surgeon, June, 1842; died, March 31, 1843.

mutiny on the evening of the 26th November, when I was called on deck at evening quarters. . . .

[*The arrest and events leading to the execution.*]

The witness said he was one of the council who examined witnesses and we came to the conclusion that it would be eminently hazardous to attempt to carry the prisoners home, for fear of a rescue being made and the vessel seized. I heard Spencer previous to his execution ask to speak to Mr. Wales, and also ask Small to forgive him. About 2 or 3 days before Mr. Spencer was arrested, as well as I can remember, he was in the Ward-Room where Purser Heiskell and myself were. I was at the table looking over charts of the coast of Africa and the West Indies, when Spencer asked me if I knew where the Isle of Pines was. I told him it was some where on the coast of Cuba, and I believe I asked him at the time if he knew any body there, and remarked that I had heard it was a great piratical resort. Mr. Spencer made no further observation that I know of, but continued for some time looking attentively over the chart of the West Indies, and then spoke of the homeward cruise of the Potomac from Brazil. I recollect he asked Cromwell, when he was on the sick list off Cape Mercerado, if he had ever been on the coast of Africa before. I think he said he had, and he then asked what vessel he was in, and he replied *in a slaver;* and also said he had been taken by a man of war. This was Cromwell who said so. On the morning of the 26th Nov. Small presented himself to me to go on the list, complaining of nausea and vomiting. I put him on the list and gave him some medicine. The same day Mr. Wales's evidence on Mr. Spencer's case, came to my knowledge, implicating also Small. The next morning Small again presented himself, when I saw the sick, and still complained of vomiting. From his appearance, tone of voice, and the quivering of his hand when I felt his pulse, I perceived he was laboring under manifest fear and anxiety. I then made some inquiries of persons on the deck as to whether he had been seen to vomit or throw up his food. Nobody having seen him do so, and believing he was feigning sickness, I refused to keep him on the list longer and discharged him. I don't think the disorder he complained of would have produced the effects he showed. Nausea is apt to produce such an effect, but I had heard of his being concerned with Mr. Spencer, and I thought his tone and manner betrayed more anxiety than sickness. I asked some of those on the berth deck, I think in Small's presence, whether he had been seen to vomit. I did not ask Small who had seen him vomit. I do not know whether he took the medicine I ordered him the previous day or not. I think he was ironed the evening of the 27th. He never requested any medical aid after his arrest, and although I had my watch over the prisoners, I never saw him in want of any. I never heard any conversations, tending to show whether there was a mutiny or not on board the Somers. The grounds which induced me to form the opinion that a rescue was to be attempted, and that the execution was necessary, were, that there were a great many

he dropped the conversation. Two or three weeks previous to his
t he was speaking of fortune-telling, and said that he could tell
nes. I asked him if he could tell mine by examining my hand. He
he could, and having examined my hand he told me that my death
ild be a violent and sudden one, my life would be short, and that I
uld be a *gambler*. He told Midshipman Thomson and Mr. Delonde's
tunes at the same time in my presence, but I do not recollect what
irs was. He was in the habit of speaking very disrespectfully of the
mmander in the steerage, but was much too obsequious in his presence.
remember his saying that if the Commander should have another S
his initials, it would spell his character. I recollect his speaking very
isrespectfully of the Commander at Monrovia, while going ashore in a
oat in which I was. I don't recollect the words. On another occasion,
shortly after leaving New York, I was in conversation with some of the
midshipmen in regard to the vessel and character of our Commander. To
some observation of mine Mr. Spencer remarked, that he did not know
that [31] he was that kind of a man. He thought he was a d—d old
granny. I have observed his familiarity with the crew, and general inattention to duty. He seemed to be most familiar with Cromwell, Small,
Green and McKee, and with most of those whose names I subsequently
found on his list. He was frequently conversing with them when he was on
duty during his watch—laughing and talking with them in a more familiar
manner than became an officer or gentleman. This familiarity had attracted
my attention previous to my discovery of the mutiny, and I had made
observations on it to my messmates. He was on my watch, and was not
attentive to the duties on deck. I frequently had to give orders several
times without their being obeyed, and was often under the necessity of
going forward myself to put my own orders in execution. On each occasion
I generally found him either standing by himself or talking to some of
the crew. On the night of the 24th, during the mid watch, the lee main
top-gallant brace parted, causing the yard to swing forward. I went on
the forecastle to discover whether it had parted or let go by mistake, and
passed Mr. Spencer standing on the lee hen-coop conversing in an apparently familiar manner with John Brunt the lookout. I called the boy
to haul in the running part of the brace that was towing overboard, when
Mr. Spencer appeared to see me for the first time. He immediately got
down and went to his station on the weather side of the forecastle. He
afterwards asked me why I had braced the yard sharp up with the weather
brace. I relate this as an instance of his familiarity to his inferiors and of
his inattention to duty. He was morose and quarrelsome in his disposition,
so much so that none of his messmates would have more to do with him
than was unavoidable. He associated more with the crew than he did
with his messmates. His manner to the crew was the same as to his
messmates. I have heard Mr. Spencer make use of mutinous expressions

prisoners on the quarter-deck, and I did not know ho
leagued with them among the crew; and also from the te
from the seamen examined before the Council, who t.
very dangerous characters. I [30] thought also that the n
in stirring and performing their duties during the time t.
prisoners were in irons on the deck. This, I think, disap
after the execution. . . .

MIDSHIPMAN HENRY ROGERS, sworn.*—I was senior M₁
board the Somers during the last cruise, and first heard of th
the 26th of November, immediately after the arrest of Mr.
evening quarters, on going forward to report the first divisio
Lieutenant ordered me to remain on the quarter deck, and at
time sent for all the officers on to the quarter deck but Mr. Ha
witness went on to describe the arrest of Spencer, his conduct,
the conversation which took place between him and the Captail
time of the arrest.]—I also assisted in searching Mr. Spencer's
where they found the razor-case with the paper in it, with writing in
characters, of words in English. This was a list of his accomplices, h
certain, doubtful, and those to be retained on board *nolens volens.*
were also three explanatory paragraphs. These the first Lieutenant t
and I shortly afterwards decyphered them for the Commander. Betw
3 and 4 o'clock on the 27th, I heard the officer of the deck give the or
to set the sky-sails, and shortly afterwards take them in again, wh
the top-gallant-mast was carried away. I went on deck, and saw Cromwel
Small, Wilson, and several others in Mr. Spencer's list, collected abou
the main-top-mast head. They were out of their stations, and were not
usually zealous on such occasions, and it therefore struck me that they
had gone aloft either for the purpose of plotting or putting in execution
some previously formed plot. As soon as it became dark the First Lieutenant armed each of the officers with pistols and a cutlass and stationed
me at the lee gangway, with orders to watch that rigging strictly, as he
expected they would come down that way. They however came down the
weather rigging, and Cromwell and Small were arrested and confined in
irons as soon as they came on deck. . . . I saw Small addressing the
crew, but did not hear what he said. I heard Cromwell call out that "he
was innocent." They were buried about 7 o'clock, the funeral service
being read over them. Mr. Spencer was a messmate of mine, and messed
in the steerage. The day before his arrest he came up to me where I was
sitting in the steerage and asked me abruptly if our chronometer was
a good one. I told him I did not know, but supposed it was a very good
one. He then asked me if I knew the rate of it. I replied that I did not,

* Henry Rodgers was midshipman, 1837; passed midshipman, June, 1843; master,
1850; lieutenant, 1851; lost in the *Albany,* September, 1854. He belonged to a distinguished naval family.

towards his commander among the crew previous to his arrest, but I don't remember the words. The substance of what he said in the boat at Monrovia was that the commander was a d—d old humbug. I don't remember any others at the time. The discipline of the crew on our arrival at Madeira appeared to be very good. After leaving there, until the arrest of Mr. Spencer, the state of the crew was growing worse, and also till the execution. The rules and regulations were enforced in the same manner as at the commencement of the cruise. After leaving Monrovia there was a marked change in the manner of the crew for the worse. This continued till Spencer's arrest, and from that time until his execution it continued to grow worse every day. The change was very marked. The elder part of the crew would collect together in knots about the vessel, and were slow to obey the orders of the officers. Their looks were sullen. If an officer approached one of these knots, they would some-times remain together and their tone of voice would become louder. While the prisoners were in irons I observed M'Kie standing forward, looking very intently on Mr. Spencer, apparently endeavoring to catch his eye, but seeing me he commenced sky-larking with one of the boys near. I saw the last four prisoners and others who were suspected, always attend to bringing the meals to the prisoners Spencer, Cromwell and Small. I ob-served no other sign of any desire to communicate with the prisoners. I have observed that within a few days previous to Cromwell's arrest his manner had become more obsequious when addressing an officer, while at the same time there was a sneer upon his countenance. I had seen Wilson looking into the ward room very intently and pretending at the same time to be engaged in the sail room. The evidence given by others who were examined by the council, led me to unite in the letter to the commander recommending the execution, with all these circumstances combined.

Q. Are these the letters found in the razor case in Mr. Spencer's locker?
A. They are.

[*At this point Spencer's "Greek papers" were produced, and Rodgers verified the translation. See facsimile of these papers below.*]

From a letter from Catharine Maria Sedgwick * to Richard H. Dana, Jr., dated New York, January 5, 1843. Here reproduced from the original letter in the Dana collection of the Massachusetts Historical Society, by permission.

In repeating some of your remarks on the Somers affair to a friend of

* Catherine Maria Sedgwick (1789-1867), one of the most popular novelists and magazine-writers of the time, was a sister of Robert Sedgwick, and an aunt of Theodore Sedgwick, Jr., who soon became Mackenzie's counsel.

SPENCER'S PROGRAMME:

The following is faithfully copied from the paper found in Spencer's locker.

Το βε κεπι νολενς τολενς

Sεplair

ΙΙ Σπενςεϱ   Σιβλευ
Ε Ανδϱευς   Σlϱεμελ
Δ Μ'κενλυ   Σκoll
U'αλες   Vαν Βϱυηl
    Σμιθ
    Uιllμoϱε
    Γαζελυ

Δουlφυλ   Βλακυεll
Uιllςον +   ϱoδμαν
Μ'κεε +   Χλαϱκ
Uαϱνoϱ   Χνενλες
Γϱεεν   Χελευν
Γεδνευ   Σελσoϱ
Vαν Vελσoϱ   Χoϱνεν
Συλλιυαν   Διχενσoν
Γoδφϱεy   Θε Δoχlεϱ
Γαλλια +   Γαϱϱεβϱανlz
'ουαϱδ +   Uαll'αμ

$\{$ ((— —)$/\backslash$ —·)$)\{$ ·$\}$

Uεελ - - - Μ'Χεε
Αϱμ χ'εσl - - Μ'Χενλυ
Χαβιν - - - $\{$ Σπενχεϱ / Σμαλλ / Uιllςoν $\}$
Uαϱδ ϱooμ - - Σπενχεϱ
Σlεεϱαγε - - $\{$ Σπενχεϱ / Σμαλλ / Uιllςoν $\}$

Θoςε δουlφυλ, μαϱκεδ + νιλλ πϱoβαβλυ βε ινδυκεδ lo Γoιν, βεφoϱε θε πϱoγεχl ις καϱϱιεδ ινlo εκεκυlιoν.

Θε ϱεμαινδoϱ oφ θε Δουlφυλ, νιλλ κϱoβαβλυ Γoιν νεν θε θινγ ις δoνε ; ιφ νol, θευ μυςl βε φoϱςεδ.

Ιφ ανυ νol μαϱκεδ δoυν, νιςʹ .lo Γoιν αφlεϱ ιl ις δoνε, νε νιλλ πιχ ουl θε βεςl ανδ διςπoςε oφ θε ϱεςl.

In the above it will be seen that the Roman Italic capital S is always used instead of the Greek *Sigma* (Σ), and the Roman Italic *l* instead of the Greek *tau* (τ). The following is an accurate translation of the characters into English—letter for letter. It will readily be understood, bearing in mind that the Greek υ υ' φ and Γ, answer respectively to the Roman y w f and j:—

Serlain	To be kepl nolens volens
P Spencer	Sibleu
E Andreus	Slremel
D McKenlu	Skoll
Uhales	Van Brunl
	Smith
	Uillmore
	Gazelu
Doulphul	Blakuell
Uillson X	rodman
McKee X	Chlark
Uarnor	Chnenles
Green	Cheleun
Gedneu	Selsor
Van Velsor	Chornen
Sulliuan	Dikenson
Godphrey	The Dokler
Gallia X	Garrebranlz
Houard X	Uallham

Ueel - - - -	McChee
Arm chesl - -	McChenlu
Chabin - - -	{ Spenker / Small / Uillson
Uard room - -	Spenker
Sleerage - - -	{ Spenker / Small / Uillson

Those doulphul, marked X uill probablu be induked lo Goin, bephore the progekl is karried inlo ekekulion.

The remaindor oph the Doulphul, uill probablu Goin uen the thing is done ; iph nol, theu musl be phorced.

Iph anu nol marked doun, wish lo Goin aphler il is done, ue uill pich oul the besl and dispose oph the resl.

The following is a *fac simile*, both as to shape and size, of Small's name, erased under the word 'Steerage' above:—

mine—a very sagacious woman—she exclaimed "Mr. Dana's opinion affects my mind more than all I have heard before and I think is entitled to more credit— What a pity it cannot be made public"!— And so I thought and think, unhappily too late—last night I might have talked it over with you. I feel deeply interested for the Mackenzies and eager that they should have the benefit of the influence of favorable opinion on the community who, as it appears to me, are more than usually disqualified on this occasion for forming an opinion.

There is not, I believe, an individual whose opinion would have, and would deserve (a rare coincidence!) so much weight as yours; if therefore there is to your mind no indecorum in the present condition of this affair in answering and permitting me to publish your answer . . . , I shall feel that you have done a great and most opportune service to an honorable man—at this moment in a most trying position. . . . Of course it will not appear who your correspondent is. I have an invincible aversion to women appearing before the public when—they can help it. . . .

From *The Diary of Philip Hone,* edited by Bayard Tuckerman
✔ ✔ ✔ (New York: Dodd, Mead & Co., 1889), II, 170-171.

[170] January 5 . . . I attended for two or three hours the court of inquiry on board of the "North Carolina." The cabin was filled with spectators and newspaper reporters, for the examination is conducted by the greatest publicity. I was received with flattering respect by the president and members of the court, who invited me to a seat at their table. The proceedings are characterized by the utmost dignity and decorum. The witnesses examined to-day were Mr. Leycock, the surgeon, and Mr. Rodgers, senior midshipman; the latter a fine, sturdy fellow, a sailor out and out. I was amused by his seamanlike reply of "Aye, aye, sir," on two occasions when requested by the judge advocate and commodore to raise his voice. The witnesses are made to give a narrative, in their own words, of the events attending the mutiny and execution on board the "Somers," after which questions are put to them in writing by Commander McKenzie [*sic*], and orally by the judge [171] advocate. Their answers are prompt and manly. The evidence looks well for the commander. He looks careworn and anxious, as well he may. God send him a safe deliverance!

Opposite: Spencer's "Greek papers." This is a facsimile of part of page 31 of *Proceedings of the Court of Inquiry* . . . (New York: Greeley & McElrath, 1843).

From a letter of Charles Sumner to Dr. Francis Lieber,* Boston, January 6, 1843. Here reprinted from Edward L. Pierce, *Memoir and Letters of Charles Sumner* (London: Lowe, Marston, Searle, ✓ ✓ ✓ and Rivington, 1878), II, 256.

. . . Of course, you will justify Slidell Mackenzie in hanging Spencer. All the circumstances make this a historic act,—so atrocious a mutiny on board a public ship, led by the son of a Cabinet minister, and the father's name not shielding that son from a humiliating death! The question is: Had Mackenzie *reasonable ground* to fear for the safety of his ship and officers? If so, he is justified in the extreme course he took. . . .

From the New York *Weekly Tribune*, January 14, as reprinted in *Proceedings of the Court of Inquiry* . . . (New York: Greeley & ✓ ✓ ✓ McElrath, 1843), pp. 32-36.

FRIDAY, Jan. 6, 1843.

[32] MIDSHIPMAN THOMPSON called and sworn.† [*Testimony agrees with that of other officers.*] . . . Mr. Spencer, on the passage between Madeira and Porto Praya, asked me if I did not think the Somers could be easily taken. He said a person could go in the cabin and murder the Captain without detection. He also asked me about pirates rendezvousing in the islands in the Pacific, and whether a vessel could not go in there and refit. I think Howard heard this conversation. . . . I am 21 years of age and entered the service in 1837. . . .

[33] MIDSHIPMAN HAYS *sworn.* . . . ‡ I am 20 years old, and entered the service 12th March, 1838. . . . I was officer of the deck when the top-gallant-mast was carried away, on the 27th. . . . I think it was carried away by design, by hauling on the weather brace, instead of letting it go, as I had ordered. I do not know who hauled it in. . . . Mr. Spencer,

---

* Dr. Francis Lieber (1800-1872) was professor of history and political economy at South Carolina College from 1835-1856. He had edited the *Encyclopaedia Americana* (1829-33) for which Mackenzie had written naval articles. He was author of *Manual of Political Ethics* (1838-39), *Legal and Political Hermeneutics* (1839), and other writings which made him a conspicuous authority on such topics. A well-known liberal, of German birth, he had fought at Waterloo, later had joined the struggle for Greek Independence, had been imprisoned in Germany as a radical, and in 1827 had sought freedom in America.

† Egbert Thompson was midshipman, 1837; passed midshipman, 1843; acting master, 1846; lieutenant, 1850; commander, 1862; captain, 1866; retired list, 1874; died, 1881.

‡ Charles W. Hays was midshipman, 1838; passed midshipman, 1844; master, 1852; lieutenant, 1853; dismissed, 1861.

some five or six days before his arrest, showed me the drawing of a brig with a pirate's flag. This was in the steerage. It had a black flag, with a skull and bones. Two or three days before Spencer was arrested a strange vessel was in sight and we beat to quarters and cleared for action. Cromwell said "there was a d——d sight of humbug about this vessel, he had been aboard vessels where shot was fired and there was not so much humbugging." . . .

QUESTIONED BY CAPTAIN MACKENZIE.

Q. . . . Was she not near us and had she not the appearance of a cruiser?

A. Yes, sir. We boarded her afterwards and found she was a French barque; a brig.

Q. Was not the Somers taken several times for a slaver and chased by supposed British cruisers?

A. She was. . . .

MIDSHIPMAN DELONDE, *sworn.* . . .* I am 17 years old, and have been a year in the service. . . . Mr. Spencer told me when we were off Cape Mesurado . . . that he should like to have command of a brig like this—would cruise off the West Indies for slavers. I never heard him talk of pirates or piracies or the Isle of Pines, or of taking the Somers. He showed me a brig which he had painted. It was not the Somers, but an hermaphrodite brig. I don't remember whether it had any flag. The Somers is a full rigged brig. [*Witness gave same general account of discipline and conduct of crew as other officers.*]

[34] JOHN H. TILLOTSON, *sworn.*† I was acting Midshipman. . . . I am 16 . . . , in the service about four years. [*He gave testimony agreeing with that of other officers.*]

OLIVER H. PERRY, *sworn.*—I was Commander's Clerk . . . , and doing duty as a Midshipman. . . . Previous to Mr. Spencer's arrest, I had heard him say that he expected to command a vessel of his own shortly. . . . Mr. Spencer said this in the presence of Mr. Gansevoort. . . . I was on the forecastle when the top gallant mast was carried away. I saw Small and a boy—I think Van Velsor—who got hold of the main royal weather brace; they jerked it hard, belayed it very hard, and in half a minute the mast went. . . . [*Further testimony was similar to that of other officers.*]

SERGEANT GARTY, *sworn.*—I was . . . doing duty as master-at-arms. . . . On the passage between Madeira and Teneriffe, I was sitting on the

---

* Adrian Deslonde was midshipman, October 1841; resigned, 1849. His sister was the wife of Mackenzie's brother, John Slidell.
† John H. Tillotson was midshipman, 30 July 1842; resigned February 1849.

combings of the main hatch, and Mr. Spencer came up. . . . He then [said] she was a fine vessel. I said she was, and he said at the same time that he could take her with six men. I told him he could not do it with three times six. He said provided he knew where every thing lay as well as I did, and the keys of the arm chest. He went on to describe how he would take her.— First he would secure the Captain and officers, then take possession of the arms, turn up the crew, and he made no doubt as soon as they saw his men in arms they would give in to him. I told him then that after the crew had been turned up they could rush on him, and before there might be 6 killed we could throw him and his 6 overboard, and that he must think us a poor crew to think he could take it with 6 men—oh no, or something like it, he muttered out as he went away. Thus ended that conversation. On or about the 6th Nov. I heard Mr. Spencer ask Cromwell how he would like to sail with him. Cromwell said he'd like it well. That was on the forecastle. About the 20th, as I was sitting on the combings of the fore scuttle, there were a number of the crew standing by, and Cromwell in front of Mr. Spencer. They were talking about one thing or another, and the Army was introduced by some one, and I asked Mr. Spencer if it would not be better for him to go in the Army than the Navy. He told me that his father told him he would get him a Lieutenant's commission in the Dragoons; that he thought he wouldn't like it, and he thought he was not going to be long in the Navy. He said he was going to have a vessel of his own shortly. . . .

SATURDAY, Jan. 7, 1843.

. . . SERGEANT GARTY. . . . Mr. Spencer asked me [*a few days after Nov. 19*] about the arms, whether they were all loaded. I told him they were with the exception of 6 or 7 muskets. . . . On the passage between New-York and Madeira, Cromwell told me Spencer had given him $15 and requested me to keep it for him. He said if there was a vessel homeward bound from Madeira he would send the money to his wife . . . to buy coal for the winter. He gave me the money with some other articles to keep for him. They remained in my possession till a few days before the arrest. Cromwell . . . said, "master-at-arms, I want my glass, I want to shave," though he never shaved himself. He took the glass with the money in it, and did not ask me to take any further care of it. . . .

[*The witness gave testimony as to the discipline similar to that of the other officers.*]

I was examined before the council and gave [35] my opinion that the brig was in a dangerous condition. I formed this opinion from the conversations with Mr. Spencer, from what I heard Spencer ask Cromwell and from Cromwell not asking me to take any further charge of the glass and money. It added to my suspicion also seeing Cromwell and Small talking . . . on the night of Mr. Spencer's arrest. Being of opinion that Spencer could not take the brig himself, gave me also suspicions that Cromwell and Small were implicated. They were also melancholy and in bad spirits as if something laid on their minds. I gave my opinion that the brig was in danger of being taken by Spencer and his associates after the arrest. I was asked whether if they were put to death I thought the brig would be safe, and said I thought she would. I believed then and I believe now that there was danger of a rescue after Spencer, Small and Cromwell were arrested. . . . I believe it might have been successful in case the officers of the watch were only on deck, for the petty officers might be up aloft. . . . I can't name any that I think would have attempted a rescue, but on the 27th Warner said there was great work going on. I said there was no more than I thought was necessary. He made a remark that the officer of the deck was armed with three pistols and the officer of the forecastle with one. He said what would *we* do if they made a rush on them in the mid-watch. I told him I thought 13 or 14 of them would drop if they did. That was all the conversation I had with him; but it excited my suspicion. . . .

[*Sergeant Garty was the first witness heard by the court among those who had testified before the council of officers on November 30 and December 1. The court now began hearing the others who were questioned then. The deposition made before the council by each was read over to him for each to affirm its correctness.*]

CHARLES STEWART, sworn.— Was . . . captain of the forecastle. . . . I had often seen Mr. Spencer talking with Cromwell previous to his arrest. They appeared to be very intimate. . . . I have not seen Spencer talking to Small. . . . Discipline was very good till arrival at Madeira. After leaving Madeira something very extraordinary occurred with regard to the conduct of the crew—it was not so good as before. Some looked very sullen. They were very slack in obeying orders. After the arrest and before the execution they used to stand three and four in number together, but I don't know what they were talking about. They spoke low. . . . Cromwell attempted at the time of [36] execution to jump overboard two or three times previous to the rope being put round his neck. I was his guard. . . . [Spencer] gave me a glass of grog (brandy) for lending him my bed or mattress when he had lost his overboard and for scrubbing a pair of pantaloons for him. . . .

CHARLES ROGERS, sworn— I was . . . Quarter-Master. . . . Before we got to the coast of Africa Mr. Spencer said to me that he wished he had the launch and ten such men as he could pick out from the crew and he would make his fortune. This was when a brig was bearing down towards them. I said, then I think your intention must be for taking the brig which was in sight, and he said yes. I told him it would be hard to find ten men of the crew to take that vessel. He said yes, he could find ten men, and

then mentioned the names of some of the crew . . . , Wilson and Cava-
naugh, and McKinley and Green. . . . One night he asked me if I had
been in a slaver, and I told him no. Spencer was very intimate with Cromwell. . . . [*At the council of officers*] I thought the older boys were engaged in the plot because I heard from Mr. Gansevoort that most of their
names were found on Mr. Spencer's list as going to join him. I had not
seen any thing in their behavior myself to lead me to such an opinion, on
account of my being most of the time aft, and not associated much with
the boys. I do not believe that the Somers could have been brought safely
into port if those men had not been executed. I thought so then and think
so now. . . .

✓ ✓ ✓ From the New York *Evening Post,* January 7, 1843.

The Late Philip Spencer.— About sixteen months since, Professor
Webster of the Medical College at Geneva, operated, for strabismus, on
this unfortunate young man. The operation, as usual, left a fixed, staring
look, that was occasionally very marked.

From the New York *Weekly Tribune,* January 14, 1843, as reprinted in *Proceedings of the Court of Inquiry* . . . (New York:
✓ ✓ ✓ Greeley and McElrath, 1843), pp. 36-37.

MONDAY, Jan. 9, 1843.

[36] . . . WILLIAM COLLINS was sworn.— I was on board as Gunner's
Mate, and, after the confinement of Cromwell, as Boatswain's Mate. The
discipline of the crew up to our arrival at Madeira was very good; from
that time till the arrest of Mr. Spencer it was very bad. . . . The state
of the crew from the arrest to the execution was about the same as before,
but rather worse if any thing. . . . After the execution the discipline was
better. . . .

MR. BROWNING, Boatswain's Mate, was then sworn, and testified, in
the same way as the others, to the discipline of the crew before reaching
Madeira—to the change for the worse afterwards—to Spencer's exceeding
intimacy with Cromwell, carried, he said, to a greater extent than he ever
saw in any other officer—to the mutinous disposition of the crew after
the arrest, and to the absolute necessity which he believed to exist for the
execution of the ringleaders. . . .

Q. by CAPTAIN MACKENZIE— Did you ever have any conversation with
Wilson about this mutiny?

A. Yes. One morning at breakfast. Anderson said that it was sure to
be found out. I said, "yes, for I would lay $1000 that some one would

turn State's evidence"; with that Wilson said, "yes, if any body knew what he [*Spencer*] had said to me it would hang him without judge or jury." I asked why he did not go and tell the Captain. He finished his breakfast and went aft. What report he made, if any, I don't know. This was the morning after Cromwell was arrested. Then McKinley asked me if I did not think it best if he should go and let the first lieutenant know what Spencer had said to him. I told him he had better go up [37] to the first lieutenant and make a report of every thing—he knew he would be thought none the worse of for it. He went up and made a report and was put in confinement. . . . I did not believe then nor do I believe now that the vessel could have been brought safely to port had the execution not taken place. . . .

ANDREW STEVENSON [sic, *for Anderson*], captain of the forecastle, testified to the same facts—to the disobedience of the crew after the arrest, &c. When the mast was carried away, witness was ordered aloft, and found Cromwell, Small, Golderman and Wilson there doing nothing but talking. He asked them several times for assistance but received no reply from any of them. . . . It was his decided opinion that if the execution had not taken place the brig could never have been brought to port.

HENRY KING, *sworn* [*Gunner's Mate*]— The discipline was very bad after the arrest and up to the execution. . . . I observed Wilson stow an African dirk about gun No. 5 . . . , and Mr. Spencer was confined on that side close by that gun. I found, also, two handspikes and three heavers which I had stowed away amidships under the boats and where I thought nobody could get at them, had been taken back to where I had removed them from. I had stowed them away under the cutter which was in the launch. There were two—Sullivan and Golderman—that I had seen about the stern of the launch. . . . It was about 10 o'clock that I found they had been removed, and I had seen these men there about 9 or 10 o'clock.— When the watch was called at 12 the first place Wilson went was to the quarter of the launch where the handspikes had been. It was dark and I could not say whether he might not have gone for his jacket. . . .

I feared a rescue would be made very much, and was afraid to turn into my hammock at night. The men were about the deck and we did not know who to trust. I thought then and do now, that had any confusion occurred a rescue would have been attempted. I think such an attempt would have been successful if made, though the officers were armed. . . . After the arrest and previous to the execution we could not get much rest; we did not get our usual rest; I was afraid to go to sleep I had such a dread on my mind; I never unbuckled my arms from me, and slept with them from the time they were given me until our arrival in New-York. . . .

THOMAS DICKERSON [*Carpenter's mate*], sworn. I have often noticed

Spencer and Cromwell talking together . . . , for the last 10 or 12 days every opportunity they could get. . . . It was in a very low tone of voice. . . . I thought Knevals, Golderman, Sullivan, Wilson, Hamilton, Garabrantz and Waltham were concerned, because they were those who gathered about the decks.— I thought Waltham was more so, because of his mumbling out threats and grumbling about the decks and cursing and swearing. . . .

> Passages from a letter of James Fenimore Cooper to his wife, dated January 10, 1843. Here reprinted by permission from *Correspondence of James Fenimore-Cooper,* edited by his grandson, James Fenimore Cooper (New Haven: Yale University Press, 1922), II, ✓ ✓ ✓   489.

Everybody [*in New York*] is talking of Mackenzie's affair. As yet it looks worse and worse for him, though they say the secretary will sustain him. If he attempt it against the evidence, it will only break him down himself. Gen. Well, Govr. Kemble, and one or two more of us, at Gen. Cadwalader's, agreed last evening. Every man of mind thinks in the same way about it. . . . I went alongside of the *Somers,* and saw the fatal yard at which Phil was swinging little more than a month since. I am told the old officers shake their heads.

> From the New York *Weekly Tribune,* January 14, 1843, as reprinted in *Proceedings of the Court of Inquiry* . . . (New York: ✓ ✓ ✓   Greeley & McElrath, 1843), pp. 37-40.

TUESDAY, Jan. 10, 1843.

[37] . . . THOMAS DICKERSON. . . . I once carried a couple of single sticks to store in Cromwell's store room and told him they belonged to the First Lieutenant, and he said he did not care a d—n, they should not stay there. On my leaving the store-room, he said, *"your time's d—n short."*— Another time he had a rule which was broke, and he said that one of the carpenters had broken it. I told him they had not, it had got broken in the chest, and as I was going up the ladder he said, "G—d d—n you, I'll fix you." Another time he had a stick of wood up in both hands and was going to knock a boy's brains out with it. He threw one stick and missed the boy. He then took up another in both hands and swore by G—d Almighty he would drive it through his heart if he was swung on the mainyard the next minute. The boy settled down on his knees, calculating to receive his death wound. I interfered and he stayed his hand, and then he repeated to me that "my time was d—n short." . . .

The witness said he had been 19 years in the service and he also gave the same opinion as all the others as to the necessity of the execution. . . .

WILLIAM NEWELL [sic, *for Neville*] sworn. I am an apprentice . . . rated . . . as ordinary seaman. The discipline was good to Madeira. I saw little difference from that time till the arrest of Mr. Spencer, except that Cromwell behaved better to the boys than he had done before.— From the arrest till the execution the greater part of the crew seemed dissatisfied, and gathered about the decks talking about Spencer, Cromwell and Small. They said they thought it was not right to put them in irons. . . . Previous to Mr. Spencer's arrest, between Madeira and Cape Mercerado, he told me he should soon have a vessel of his own, and asked me if I would not like to sail with him. I told him I didn't know. . . .

I saw Mr. Spencer and Wales talking together on the booms the night before Mr. Spencer was arrested. I should think they were there two hours. I did not hear what they said. I also saw Small come up and speak to them. I saw Spencer show Cromwell a paper about two weeks before his arrest. . . . It appeared to be about half a sheet of letter paper. He appeared as if he was pointing with his pencil and explaining something to Cromwell. There were marks with a lead pencil on the paper. It was not common English letters, but looked like crosses, or something like it. I could not tell whether it was only writing or only marks Mr. Spencer had been making. . . .

[38] PETER TYSON sworn.— I am in my 19th year. I was third class apprentice . . . and this was my first voyage. The first I heard of the mutiny was a conversation the night before Mr. Spencer was put in irons. I was laying aft on the spar deck, between the 4th and 5th guns to the leeward side, about 7 o'clock in the evening, and Wilson and McKinley came aft. Wilson had his battle axe in his hand and a sharpening stone and no hat on. McKinley said to Wilson he had just told me that we have spies and we had better be careful. Wilson replied no, he need not fear that; he knows me and knows what I am, and that I have been in too many scrapes. McKinley then said to Wilson, "Would you join them?" He answered, "He would not mind it." McKinley then said, I don't know, I think I would rather go on a regular slaving expedition, for there they had $25 a month and prize money, and when we got to St. Thomas we would be fitted out. It was against the orders to lie on the leeward side of the vessel and they had come up to me and saw who I was before they began this conversation. Had a pea jacket on. I was drowsy, and I think they thought I was asleep. I had gone there to try to sleep, and I laid still till this; and I then asked McKinley what was that he was saying about a slaver? He replied that he was talking about a slaver that left St. Thomas, and had been gone about 3 months, and had taken three or four vessels. He said she was fitted out with about as many guns as the Somers. I said I had heard of a slaver being fitted out there; and he said it was a free port,

and they were often fitted out there. There was nothing said about pirates, only McKinley said, *"he would rather go in a regular slaver."* I never noticed there was any slackness about duty till after we left Teneriffe, and after that Wilson, who was Captain of the afterguard, has often said to me, "D—n them, they have got plenty of men forward, let them do it themselves." The discipline grew a little better after the arrest, but much better after the execution. . . . I was afraid they would attempt to take the vessel after Spencer, Cromwell and Small were arrested. I recollect Wilson's saying he would take the boy Weaver's life, and would pay the Master, Mr. Perry, and the Commander, for having him flogged. . . . In the conversation between Wilson and McKinley, Wilson said, *"He* knows well enough that I did not come on board this vessel willingly." He also said that when they got to St. Thomas he would run away and join a slaver. I do not believe that if the execution had not taken place, the vessel could have been brought safe to any port. . . .

MATHIAS GEDNEY, sworn. I was seaman on the Somers; an apprentice. I am 20 years old, and have been over five years in the service. I heard a conversation between Cromwell and Spencer on the passage between Porto Praya and Monrovia. . . . I heard Mr. Spencer say he would try that plan—if he succeeded well and good, if not, he'd burst. I don't remember that Cromwell made any answer, and Spencer turned and went away. They were talking about a voyage to the Northwest Coast. A few evenings after I heard Spencer say to Cromwell he hoped he would not forget what he had spoken to him about. Cromwell said, "Oh, no, sir," and walked away. . . . At the time of the conversation about the North-West Coast Cromwell seemed to have been talking louder than he intended and not to be aware that we were so near. Two or three boys were laughing and Cromwell looked round several times and seemed frightened. I asked Van Velzer what Cromwell had been talking about, and he said that Spencer was going as Captain of a vessel and Cromwell was going as his mate. . . .

GEORGE W. WARNER sworn. I was Captain of the forecastle on the Somers. I am an apprentice and have been 5 years in the service. I once heard Spencer ask Cromwell what kind of a slaver the brig would make, and he said she would make a good one. I never heard them talking together at any other time but I have frequently seen them. . . . Mr. Spencer has never said anything to me about taking the brig. He never asked me if I had been in a slaver, and never asked any of the boys in my hearing or said anything to them on the subject. After Spencer, Small and Cromwell were put in irons I did not think any attempt would be made to take the brig. After Mr. Spencer was put in irons, I thought there was a mutiny on board and that there were others concerned in it. I didn't know then who to think was concerned in it. After Cromwell and Small were put in irons I thought both of them were concerned in it; I thought so from

Cromwell's intimacy with Mr. Spencer, and his general character:— By that I mean his general treatment of every body; he was of a quick temper, and would often attempt to strike you, and if you did not get out of his way he would do so. I thought Small was concerned in it because on the night of Mr. Spencer's arrest he was called aft and when he came forward again he appeared to be discontented about something, as if he had something heavy on his mind; the evening we were sending up the top-gallant-mast he was in the top; I went up with the mast, and he was sitting there apparently thinking about something which was not concerning his duty. I have no reason to believe that any other persons were engaged in the mutiny.

[39] The morning after Cromwell and Small were arrested Wilson told me and the carpenter that he had had a conversation with Mr. Spencer. The carpenter advised him to go and report it to the 1st Lieutenant. He told us that Mr. Spencer called him one evening, when he was alone, and asked him what was the occasion of his coming into the service, and Wilson told him it was on account of a small spree he had had on shore. Mr. Spencer said he knew all about it, and Wilson replied he must have overheard something. Spencer said no, that there were one or two on board that had told him something about it, or something to that effect. He then put an end to the conversation, by saying "never mind." That is all that Dickerson told him to report to the 1st Lieutenant.

I did not hear him say any thing to Dickerson about the mutiny or about Spencer's having said any thing about it. I have not heard any declarations from the crew to lead me to believe they were engaged in it. I was passing along the forecastle one day and Green and some others were talking about Spencer, and I said if I had my way I would hang them. I said, too, that I thought Spencer was as bad as either of the two others, and Green remarked that he thought Mr. Spencer was a nice man. My remark was merely an idle one about hanging them. I had not heard of any conversation at that time about hanging them. I did not believe that any attempt would be made to rescue the prisoners when I made that remark. I think if these men had been kept in confinement no attempt would have been made to rescue them. . . .

WEDNESDAY, Jan. 11, 1843.

. . . GEORGE W. WARNER [*continues*]. . . . I suppose Spencer intended to take the vessel to the Northwest Coast, because he had often said in my hearing that he liked that country the best. . . . I said to the Council that *I had no doubt* Spencer intended to take the vessel, from what I had heard among the crew. I had heard the carpenter say that he had seen Spencer talking with Cromwell out of sight of every body, and from that, and hearing the Captain, when he flogged Waltham, read off part of the plot, I believe Spencer intended to make the attempt. . . .

Q. Is that or was that a serious opinion of yours that "Cromwell deserved to be hung"?

A. If he was guilty, he deserved to be hung.

Q. Did you think he was guilty?

A. I did think he was guilty. I had no other reasons for thinking he was guilty than those I have given. . . .

I do believe the brig could have been taken to St. Thomas at any rate without the execution taking place. . . .

This witness was one of those who were confined by Captain Mackenzie on his arrival in this port. . . .

[39] . . . CHARLES VAN VELZER, also a prisoner since his arrival here, was next sworn.— I was Captain of the Foretop on the Somers. I am 18 years of age, and have been 4 years and some months in the service. Spencer never conversed with me previous to his arrest. I have often seen him talking with Cromwell. . . . I never heard them but once. . . . I then heard Spencer tell Cromwell that he should like to have a vessel to go out on the North-West Coast with, and he thought he could raise money enough to get one. Cromwell said he was well acquainted with the N. W. Coast. That was all I heard. Mr. Spencer was most familiar with Cromwell and some of the small boys—Scott, Stranmels [*sic*], Blackman [*sic*], Gazeley. . . . The discipline was very good until our arrival at Madeira. . . . There was no change before the arrest; after there was. . . . The boys collected about the gangways talking, in twos and threes, and wondering what Spencer was in irons for. . . . Never saw any one refuse an order. . . . I did not see them collect in knots . . . after they found out what he was ironed for. . . . I believed that if there was any plot Cromwell was concerned with Spencer, but I did not know of any plot. . . . I think the brig could have been brought safe into port without executing those men. I thought so at the time, and I think so still.

The Judge Advocate here stated that the last witness finished the number of those who had been examined by the council of officers, and he now proposed . . . to commence . . . and examine each of the boys . . . except the remainder of those in confinement. He further said he should not have examined the two last witnesses had [*they not*] been previously examined before the council of officers.

EDWARD FOWLER, *sworn*— I am 15. . . . One evening I heard Cromwell . . . ask Small if he had ever been at the Isle of Pines. Small said no, and Cromwell said he had been there once in a man of war, and it was a very nice place. Cromwell said as how as there was a good many man of war's men and pirates there, and he then said never mind we'll soon see the times when we'll see it again. Small never spoke to that. . . .

[40] MANUEL HOWARD . . . sworn. I was steerage steward. . . . One

day . . . Spencer . . . came down in the steerage and said, "The Captain has been reprimanding me, but he sha'n't do it much longer." I have often heard him say he would soon have a ship of his own, but don't know where he was to get it from. One day I was rubbing his head, and he asked me if I would go with him—he did not say where. I told him I would, and he said I should have nothing to do but rub his head, and brush his clothes, and clean his boots, and he would give me good wages. He did not say where the vessel was to come from or whether he was to be Captain. He did not say he wanted me to go in a *vessel* with him. One day afterwards Mr. Rogers asked me if I would go on his farm as overseer, and Mr. Spencer overheard it, and asked him, I think, if he wanted me, and he said, "Oh, d—n you now, you're going with Mr. Rogers, not with me." I have seen him with a piece of paper on which he seemed to be writing some names, and he asked Mr. Rogers if he understood Greek. Mr. Rogers said he did, and Mr. Spencer then said "then you can't see it, or any one else." After Spencer was arrested, McKie came to me and said "I'm sorry Mr. Spencer is arrested—I'm d—d sorry." . . . McKie appeared to be interested, and as if something was going on that was not right. The sailmaker [Small] and Wilson also appeared dissatisfied. I thought the vessel was not safe before the execution. . . . That is my opinion now also. . . .

[*Nothing significant added by eight further witnesses.*]

༈ ༈ ༈ From a letter to the editor (William Cullen Bryant) of the New York *Evening Post,* January 11, 1843.

. . . Mr. Mackenzie is one of those men whose history and character afford the best practical evidence of the moral advantages of political equality. His father was, at one time, wealthy; but, before his death, lost his property, and became the Secretary of an Insurance Company. Some of the older frequenters of Wall Street, still cherish his memory as that of a singularly urbane and scrupulously honest man. . . . The eldest [son, John] after fighting a very desperate duel, went to New Orleans, where his talents soon recommended him to General Jackson, by whom he was appointed District Attorney of Louisiana. . . . Alexander entered the navy at the age of ten. . . . Mackenzie is essentially a self-made man. . . . He has ever been a thorough democrat in principle. His writings indicate this. . . . His republican spirit might be inferred from the rare simplicity of his character. This trait, while it endears him to his friends, often betrays itself in a singular absence of worldly wisdom. . . .

T.

A letter from Commander A. S. Mackenzie to George L. Duyck-inck,* dated from U. S. Brig *Somers,* New York, January 11, 1843. Reproduced here from the original letter in the Duyckinck Collection of the New York Public Library, by permission.

Understanding from your friend Mr. B. W. Whicher that you had been a fellow collegian of the late Mid. P. Spencer at Geneva College, and as attempts have been made to prove him a mere boy incapable of the murderous purpose imputed to him and to denounce those whom necessity compelled to pass upon him the sentence of the law without all its forms, I take the liberty of calling upon you as a friend of truth and justice to state what you know of the character, tastes, and acts of Mr. Spencer, in case it should be necessary for me to use it for my own justification before the court of enquiry or to repel future attacks.

From a letter of Richard H. Dana, Jr., to an un-named "Friend" [Catharine M. Sedgwick], first published in the New York *Evening Post,* January 13, 1843, and widely reprinted in other newspapers. Here reprinted from Charles Francis Adams, *Richard Henry Dana* (Boston: Houghton Mifflin, 1890), I, 50-58.

Boston, *January* 11, 1843.

[I, 50] . . . Short as my stay was, I could not refuse ———'s invitation to attend the court-martial, and to visit the little brig which had been the scene of the exciting tragedy.

[I, 51] We had a fine, clear, cold day [Jan. 4], and the Brooklyn ferry-boat zigzagged us across the river, to avoid the floating ice, and a lively sleigh took us to the navy yard. The court is held on board the North Carolina, a large ship of the line, which lies moored a few rods from the wharf. A little wherry, in which were two sailors with the naval jacket and shirt collar, was passing and repassing by a tow-line or guess-warp, taking passengers off and on.

It was interesting to see these poor fellows attending about a ship in which a court of great personages was sitting to determine whether a commander can string them up at a yard-arm at sea for a mutiny; and I felt a strong inclination to learn what impression the whole affair made upon them; but it would have been improper for me to touch upon the subject with them if I had had an opportunity, as I did not. The marine on guard at the cabin door let us pass, and we found ourselves in the upper cabin, and in the midst of the grave and rather imposing assembly.

A long table filled the middle of the room. On one side of it sat the three commanders who compose the court; Mr. Mackenzie sat at one

* George Duyckinck (1823-1863) was the younger brother of Evert Duyckinck, whom he assisted in various editorial and literary projects.

end, Mr. Perry (the witness under examination) stood at the other end; and opposite the court sat the clerk and Mr. Hoffman, the judge advocate. There were a number of auditors, and the reporters of the principal papers had a table to themselves. The clerk was reading Mr. Perry's testimony, and all was silent, so that I had a good opportunity for observation.

Notwithstanding my desire to see Mr. Mackenzie, my eye rested for some time upon the venerable president of the court, Commodore Stewart, one of the [I, 52] Old Ironsides' heroes, and the manager of what always seemed to me to be the best manœuvered battle in our late war. He has a good head, and carries the appearance of a man who can command himself as well as others, and has that calm manner which usually attends one who feels that his reputation is settled. The whole court is one in which great confidence must be placed, for they have the name and appearance of possessing clear heads and right minds.

I next carefully observed the features and expression of the party on trial; for this case is one which receives its complexion very much from the character of the chief actor: the facts being such as can never come to us with the same force and meaning with which they came to him at the time. It is not questioned that he acted upon the best of his deliberate judgment. How is he qualified, then, in moral and intellectual character, for forming a judgment?—becomes an important question. On this point his appearance is very much in his favor. He is apparently about forty years of age, and I am told that he entered the service at ten, and he says he has served thirty years. He has every mark of a calm, self-possessed, clear-minded man, entirely free from any of that dashing, off-hand or assuming manner which sometimes attends the military button. I felt much confidence in him from the moment I had carefully observed him, and this confidence has increased by my being informed that he is more noted for conscientiousness, order and thoroughness, than for imagination or enthusiasm.

I remained but a short time, as I knew that I could read the evidence more carefully the next day [I, 53] in the papers than I could get it while looking so many different ways.

From the North Carolina I went to the Somers; and here I must say that no one ought to form an opinion upon the issue of this conspiracy without first seeing the Somers. You have been on board a man-of-war, and you have, doubtless (as I find others have), formed your notions of the state of things in the Somers by what you have seen before. In the ships of the line, frigates, or sloops of war which you have visited there is great appearance of protection, defence, and imposing authority connected with the after end of the ship. There is a poop deck, a cabin built above the main deck, with doors and windows looking forward, a marine with bayonet and loaded musket at the door, another at the gangway, and others on guard at various parts of the ship, clear, roomy decks, a plenty of officers about, and the quarters of officers furnished with arms, and well guarded. But you must make a revolution in all your ideas upon these particulars to judge of the Somers. You would hardly believe your eyes if you were here to see, as the scene of this dreadful conspiracy, a little brig, with low bulwarks, a single narrow deck flush fore and aft, and nothing to mark the officers' quarters but a long trunk-house, or companion, raised a few feet from the deck to let light and air in below, such as you may have seen in our smaller packets which ply along the seaboard. You feel as though half a dozen resolute conspirators could have swept the decks and thrown overboard all that opposed them before aid could come from below. And in coming on deck (which seemed to me more fearful than anything else in the officers' [I, 54] condition) the officers would have to come up the steps and through the small companion scuttles, at which a couple of men could easily have cut them down, or shot them as they appeared. The officers' quarters and the cabin are on the same floor with the berth deck of the crew, separated only by bulkheads, and there was not a marine on board to keep guard at the doors, in the gangways, over the spirit room, powder magazine, or arm chest. All these places, and others of hardly inferior importance, have to be guarded by the officers themselves, or intrusted to such of the petty officers and men as they could place confidence in. We were not permitted to go below, but I could easily believe that, allowing sufficient space between decks for the accommodation of the officers and men, the hold might be so occupied by stores, ammunition, ballast, and the numerous necessaries of a ship of war in actual service, as to leave no place where half a dozen conspirators could be safely confined, apart from the crew, even if retaining them on board at all had been possible. In short, no one at all acquainted with nautical matters can see the Somers without being made feelingly aware of the defenceless situation of those few officers dealing with a crew of ninety persons, of whom some were known to be conspirators, while of the rest they hardly knew upon whom to rely for active and efficient aid in time of danger.

Indeed, I would go farther and say that one must either have been at sea, or be willing to receive something on faith for [*sic*] those who have, to judge fairly of this case. The difficulty in the public mind is to be satisfied that there was such a state of things on board, after the arrest, as would render it all but certain [I, 55] to men of reasonable firmness and discretion, that the arrested persons could not be taken into port in irons. For this must be made out, or the execution was unjustifiable. I do not yet mean to give you an opinion upon which I am willing to be held, for the facts are not yet all in; but I should not be surprized if the facts and demonstrations which satisfied Mackenzie and his officers should have less effect upon the general observer and reader on shore. The crew were under some fear after the arrest, and would be careful not to do any overt act, or commit themselves at all, until they were ready to attempt the rescue. They would conceal every sign until the moment of the outbreak.

The American fleet, off the coast of Santiago. This illustration shows the *Somers* (third ship from the left) in company with larger ships and gives some idea of its relative size. [Fitch W. Taylor, *The Broad Pennant: or a Cruise in the United States Flagship of the Gulf Squadron during the Mexican Difficulties* (New York: Leavitt and Trow, 1848), *frontispiece*]

If the officers had waited for that evidence, they would have waited just too long for their own safety, and for the prevention of dreadful crimes on the whole ocean. They were obliged to judge from a variety of small circumstances, of which some are significant only to naval men, and others can hardly be made to appear on paper as they did on the deck. For instance, the refusal of three men to muster. If this was, as the officers believed, a deliberate combination to disobey a lawful order, and carried out, it was of itself a mutiny, and would forfeit the lives of the parties by the martial law: for I know no other definition of mutiny than would cover that act. It is an open defiance of authority, and, connected with the event of the others, would alone go far to make out the required case. The suspected contrivance to carry away the mast; the gathering of the men about the mast-head, away from their stations; their rushing aft to the boom-brace, and refusal to go forward when ordered; the crowding into and blocking up of the [I, 56] narrow gangways; their neglect and disobedience of orders; that "indescribable something," which Mr. Perry mentioned, in their looks and manner, denoting defiance and preparation for worse; the concealing of deadly weapons in convenient but secret places; the hiding a dagger in the gun carriage, near Spencer; the midnight alarms; and above all the fact of these demonstrations becoming stronger, more apparent, and more frequent as they drew nearer to port and the chances of escape for the guilty were lessening; all these might make out a case which would satisfy a conscientious, humane and brave man in taking life, when yet a landsman, reading the articles in the papers by his fireside, in the heart of a city, surrounded by watchmen, a police and a *posse comitatus,* before whom he can "swear the peace" against a suspected assaulter, and have him put into the "Tombs," might think the judgment not sustained by evidence of sufficient danger. If the officers were morally certain of an outbreak, which no confinement could prevent,—recollect, they could call in no aid from abroad,—there was no place for them to retreat, and no concessions would avail them. Must they then wait the onset and its chances? Perhaps, so far as personal danger to themselves was concerned, Mr. Mackenzie and his officers would have been willing to run the risk of the contest, or (as would have been more probable) of being taken by surprize and at a disadvantage, rather than to take life beforehand; but they had also a solemn duty as public officers, at all hazards to prevent this vessel's becoming a pirate, in the hands of men who would have the power and the will to commit the most dreadful atrocities of which we can form any imagination; [I, 57] and if, from any over-humanity, or a fear of the consequences of an execution to themselves professionally, or before the public, or from too much confidence in their own power, they had suffered the conspirators to prevail, and the dreadful consequences had come to our ears—not even the personal sufferings and death of these officers would have saved their memory from our reproaches. . . .

From a legal document reprinted by the New York *Weekly Tribune,*
✓ ✓ ✓ January 12, 1843.

January 11, 1843. . . . Samuel R. Betts, District Judge: Two affidavits were presented me yesterday . . . for a warrant to arrest Alexander Slidell Mackenzie and Guert Gansevoort, for murder on the high seas. . . . By Margaret R. Cromwell and Charles Cleveland. . . . I decline granting the warrant. . . .

From a letter from Lieut. Charles H. Davis to Charles Sumner, dated Washington, January 12, 1843. Here reproduced from the original letter in the Sumner Papers, in the Houghton Library of
✓ ✓ ✓ Harvard University, by permission.

I must thank you very kindly for your last letter giving me the opinions of Judges Story, & Prescott in Mackenzie's case—
It was very comforting, particularly as I am assured that it is the intention of those concerned to bring M. before a civil tribunal as soon as the Court of Enquiry has closed its investigation— Mr. [Rufus] Choate [*U. S. Senator from Massachusetts*] has expressed to me the same views—
The friends of Mackenzie are desirous that a Court Martial should immediately follow the C. of Enquiry—& they are now convinced that it would have been more judicious to have commenced with the Court M.
This course would have saved much future trouble. . . .

✓ ✓ ✓ From the New York *Weekly Tribune,* January 14, 1843.

A pamphlet containing the full Proceedings of the Court of Inquiry in the case of the Somers Mutiny, with Diagrams, Cuts, &c. will be published at this Office next week. Price 12½ cents.
[*This is the pamphlet,* Procedings of the Court of Inquiry . . . , *from which extensive excerpts are reprinted in this Part. Its text is taken directly from the* Tribune's *regular reports.*]

From the New York *Weekly Tribune,* January 21, 1843, as reprinted in *Proceedings of the Court of Inquiry* . . . (New York:
✓ ✓ ✓ Greeley & McElrath, 1843), pp. 40-42.

THURSDAY, Jan. 12, 1843.

[40] . . . HENRY STREMMELL, 1st class apprentice, 15 years of age . . . saw Mr. Spencer and Mr. Wales on the booms talking, and saw them call Small up to them, but did not hear any thing that was said. . . .

WARD M. GAZELEY, 1st class apprentice, 15 years of age. . . . Witness was sitting on the bitts and saw Spencer and Wales in conversation on the booms, when Small was called and Spencer said something to him at which he drew back and seemed frightened and Spencer then said, "It's all one, and he would have another conversation with him that night." . . .

[41] WILLIAM CLARK, first class apprentice, 16. . . . Some three days before Spencer's arrest he asked witness whether he had a knife, and he said no, not yet. At night he was sitting forward and Spencer came to him with a sheath knife with brass on the handle, and said here's a knife for you. Witness told him Charley Stewart had given him one, and Spencer said never mind, *take this and keep it sharp and ready*. Witness did not take it. . . . Saw Spencer show Cromwell a piece of paper . . . asking him if it would do. Cromwell said it would do very well. . . . The letters were an old fashioned alphabet. . . . Witness saw Spencer show Cromwell that paper again at supper time. Cromwell said it was better. . . . One day Cromwell . . . was finding fault [with the boys] when Mr. Spencer said—"Yes, the sooner we get shut of these little devils the better, for they eat bread and are of no use." This was on the passage to St. Thomas, before his arrest. Saw Wilson one day trying to approach Mr. Spencer when he was in irons. . . .

JAMES MITCHELL, 2d class apprentice, 16. . . . One day after the execution I was sitting in the main-top with Sullivan, and I asked him if he thought they could have took the vessel. He said he thought they could, and I then asked him what they would do with it if they had taken it, and he said they would kill all hands and then sink the vessel. . . . He said, "Dead men tell no tales, kill all and sink the vessel."

JOHN WILSON, second class apprentice, 16. . . . Was in the mess with McKinley and Wilson, and heard Wilson say if Lt. Gansevoort and the Captain knew what he did about Spencer, it would hang him. Heard McKinley say, after Spencer was arrested but before his execution that he expected he should be in irons before night. He said so two or three times but gave no reason for saying so. . . .

[*Nine other boys added no new testimony of importance.*]

FRIDAY, Jan. 13, 1843.

. . . [Sixteen] lads were examined and testified to what has been repeatedly before the public. . . . They were all asked their opinions as to the necessity of the execution. Several had no opinions and others thought that the vessel was not safe until the execution had taken place. . . .

SATURDAY, Jan. 14, 1843.

[42] . . . WILLIAM INGLIS, 2d class apprentice, 17. . . . Spencer had a paper . . . ; he would write on it with a pencil, and then show it

to Cromwell, who would say Yes, sir. Witness went past, and as he passed looked over his shoulder at Mr. Spencer, who got up, and shook his fist at him—called him a d——d son of a b——h, and if he looked at him in that way again, he would have him at the gangway and get him flogged. Thought that there were more than three engaged in the mutiny, and had seen Wilson making motions to Spencer, who returned them. He had also seen Wilson, McKinley and McKie standing about the main mast and whispering, while . . . Mr. Spencer was in confinement. . . . I think Spencer was writing names on the paper. He was writing straight down, and very few words on a line. At the time he was writing he was looking round at the boys. He would first look round then write down, and then show the paper to Cromwell. . . .

[*John* (sic *for Edward*) *English, 17, witnessed this scene, according to his testimony. Spencer* "seemed to be putting down something Cromwell was telling him." *Nine other boys were examined.*]

MONDAY, Jan. 16, 1843.

[*Twenty-one boys were examined, none of whom threw any additional light on the subject, except* JONAS HUMBER] who testified that on the day of Spencer's arrest he (witness) was handling an African dirk knife belonging to Wilson, when he said he had just been sharpening it up, and would as soon cut his throat with it as look at him. He also saw Wilson have that knife near No. 5 gun (the one next to where Spencer was confined,) and he said he should like to put it into Mr. Spencer's hand. The Tuesday previous to Mr. Spencer's arrest, he heard Mr. Spencer ask McKie [*sic*] if he knew how to cut out clothes and sew them. McKie said he did. Spencer then asked him if he would like to sail with him, to which McKie replied that he would. Mr. Spencer said all he would have to do would be to cut out and make clothing for the crew, and that he would not have any winter clothing to make, because they were going to a warm place. . . .

✓ ✓ ✓ From the New York *Herald,* Tuesday morning, January 17, 1843.

. . . We would not hastily condemn Captain McKenzie, nor do we think he would have proceeded to such an extremity without being persuaded that there was a necessity for such rigor. But still he must be satisfied on such strong grounds as will also satisfy the law, the community and the age. . . . We think he has not yet shown facts strong enough—and his exculpation is therefore incomplete. . . . It would seem . . . that a panic or mania prevailed . . . on board the Somers—the captain, officers, and crew being afflicted with it in one way, seeing mutiny in everything—and Midshipman Spencer afflicted with it in another shape—concocting mutiny out of Greek letters and nothing. It is probably the greatest farce, ending in an awful tragedy, that ever was enacted since the creation.

> From the New York *Weekly Tribune,* January 28, 1843, as reprinted in *Proceedings of the Court of Inquiry* . . . (New York: Greeley & McElrath, 1843), pp. 43-47.

TUESDAY, Jan. 17, 1843.

[43] . . . WILLIAM CONGER, 2d class apprentice, 18. . . . About half an hour previous to Spencer's arrest, witness passed him—he appeared agitated, and witness heard him say *"The die will shortly be cast."* Witness remarked it at the time to some boy, and wondered what was the matter with him. After Mr. Spencer's arrest, the witness asked what he was confined for, and one of the boys answered it was for fighting with Mr. Thompson. . . .

[WM. NEVILLE, WM. CLARK, WM. ENGLES (sic), *and* EDWARD (sic) ENGLISH, all *recalled to stand, and first three identify one of papers found in Spencer's locker as that they saw him showing to Cromwell; Edward English cannot tell whether either is that paper he saw. Seven more boys tell nothing new.*]

WEDNESDAY, Jan. 18, 1843.

[45] . . . Commander Mackenzie . . . presented the following Document:

. . . I am prepared to prove that more than a year ago, it was one of the amusements of Mr. Spencer to relate to the young children of one of the professors of Geneva College, in whose family he was domesticated, "murderous stories and tales of blood;" that the chief and favorite theme of his conversation was piratical exploits, and the pleasures of a pirate's life; that the great object of his ambition was renown as a pirate; that the book which he oftenest read, and which, on leaving Geneva College to embark in a whaler, he presented to the student's library, was the "Pirate's Own Book," and that it still remains there with his name in it; that on stepping into the stage coach to leave Geneva, the last words he said to a friend . . . were, that he would next be heard of as a pirate.

Witnesses are now in attendance upon the Court, to prove that throughout the period of his service in the Potomac, from Rio to Boston, the possibility of capturing her, and the use to be subsequently made of her as a pirate, were the object of his thoughts, and the theme of his conversation to at least three of her forward officers and [at least three of the crew]. . . . When he found his plans for carrying the Potomac could not be matured, he proposed to equip . . . a clipper brig at Baltimore, and arranged all the details for manning and arming her after he should be dismissed from the naval service. . . .

[*He is also prepared to prove previous mutinous and piratical tendencies of Cromwell.*] . . .

The Court . . . could not admit or receive [this] testimony. . . . [46-47] [*Further testimony by several officers about taking testimony at the Council of officers. Commander Mackenzie submits a brief summary statement of his reasons for the executions.*]

✓ ✓ ✓ News item in the Chicago *Express,* January 18, 1843.

U. S. Brig Somers.—The occurrence on board of this vessel has been dramatized and brought out in defiance of all good feeling and taste, at the Bowery Theatre, New York.

✓ ✓ ✓ From the New York *Weekly Tribune,* January 28, 1843, as reprinted in *Proceedings of the Court of Inquiry* . . . (New York: Greeley & McElrath, 1843), p. 48.

THURSDAY, Jan. 19, 1843.

[48] . . . The President . . . stated that the testimony being now closed the Court would be cleared, which was accordingly done. The Court will deliberate and frame their decision in secret, and it will then be sent to Washington for approval.

[*End of the Court of Inquiry.*]

✓ ✓ ✓ From the New York *Courier and Enquirer,* January 21, 1843.

The Somers. N. Currier, No. 2 Spruce Street, has published a *portrait* of the U. S. brig Somers [*see frontispiece*], now the object of so much interest in all parts of the country. It is finely lithographed by Napoleon Saroney, a very promising young artist of this city, and coloured by himself. The brig is correctly drawn except in the rake of the mainmast, and the picture is in all respects a very handsome one.

✓ ✓ ✓ From the New York *Herald,* Saturday morning, January 21, 1843.

. . . Mr. Fennimore [*sic*] Cooper, . . . is now in this city, and was very busy in Wall Street, a few days ago, examining certain charts in one of the insurance offices. Mr. Cooper, whose judgment is one of the best

INQUIRY

INTO

THE SOMERS MUTINY.

WITH A FULL ACCOUNT OF THE EXECUTION OF

SPENCER, CROMWELL AND SMALL.

NEW-YORK:

GREELEY & McELRATH, TRIBUNE BUILDINGS.

PHILADELPHIA: BURGESS & ZIEBER.

BOSTON: REDDING & CO.

Tribune Print.   160 Nassau-st.

The above illustration, and the four following, are from the New York *Weekly Tribune*, January 21, 1843, as reprinted in *Proceedings of the Court of Inquiry* . . . (New York: Greeley & McElrath, 1843).

THE UNITED STATES BRIG-OF-WAR SOMERS.

THE above engraving accurately represents the appearance of the SOMERS as she sits upon the water. She is a beautiful craft of 266 tons measurement, though she is so sharply built that she carries only 120. She is a very swift sailer, and is pierced for 14 guns, though she mounts only 10. Her mainmast and foremast are each 21 inches in diameter at the deck. The dimensions of the several parts of the vessel are as follows:

Mainmast	60 from deck.	Foremast	56
Main topmast	36	Fore top-mast	33
Main top-gallant-mast	18 3 inches.	Fore top-gallant mast	16 9
Main royal top-gallant-mast	12 3 "	Fore royal top-gallant mast	11 3
Pole	4	Pole	3 8
Total hight from deck	130 6 "	Total hight	120 9

Length of Bowsprit outboard .... 21 feet.
Length of the Jib-boom .... 17 "
Length of Flying Jib .... 10 " 9 in.

Total length .... 43 " 9 "

Whole length of keel .... 85 ft. 3 in.
Length between perpendiculars .... 100 "
Breadth of beam moulded .... 25 "
Extreme breadth .... 25 " 7 "
Depth of hold .... 11 "
Length from knight-heads to taffrail .... 105 "

The following is a table of the distance run by the Somers on each day after the first discovery of the mutiny, up to her arrival at this port—copied from her log-book :—

Nov. 26 ....(day in which Spencer opened the plot to Wales) ....210 miles.
"   27 ....(day on which Spencer was arrested) 206
"   28 ....(day of the arrest of Cromwell and Small) 184
"   29 184
Dec. 30 ......(day of the arrest of McKee, McKinley, Wilson and Green) 177
Dec. 1 ....(day of the execution of the three ringleaders) 190
"   2 153
"   3 155
"   4 ....(arrival at St. Thomas) 174
"   5 ......(left St. Thomas) ....114 | Dec. 10 143
"   7 ....179 | " 11 116
"   8 ....175 | " 12 118
"   9 ....116 | " 14 ....(arrived at New York) 106

SECTION REPRESENTING THE SPAR DECK.

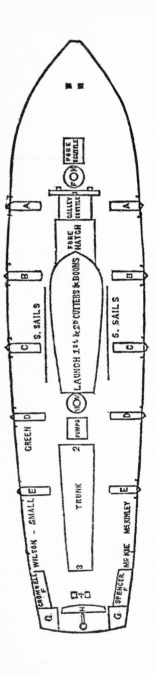

This cut represents the upper deck of the Somers and exhibits the position of the prisoners while in irons, the space left for working the vessel and the entrances to the rooms below. The following will sufficiently explain the whole:

No. 1—Just behind F. M., the foremost represents the place of the bitts. The whole space behind this to M. M. the mainmast, to the dotted lines at the sides is occupied by the launch cutters, and over them the booms, spare spars, sails, &c.

No. 2—Is the entrance to the steerage from deck, and the space to 3 is occupied by the trunk raised about two feet from deck, in which are two sky-lights.

No. 3 is the entrance to the Cabin, and from 3 to 4 is the only clear passage across decks.

No. 4 designates the position of the binnacles.

A. B. C. D. and E. show the position of the guns and gun-slides.

F. F. are the arm-chests on which Spencer and Cromwell were kept after confinement. The places of the other prisoners are marked by their names.

G. G. Roundhouse—the top being on a level with the bulwarks.

H. The wheel and fixtures.

It will be seen from these engravings that the only space in the vessel where prisoners could be kept was that which those in confinement occupied. After having disposed of the officers on deck the entrances from below by which officers could have come up could easily have been guarded by two men. Below there was, of course, no place to confine the prisoners as will readily be seen.

By the extract from the log book given above it will be seen that at the time of execution the Somers was four days sail from St. Thomas, and there was reason to fear that her arrival might have been retarded by adverse winds.

The following are the ages of the Officers and Men on board:

Officers, of 20 and upwards	8	Men, of 19 and upwards...18
" 19 "	"	" 18 " 20
" 17 "	"	" 17 " 23
" 16	1	" 16 " 16
Petty Officers, of full age.:	8	" 15 " 15
Cook and Stewards, of do	2	" 14 " 3
Men, of 20 and upwards...	51	" 13 " 3
SPENCER, CROMWELL and SMALL........	3	
Total number of the Crew...............	120	

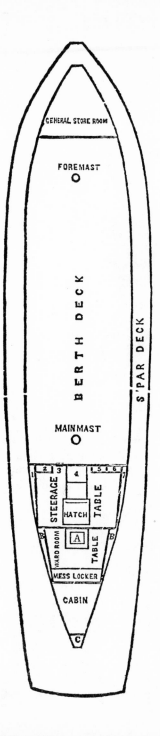

SECTION REPRESENTING THE BERTH DECK.

The above is a longitudinal section of the vessel giving an accurate representation of the Berth Deck, which is 50 feet long, by 17 wide. On this deck the great body of the crew slung their hammocks. The steerage is four feet long and 14 wide. Mr. SPENCER's hammock was slung in the steerage over the door leading from the berth deck through the steerage to the ward-room. A space of six feet by three in the steerage is taken up by the pumps and a table; and seven midship-men were confined to the remainder. The ward-room is ten feet by six, and in it a space of four feet by three is occupied by a table under which is the entrance to the magazine occupying the whole space beneath the ward-room.

In the ward-room were four officers; on the starboard side Lieut. Gansevoort slept on a bunk; on the larboard slept the Doctor, while the Purser and Master swung in hammocks. In the cabin slept the Commander—the rear being occupied by pantries, lockers, &c. The vacant space in the cabin was eight feet in width at the broadest end, and four at the narrowest; the length being eight feet. The following references will sufficiently explain the engraving above:

A...An Entrance to Magazine.
B, B...Bunks.   C...Pantry.
1...Breadroom.   2, 3...Lockers.
4...Pumps.   5...Door into Steerage.
6...Locker.   7...Sail-room.

Captain A. S. Mackenzie

on naval affairs, was about concluding a naval work, but has delayed it till this case can be terminated, in order to embrace in his book a correct history of all its details. We learn also that Mr. Cooper's opinion is decidedly against the propriety or necessity of the course pursued by Capt. McKenzie. . . .

↗ ↗ ↗ From a letter to the editor, Boston *Courier,* January 21, 1843.

I read with some regret, Mr. Editor, and not a little surprise, in a New-York paper . . . a letter from Mr. R. H. Dana, Jr. . . . There is some mystery in this affair. Mr. Dana goes to New-York,—possibly for this very purpose,—visits the Somers, with a friend—returns to Boston—thence, we know not why, writes a long letter to a friend in New York . . . as if he went on board for that purpose and no other . . . , and then the public are presented with a document . . . evidently intended to affect the public favorably . . . in regard to Commander Mackenzie. . . .

Mr. Dana, while a very young man, if not while a mere boy, went out *one voyage* from Boston, before the mast, in a merchant vessel. . . . He published a very interesting account of that voyage. . . . What possible advantage could such a voyage, in such a capacity, give a very young man over any landsman, in judging of the practicality of bringing home for trial Spencer and his associates in irons? Not the slightest. The opinions he has expressed are worth just as much as those of any other person and no more. . . .

Mr. Dana says, "with us in Boston, I have heard but one opinion." . . . It is not, however, true, that there *is* but one opinion in Boston. A writer in one of our papers has since stated that he has ten times the means of hearing the opinions of people—especially seafaring people—that Mr. Dana has, and he finds most of the shipmasters he has conversed with, think the prisoners might have been safely brought in. . . . The letter of Mr. Dana has not, in *my* mind, much weight. . . .

From a letter from Mrs. Robert Sedgwick to R. H. Dana, Jr., New York, January 23, 1843. Here reproduced from the original letter in the Dana Papers of the Massachusetts Historical Society, by permission.

. . . My sister [Catharine M. Sedgwick], I presume, has told you how much satisfaction your letter gave to the Community and particularly to Capt. MacKenzie [*sic*]—to use his own words "it was just the thing"— He called here a few days after with his wife & sister to express his acknowledgments—and to beg, that if any chance should bring you to the City, he might have the pleasure of seeing you— It is many years since I have seen him and Time, which is the destroyer of beauty, has kindly mellowed his ugliness—and there is a simplicity & manliness about him, which is very interesting now—when his name is in every mouth either for praise or blame— We all went over on Friday to see the Somers. It is now understood that McKenzie [*sic*] has applied, very wisely, for a Court Martial— It is expected that the Court of Enquiry will clear him— but the populace will not be satisfied—something more will be demanded — You have read Judge Betts' opinion on the indictment of Cromwell's wife, which is supposed to be instigated by the Secretary of War. . . .

From an editorial by James Watson Webb in the New York *Courier and Enquirer,* January 23, 1843.

JAMES F. COOPER.—This somewhat notorious character is now in our city, and it is said, has openly avowed his determination to write a review of the *Somers* case which will "annihilate MACKENZIE." That he will make the attempt no one can doubt, who is at all familiar with the unforgiving nature of the man. . . .

For years past he has hunted us [James Watson Webb] from court to court with indictments. . . . MACKENZIE . . . wrote a life of the late gallant OLIVER H. PERRY, who he believed . . . had been grossly misrepresented . . . by COOPER. That defence of the memory of the gallant PERRY, was a most acceptable offering to the patriotism of the American people, and precisely as it was acceptable to them and demonstrative of Mr. COOPER's unfairness, has it rankled in the bosom of that *amiable* personage. The time has now arrived for *revenge;* and it is said that pending the session of the recent Court of Inquiry, Mr. COOPER remarked that the execution of the mutineers by MACKENZIE, was a cold blooded MURDER! or some similar expression. Such is the story. If not true, we shall cheerfully correct the rumor; but if true, it very clearly exhibits the feelings with which Mr. COOPER will undertake the task of a *Reviewer.* He is a man of unquestionable talents; and knowing as we do his unforgiving nature and his resemblance in some respects to his unfortunate cousin, KELLY, who was executed for *murder* in Otsego, we doubt not but his proposed review . . . will be a very able and specious paper. We therefore caution the public in advance that Mr. COOPER bears Mr. MACKENZIE no good will. . . . That gallant officer has an enemy of no ordinary character to contend with—albeit, he [Cooper] cannot clothe his vigorous thoughts in as good English as we ordinarily meet with from the members of the Freshman Classes of our colleges.

But Mr. COOPER is the very last man in the United States who should condemn Mr. MACKENZIE, he having by his writings, done more to foster a taste for *Piracy* than any other person in it. His *Red Rover* and his *Le Feu Follet* [*Wing and Wing*] are works in which a Pirate's life is painted in the most fascinating colors, and could young SPENCER now be heard, we doubt not but he would point to Mr. Cooper's *Red Rover* as one of the prominent causes for his determination to war against civilized society. . . .

>   From a special article by "C. K. W." in the *Liberator* (Boston),
> ✓ ✓ ✓ January 27, 1843.*

NON-RESISTANCE. Case of The *Somers.* . . . Was it justifiable for Mackenzie to kill Spencer and his associates? . . . The precepts of Christ . . . forbid the treatment which Spencer received. . . . The execution was therefore . . . MURDER. . ʾ. . Will it be said that his death is justified by the laws and customs of the navy? Then those laws, being anti-Christian, should be abolished. . . .

 . . . Spencer . . . would probably have killed multitudes of people

---

* Edited by William Lloyd Garrison, the *Liberator* was the organ of his uncompromising antislavery views. Garrison was founder of the American Antislavery Society and of the New England Nonresistance Society.

with great honor to himself and his country, if he had waited a little while for the President's certificate empowering him to do so. His action was premature. . . . Spencer and Mackenzie acted on the same principles. . . .

. . . The application of the Christian rule to Mackenzie shows us that he had no right to be in the navy at all. . . . If [he] ever becomes a Christian, he will of course renounce and abandon the navy. . . .

From a letter of James Fenimore Cooper to his son Paul at Geneva, New York, dated January 28, 1843. Here reprinted by permission from *Correspondence of James Fenimore-Cooper*, edited by his grandson James Fenimore Cooper (New Haven: Yale University Press, 1922), II, 491-493.

✓ ✓ ✓

The *Somers* affair makes much conversation. The better opinion is everywhere against him, though there is a desperate effort making to get Mackenzie out of the scrape. Of the final decision of the country I entertain no doubt, though there is an evident desire to shield him among certain officials. All relating to the Court of Inquiry has been badly managed, and leaves a suspicion of favoritism. Still all the captains with whom I have conversed think him wrong.

The leading points are these: Spencer tells Wales his plans, to induce the latter to join him. He says he has about *twenty* men concerned. These, then, were the most he had engaged. Mackenzie reasons exactly the other way; he thought twenty was the *least* number opposed to him. *This fact, alone, proves the frame of mind under which he acted.* Of course Spencer, in cajoling a recruit, [492] put his best foot foremost—he boasted of all he had, and, as his own muster-roll subsequently showed, he boasted of *more* than he had. This paper has four down as certain. One of these four was Phil, himself, and another was Wales. Wales was clearly uncertain. He enlisted at nine o'clock at night, after the lights were out, and he swears that this was the first he had heard of the mutiny. Of course his name was put down next morning, the day Spencer was arrested, and this list was then complete. Three men *certain,* did not make a formidable mutiny—but there were *nine* doubtful. The doubtful were sure to join the strongest side. But four of these doubtful were marked as likely to join before the rising. Well, this makes but seven in all, and surely a brig of 266 tons could hold seven, or seventeen, or seventy prisoners, if necessary. Suppose she had taken a pirate; what would she have done with the crew? Hang them, by way of precaution? Mackenzie had all the evidence in his possession of the feebleness of this plot, and yet he hangs one man, whose guilt, to say the least, was questionable! . . .

[493] . . . I met Professor Webster in Albany, and was much gratified by his account of you. . . . I saw a person in Albany, whom I took to

be an employe of John C. Spencer, that had been at Geneva obtaining testimony as to Phil's character. He told me it was not so very bad. I told him, in answer, that I had received the worst accounts of it. He then told me that a letter desiring Phil to call on the writer, before the *Somers* sailed, and signed "Eliza," had been found in Phil's trunk. This letter was sent to Washington with an endorsement on the back, to say that it was a *proof of his dissolute habits, etc.* This letter was written by a female relative, who had already given poor Phil, and wished still to give him, good advice!

✓ ✓ ✓ From the New York *Weekly Tribune,* January 28, 1843.

It affords us much pleasure to be enabled to state that Captain Mackenzie has been unanimously and triumphantly justified from all blame by the Court of Inquiry. This result must have been anticipated by everyone who has given a candid attention to the testimony.

[Philadelphia Gazette]

END

OF PART TWO

✓ ✓ ✓

Part Three

THE COURT MARTIAL

January 28 to
March 31, 1843

Even before releasing the findings of the court of inquiry, the Secretary of the Navy ordered a court martial of Commander Mackenzie. The charges were murder, oppression, illegal punishment, conduct unbecoming an officer, and general cruelty and oppression. As various documents make clear, Mackenzie himself had requested this court martial. For one thing, he and his advisers saw that public opinion was not going to be satisfied with a favorable finding by the court of inquiry. For another thing, he was well aware that John C. Spencer was moving to have him and Lt. Gansevoort brought to trial in the civil courts. He preferred a military trial, both because it was to his advantage to be judged by brother officers rather than by a jury of landsmen, and because he believed it the proper court. Which court indeed had jurisdiction, became a legal issue that was argued at length even as the Court Martial proceeded.

The bulk of the testimony before the court martial merely repeated the substance of that already given. For his defense, Commander Mackenzie brought out some new evidence, mostly reports concerning the talk and behavior of Spencer, Small, and Cromwell. But now the Judge Advocate closely cross-examined defense witnesses, and also called three of the arrested men who had not been heard by the court of inquiry. It was his duty to prosecute the case in such a way as to elicit the truth on both sides; but to Mackenzie's friends it seemed that he was acting as a tool of John C. Spencer. He managed to get much new light on various matters: on the carryaway of the main-top-gallant mast, on the rush aft that night, on the timing and motivation of the death decision, on the conduct of the council of officers, on the question of whether or not Spencer dictated a last letter to Mackenzie, on Wilson's knife, and on other points.

Only that testimony is reprinted here which adds something to that already given. By the end of this Part, all the important evidence, the editor believes, is before you. No further facts of great significance ever transpired concerning what happened on the cruise, or why. Yet before making up your mind about the men and events, you should weigh the collateral testimony, in the remaining Parts, concerning the career and character of Commander Mackenzie and of Philip Spencer.

From *Proceedings of the Naval Court Martial in the Case of Alexander Slidell Mackenzie* (New York: Henry G. Langley, 1844), ✔ ✔ ✔ pp. 1-6.

[In documents dated January 23, 1843, the Secretary of the Navy, A. P. Upshur, brings charges against Commander Mackenzie and orders a court martial to convene at New York on February 1, 1843, to try him and such other involved persons as may be brought before it.]

[1-4] CHARGES AND SPECIFICATIONS. . . . I. MURDER ON BOARD A UNITED

STATES VESSEL ON THE HIGH SEAS [*murder of Spencer, Cromwell, and Small*]. . . . II. OPPRESSION. . . . III. ILLEGAL PUNISHMENT. . . . IV. CONDUCT UNBECOMING AN OFFICER [*use of "taunting and unofficer-like language" to Spencer at time of execution*]. . . . V. CRUELTY AND OPPRESSION [*cruel and oppressive treatment in general on the cruise*]. . . . [5] [*The following officers appointed to compose the Court: Captains John Downes, George C. Read, William C. Bolton, Daniel Turner, John D. Sloat, Joseph Smith, Isaac McKeever, John H. Aulick, Bladen Dulany, John Gwinn, Thomas W. Wyman; Commander Henry W. Ogden, Commander William W. McKean; president of Court, Captain John Downes; Judge Advocate, William H. Norris, Esq.*]
[6] [*Commander McKean, Captain Aulick, and Captain Dulany are excused from serving; Commander Irvine Shubrick, Captain George W. Storer, and Captain Benjamin Page are ordered to serve in their places.*]
[*First meeting of Court,* February 1, 1843.]

[FEBRUARY 2, 1843.]

[6] . . . Commander Mackenzie pleaded as follows:
I admit that acting midshipman Philip Spencer, boatswain's mate Samuel Cromwell, and seaman Elisha Small, were put to death by my order . . . ; but, as under the existing circumstances this act was demanded by duty and justified by necessity, I plead not guilty to all the charges. . . .

From a letter of James Fenimore Cooper to the editor [William
✓ ✓ ✓ Cullen Bryant], New York *Evening Post,* Friday, February 3, 1843.

The *Courier and Enquirer* [January 23] has falsely and indecorously dragged my name into the *Somers* affair. . . .
It is not true that I have suspended any work in order to include the facts of the Somers mutiny, as stated in the New York *Herald* [January 21]. I have no such work in view even. . . . There is, certainly, a grave collision between Capt. Mackenzie and myself, in our character as historians. That gentleman has had his say, it remains to hear me. I have several times announced an intention to publish my side of this case [the Battle of Lake Erie] and this was the very moment when I expected to lay it before the world. I do not wish *now* to publish what I may have said on the subject of this controversy, but, I will add, that, while last in New York, I acquainted several friends with my intention to *defer it, until the investigation of the affair of the Somers had terminated!* I presume that Mr. Webb, like others who fetch and carry, has made a material mistake in his facts. I certainly have no recollection of having made the remarks he quotes, in connection with the mutiny; while, as certainly, I

have often said something very similar to it in relation to the other affair. As I have no intention to publish what I *do* think, or may have said of Capt. Mackenzie's course . . . , I do not feel called upon to publish what I do *not* think, or may *not* have said about it. . . . I will only add, that my opinion has undergone a material change, with the change in testimony.

✓ ✓ ✓ From the New York *Weekly Tribune,* February 4, 1843.

Naval Court Martial . . . to Assemble Wednesday.— . . . A Washington correspondent of the Boston Post writes this. . . . It will be difficult to organize a Court Martial, as almost every officer . . . has made up his opinion. . . . One Commodore, who was named as a member, sent back word that if he tried Mackenzie he should bring him in guilty and recommend that he should be hung forthwith. . . .

✓ ✓ ✓ From *Proceedings of the Naval Court Martial* . . . (New York: Henry G. Langley, 1844), pp. 9-10.

FEBRUARY 6, 1843.

[9-10] [*Midshipman Charles W. Hays* (sic) *was called by the Judge Advocate and questioned to establish the fact of the execution of the three men at Mackenzie's order. This constituted a demonstration of Mackenzie's act, in the procedure followed by the Judge Advocate. Commander Mackenzie then began the presentation of witnesses to demonstrate that his act was demanded by duty and justified by necessity.]* . . .

✓ ✓ ✓ From a long rejoinder to James Fenimore Cooper's letter of February 3, by James Watson Webb, editor, New York *Courier and Enquirer,* Friday, February 10, 1843.

. . . From the most abject fear he [Cooper] has virtually recalled all he has heretofore said on the subject of the *Somers* execution. . . . When informed that in a large assemblage of gentlemen MR. COOPER had virtually called MR. MACKENZIE a *murderer,* we thought it proper to point out who it was that ventured on such a declaration. . . . His reported language, was communicated to us by a near relative of Commander MACKENZIE; and we have reason to believe, that the apprehension of being invited by a friend of MACKENZIE'S to *visit another state,* [*fight a duel*] and the threatened prosecution for libel, has induced this partial retraction. . . .

From *Proceedings of the Naval Court Martial* . . . (New York:
✓ ✓ ✓ Henry G. Langley, 1844), pp. 36 ff.

[FEBRUARY 11, 1843.]

[36] [*Lieut. Gansevoort . . . examined by Commander Macken-zie.*] . . .

Q. Had you any conversation with Mr. Spencer with regard to the papers found in the razor case . . . about the name of E. Andrews, which appeared in the list of the certain next his own? . . .

A. Yes, sir; I asked him if that name did not stand for Cromwell; he said no, that it meant Small—that was his real name; I said, "Ah! how is that, when you have Small's name twice on the list?" . . . Mr. Spencer appeared to be surprised, and said, "Ah! I did not know I had written it in that way." . . .

[37] *Q.* Do you remember whether, on the day following the arrest of Mr. Spencer, the maintop-gallantmast was carried away? were you on deck at the time?

A. . . . I was in the ward-room.

Q. Did, or did not, the whole crew rush aft on that occasion . . . ?

A. I heard a movement on deck; looked up the hatch, and found that the maintop-gallantmast was gone; went on deck, and the commander ordered me to take charge of the deck. The rush took place when the mast was pointed, or about to be swayed from the deck. The commander and myself were standing on the larboard side of the quarter-deck, at the after end of the trunk; we were in conversation; it was dark at this time. I heard an unusual noise—a rushing on deck, and saw a body of men in each gangway rushing aft toward the quarter-deck; I said to the commander, "God, I believe they are coming." I had one of Colt's pistols, which I immediately drew and cocked; the commander said his pistols were below; I jumped on the trunk, and ran forward to meet them; as I was going along I sung out to them not to come aft. I told them I would blow the first man's brains out who would put his foot on the quarter-deck; I held my pistol pointed at the tallest man I saw in the starboard gangway, and I think Mr. Rogers sung out to me, that he was sending the men aft to the mast-rope. I then told them they must have no such unusual movements on board the vessel . . . ; they knew the state of the vessel, and might get their brains blown out. . . .

[FEBRUARY 13, 1843.]

[41] . . . Cross-Examined by the Judge Advocate.

Q. When did you first suppose it would be necessary to execute Mr. Spencer, Cromwell, and Small, for the safety of the vessel, officers, and crew?

A. When we made more prisoners than we had the force to take care of, and I was more fully convinced after the examination in the ward-room before the council of officers. . . .

[42] *Q*. When did you first hear the mutiny was to break out before the arrival of the Somers at St. Thomas?

A. I don't recollect that I did hear it.

Q. Did Wales swear before the council of officers, that Mr. Spencer had told him that the mutiny was to break out before you reached St. Thomas?

A. The evidence will show; I am not positive. . . .

[FEBRUARY 14, 1843.]

[45] *Q*. Why, and on what day, did you take Mr. Spencer the papers found in his locker?

A. I am under the impression that it was on the 30th; for the purpose of his proving more clearly his guilt; I took him the paper that he might translate it, so I could understand it; my object was to obtain from him an acknowledgment of his guilt. . . .

[49] *Q*. Had you any consultation with the commander about his writing a letter to the officers, before you saw the one that was sent?

A. I am not positive as to the time he spoke to me of addressing a letter to the officers, but I believe I knew there was one to be addressed to them before I received it.

Q. Did you not, on the 28th or 29th of November, advise him to send such a letter to the officers?

A. I don't recollect that I gave him any advice about it. . . .

Q. Was not the letter of the commander to the officers prepared before Wilson, M'Kinley, and M'Kee were arrested?

A. I don't recollect.

Q. Did you on the 28th, and at what time of the day, advise with Mr. Perry, the master, as to whether Cromwell, Small, and Mr. Spencer should not be put to death, if you had to take more prisoners? and what was his conclusion?

A. I don't recollect as to the day; I think I spoke to the doctor, Mr. Perry, and Mr. Rogers, and I think their conclusion was that they should be disposed of.

By the Court.

Q. Was that before the council of officers was held?

A. Yes, sir.

By the Judge Advocate.

Q. Was it a day or more before the holding of the council of officers?

A. I don't think it was more than a day; I am not positive as to the time.

Q. Did you communicate the opinion of these officers to the commander, and when?

A. I am under the impression I did, a short time after I had the conversation; I am not sure I spoke to them all the same day.

Q. As you would have the opinion of each officer, did you communicate it to the commander?

A. I think I did, sooner or later. . . .

[FEBRUARY 15, 1843.]

[LIEUTENANT GANSEVOORT . . . CROSS-EXAMINED BY THE JUDGE ADVOCATE.] . . .

[51] *Q.* When you saw Mr. Wales's name on the list found in Mr. Spencer's locker, did you conclude that it was put there without Mr. Wales's authority, or put there after the conversation on the booms?

A. I supposed it was put there after the conversation on the booms, and without his authority.

Q. If it was put there after conversation on the booms, what was there in the paper to excite alarm? Were not only four names down as certain, and Mr. Wales among them?

A. . . . My alarm was not excited by the paper, but from the manner of those that were on that paper, and the manner of those that were not on it. . . .

[52] *Q.* During the time the investigation was going on before the council of officers, were Mr. Spencer, Cromwell, and Small, informed of it, and desired to state if they had any questions to put? or was the evidence in particular of any witnesses reported to them, or either of them?

A. I don't know that anything of that sort was done.

Q. From the time of his arrest to the time of his execution, did any officer apply to the commander or yourself, for permission to explain to Mr. Spencer his situation, and what was contemplated in respect to him, that he might afford him any friendly services, to take care of his rights?

A. I don't recollect that he did.

Q. Was anything of the like kind asked or proposed by any of the crew, in respect to Cromwell and Small?

A. Not that I know of. . . .

[FEBRUARY 17, 1843.]

[65] [ACTING-MASTER M. C. PERRY, JR., CROSS-EXAMINED BY THE JUDGE ADVOCATE, WM. H. NORRIS.] . . .

Q. When did Mr. Gansevoort first consult you, as to the propriety of executing Mr. Spencer, Cromwell, and Small, and what did you tell him?

A. He asked me, during the day before the council of officers was held. . . . I told him that I did not think we could take charge of any more prisoners with safety to the vessel, and, if necessity required more to be taken, the first three ought to be disposed of, that is, put to death. . . .

Q. Did you not swear before the court of inquiry that this conversation with Mr. Gansevoort was on the 28th of November?

A. I may have done so; I don't remember; if I did so, it was correct. . . . I do not mean to be positive as to dates, except when I refer to the log-book. . . .

[66] *Q.* Was it discussed in the council of officers as to whether the vessel could be carried into St. Thomas or any nearer port? . . .

A. It was discussed as to whether she could be taken into St. Thomas, and I, in answer, said that I would rather go overboard than go into St. Thomas for protection—that I would never agree to a thing of the kind, and I also said it would be an impossibility to take the vessel into any port. . . .

Q. Why did you say you would sooner go overboard than seek protection at St. Thomas, and that you would not agree to such a thing?

A. Because I thought it would be a disgrace to the United States, the navy, and particularly the officers of the brig; my reasons were that if an American man-of-war could not protect herself, no use in having any. . . .

Q. How was the vote and opinions asked of the members of the council? . . .

A. I was absent when the final opinion was given in; I had given in mine the night before; and as some officer had to be on deck, I took charge of the deck on the morning of the 1st of December, when the opinion was given in. . . .

[FEBRUARY 18, 1843.]

[69] *Q.* What time of the day was it when you saw M'Kinley filing his battle-axe? . . . What day was it . . . ?

A. To the best of my recollection, 'twas during the afternoon. . . . What day I can't remember; I think it was after the arrest of Mr. Spencer? . . .

Q. You have stated that Wilson was arrested on the 30th. If you thought his conduct so suspicious, why did you not report it before?

A. I did not think his cleaning his battle-axe suspicious at that time— 'twas a usual occurrence. . . .

[FEBRUARY 20, 1843.]

[72] [*Document put on record by Mackenzie*] . . . Commander Mackenzie takes occasion to mention, that the idea was never entertained by him of seeking protection against his crew in any foreign port, from any foreign power whatever, or from any foreign ship in port, or at sea, or anywhere, save in a port of the United States, or under the guns of an American man-of-war; it being his deliberate opinion, that a naval commander can never be justified in invoking foreign aid in reducing an

insubordinate crew to obedience; . . . his views in this particular were well known at the time to the 1st lieutenant of the Somers, were shared by him, and by him communicated to others of the officers.

Believing that the United States ship Vandalia, or some other American man-of-war, might be at St. Thomas, Commander Mackenzie was very desirous of reaching that port without the execution of the ringleaders in the mutiny, and the execution took place when the daily and hourly increasing insubordination of the crew, rendered it imperatively necessary. . . .

From a letter from Willam Watson to R. H. Dana, Jr., New York, February 22, 1843. Reproduced here, by permission, from the original letter in the Dana Papers in the library of the Massachusetts ✓ ✓ ✓ Historical Society.*

. . . In regard to your letter [in the *Evening Post*] about the Somers . . . , I was before Judge Oakley on a habeas corpus case sued out by one of the men; when he fell into conversation after it was through & said that his opinion was that Mackenzie's acts could not be justified— until he read a letter in the Post by a young man by the name of Dana which placed the matter in such a light as totally to change his views. But I perceive that the current is setting pretty strongly against Mackenzie now that the facts are more fully developed. The notion is getting horridly prevalent that he was unnecessarily frightened & I must say from an examination of these boys [of the *Somers* crew] all of whose discharges on writs of Habeas corpus I have had to oppose, I do not believe a soul of them had any hand in it. I think he had a right to hang the three, but I fear that it was unwise, & that he will be involved for the rest of his life hereafter in a great deal of trouble. If he is acquitted by this court-martial, there is a power [*i.e.,* John C. Spencer] through whose instrumentality he will be harassed by all sorts of [charges of] false imprisonment of the seamen & apprentices. I say to you *in confidence* that they are very willing to let the boys go—the opposition, by instructions, not being very strong. . . .

From *Proceedings of the Naval Court Martial* . . . (New York: ✓ ✓ ✓ Henry G. Langley, 1844), pp. 90-96.

[FEBRUARY 23, 1843.]

[90] Billinger Scott [*age 15, 2d class apprentice*] . . . EXAMINED BY COMMANDER MACKENZIE. . . .

---

* William Watson was a friend of Dana, and assistant to the U.S. District Attorney, Ogden Hoffman, at New York.

A. . . . I heard Mr. Spencer ask Cromwell if he could disguise the brig; Cromwell said "yes;" Mr. Spencer asked if he could disguise her so as to bring her into New York; Cromwell said he could; Mr. Rogers was coming forward at the time; he said he "could do it in damned short order, by shipping the bowsprit aft;" then Mr. Spencer told me to take his hammock down, and I heard no more.

Q. Were Mr. Spencer and Cromwell serious when this conversation began?

A. Yes, sir, they appeared to be.

Q. What was the manner of Mr. Spencer when Mr. Rogers came up?

A. Cromwell turned it off, and Mr. Spencer went over to the larboard side.

Q. Did you ever see Mr. Spencer, Small, and Cromwell, in conversation? . . .

A. Yes, sir; I heard them talking about slavers; I heard Mr. Spencer ask Small how they got the slaves; Small said they went up the rivers in Africa; they would anchor off in the brig they went up in, and take the long boat and go ashore. . . .

[91] *Q.* Were you Mr. Spencer's hammock-boy? Has he ever asked you if you liked to sail with him? . . .

A. Yes, sir; he asked me how I would like to sail with him; I told him I would like it very well. . . . I told him I was second class boy; he said when he got to be commander he would rate me "seaman." . . .

[94] Samuel Van Norden [*age, 15; 3rd class apprentice*] . . . Examined by Commander Mackenzie. . . .

Q. Were you on deck when the main-top-gallantmast was carried away?

A. Yes, sir.

Q. Did you hear the order given to let go the weather-mainroyal-brace? and did you see where Cromwell and Small were then sitting?

A. I heard some order given, I am not sure what it was; Cromwell and Small were sitting on the bitts together. . . . Small got up and hauled on the brace, and the mast was carried away. . . . He hauled violently.

Q. Did you ever hear any conversation . . . about disguising the brig? . . .

A. They were on the forecastle in the dog watch; Mr. Spencer asked Cromwell how he could disguise the brig; he said, "by shipping the bowsprit aft," that is all; there was an officer coming forward at the time . . . ; he (Cromwell) seemed as if he tried to turn it off. . . .

[FEBRUARY 24, 1843.]

[96] Samuel Van Norden . . . Cross-Examined by the Judge Advocate.

Q. If the bowsprit of the Somers had been put aft, would she have been disguised so that you would not have known her?

A. No, sir; I don't think I should, or anybody else.

Q. If one of the seamen had told you he could have disguised the Somers by putting the bowsprit aft, so that she could come into New York and not be known, would you not have supposed he was laughing at you?

A. Yes, sir. . . .

Q. [*by Commodore Downes*]. . . . Did you or not think [Cromwell] said to turn it off as a joke, in consequence of an officer coming forward at the time? Did Mr. Spencer appear serious when he asked Cromwell how he would disguise the Somers?

A. I thought he intended to turn it off as a joke. . . . Mr. Spencer appeared serious. . . .

✓ ✓ ✓ From the New York *Herald,* Friday morning, February 24, 1843.

. . . [M. C.] Perry [Jr.] says the honor of the flag forbade seeking protection elsewhere than from the ship herself. . . . But is the "honor of the flag" to justify the hanging of three human beings, unarmed, in irons, without trial. . . ? The tragedy of the Somers discloses a tissue of barbarity, insolence, cowardice, farce and folly, that seems unparallelled in the history of human nature.

✓ ✓ ✓ From New York *Weekly Tribune* report of proceedings of the Court Martial on February 24, report published on March 4, 1843.

. . . Before the next witness [Henry Corny] came into Court the Judge Advocate . . . said, that Mr. Norris, the son-in-law of Mr. Spencer, had arrived, and in obedience to instructions from the Secretary of the Navy he (the J. A.) was prepared to receive any suggestions he might have to offer. . . .

✓ ✓ ✓ From *Proceedings of the Naval Court Martial* . . . (New York: Henry G. Langley, 1844), pp. 97 ff.

[FEBRUARY 24, 1843.]

[97] Henry Corny [*age, 15; 2nd class apprentice*]. EXAMINED BY COMMANDER MACKENZIE. . . .

Q. Were you at the weather-main-royal-brace, the day the main-top-gallant-mast was [98] carried away? If so, state who was there with you, and all that occurred.

A. Small was with me, the officer of the deck said, "A small pull at the weather-main-royal brace;" I went to it, and Small came too, and we were hauling on it, and the officer of the deck said, 'Belay," and the commander, too. I let go and Small kept hauling on it; I told him to stop, but he paid no attention; he hauled with a jerk and then belayed it; about five minutes after the mast carried away. . . .

CROSS-EXAMINED BY JUDGE ADVOCATE. . . .

Q. Where was you before the order was given to take a pull?

A. I was at the bitts. . . . Small stood alongside. . . . He was standing about two feet off. . . .

Q. Did you see Cromwell there?

A. No, sir.

Q. Are you sure Cromwell was not there?

A. Yes, sir, I am sure he was not there.

Q. Did you see Van Norden?

A. No, sir. . . .

[99] BY COMMANDER MACKENZIE. . . .

Q. Were not the greater part of the crew usually about the foremast and forecastle, in fine weather or Sundays?

A. Yes, sir.

Q. Might not Cromwell have been seated on the other side of Small . . . without your recollecting it?

A. I don't know whether or not; I can't say. . . .

The engagements of Mr. Duer not allowing [100] his longer continuing as counsel for the accused, he was relieved . . . by Mr. Theodore Sedgwick. . . .*

[100] [*Jonas E. S. Humbert, age 16, 3d class apprentice,* EXAMINED BY COMMANDER MACKENZIE.] . . .

Q. Have you ever seen Mr. Spencer in conversation with Cromwell? . . .

A. . . . Mr. Spencer asked Cromwell what kind of a piratical vessel he thought the brig would make; Cromwell said he thought she would make a very good one—she was a fast sailer—but if he had anything to do with her he would throw the launch overboard: I saw them talking another time. . . . Mr. Rogers gave the order to haul in the braces and square the afteryards; neither Mr. Spencer [101] nor Cromwell seemed to take any notice of it; it was their watch; Mr. Rogers came forward and gave the order again; they then got up and had the yards squared; when they were done, they went and sat on the chest again; then Cromwell said to Mr. Spencer, "I wish the yards, braces, and all were in hell;" Mr. Spencer told him not to say that, that they would have some fun with

---

* Theodore Sedgwick, Jr. (1811-1859), a prominent lawyer, Democrat, and writer on legal subjects. He was a nephew of Catharine Maria Sedgwick, and a friend of Charles Sumner.

the brig yet; then Mr. Spencer asked Cromwell for a chew of tobacco, and then went off. . . .

[FEBRUARY 25, 1843.]

[103] BY THE JUDGE ADVOCATE. . . .

Q. What was Mr. Spencer's manner when he said, "Don't say that— we'll have some fun out of her yet?"

A. He was laughing.

Q. Do you remember when the rush aft took place, on the 27th, the evening of the mast accident?

A. Yes, sir; I was forward on the forecastle.

Q. Was you lying down there?

A. Yes, sir.

Q. About how many people were lying down there then?

A. About five or six, and the biggest part of the crew standing around.

Q. Did Browning come in among them with his colt? *

A. Yes, sir. . . . He flourished his colt about, told them to go aft and take hold of the top-gallantmast rope. . . . They went aft with a great deal of noise.

Q. Was there or not any scrambling and pushing to get out of the way of the colt?

A. Yes, sir. . . .

✓ ✓ ✓ From a letter to Thurlow Weed from Lewis Benedict [Washington, February 25, 1843]. Printed here from the original letter in the Weed Papers, University of Rochester Library, by permission.†

Before McKenzie sailed in the Somers he was at Washington & had command of the Mississippi Steam Frigate. She and the Missouri was at Washington, Mrs. Upshur & Mrs. Spencer were on board in company and were introduced to Capt. McKenzie—is it not strange that he should say in his despatch that he did not know that *Spencer had* a Mother living until Spencer mentioned to him that it would kill his mother meaning his conduct—I want you to write an article on this subject or at least state the *fact*—

Your letter about the Somers—1st written from N. York gave no offense to Mr. [J. C.] Spencer as I think. It was alluded to by Mr. [Henry] Morris today & I gave him a history of our doings in N. York *on Sunday.* I told

* *Colt:* a short length of rope used as a whip—on the *Somers,* "not so large as your little finger," according to Lieut. Gansevoort's testimony (p. 55).

† Lewis Benedict was an Albany merchant and a close friend of Thurlow Weed. He served on the Whig State Committee for over twenty years.

him you did not intend your first letter should be published & fully explained your feelings on the subject of the Somers affair & the object of our visit. The prevailing opinion of all we conversed with & the advice of friends that we should call as we did and advise Mr. S. to disavow the article signed S. if he could. I think I changed their views. Mrs. S. said it was kind in you to write the article you did about John *—he will be home in May.

From *The Diary of Philip Hone,* edited by Bayard Tuckerman (New York: Dodd, Mead & Co., 1889), II, 174-175.

[174] *February 25.*—The court-martial at Brooklyn, on the "Somers" case, drags along its tedious length so slowly, and there is such an everlasting sameness in the examination, that the public here appears to have lost all interest in the matter, and you scarcely hear an inquiry made as to its progress, or the probability of its termination. Not so with our kind, officious brethren in the "mother country." One universal burst of vituperation comes from the pack of hireling papers published in London; not only is Commander McKenzie saluted with the epithets of "murderer," coward," fool," "bully," and all others which may be supposed to be most offensive to a gentleman and an officer, but the navy is vilified, the civil institutions of the country derided, and the country itself insulted by the blackguards of the British press, and their coadjutors and supporters here. The editor [James Gordon Bennett] of the infamous "Herald" blazons these offensive articles in the public view with evident satisfaction, and makes their publication the ground of insulting remarks to the court. When the court's actions were subject to the supervision of the American people only, it was not of much consequence how the proceedings were conducted; but now that they come under the notice of the "British press;" that the Bennetts of St. Paul's churchyard have honoured the country by their animadversions, and established a tribunal in the slums of St. Giles for the trial of the triers,—it behooves them to be circumspect. They must blacken the character of McKenzie if they wish to preserve their own, and hang him if they would escape the gibbet themselves. So says Mr. Bennett. The vile bribe, which there is good reason to believe has set him in motion, shines through every line he now writes on this melancholy subject. The interest of the protracted affair has given place in the public mind to new subjects, and the character of an honoured American officer [175] is left to be worried and mangled by as filthy a cur as ever barked in foreign accents at the bidding of a corrupt employer.

I am not as clear as I could wish to be in my opinion of the absolute

---

* This may refer to the letter to the editors of the *National Intelligencer,* December 24, 1842, reprinted under that date above.

necessity of the dreadful act of discipline resorted to by McKenzie, and for his sake, as well as for the sake of national justice, I sometimes think I should like to have evidence of some clearly overt act of mutiny; but I do most entirely believe that he proceeded in his extremity with good motives, in a full conviction of the existence of the mutiny, and a persuasion that the execution was necessary for the safety of his vessel and the preservation of his men. Be this, however, as it may, I am indignant that this "scum of Britons" should avail themselves of this distressing occurrence to cast the contents of their "stink pots" upon my country, and that a wretch should be found among us base enough to ladle them out to the last loathsome drop. But, above all, am I humiliated that my fellow-citizens should give to this infamous journal [New York *Herald*] a circulation greater (if the mendacious sheet may in any sort be believed) than that of any other daily newspaper in the country.

From *Proceedings of the Naval Court Martial . . .* (New York: Henry G. Langley, 1844), pp. 111 ff.

[FEBRUARY 28, 1843.]

[111] Peter Tyson . . . EXAMINED BY COMMANDER MACKENZIE. . . .

A. Immediately after quarters on the night of Mr. Spencer's arrest, me and Sears went forward, and Cromwell and Small were in conversation together; Sears asked Small what Mr. Spencer was confined for; Cromwell replied for a supposed mutiny; Sears asked him the meaning of mutiny; he said it was a plan to kill the captain and officers and take the vessel; Small said he (Small) thought like the commander did, that Mr. Spencer was half crazy and childish; they parted then, and we went away. . . .

[113] CROSS-EXAMINED BY THE JUDGE ADVOCATE. . . .

Q. . . . What time of day was it?

A. Immediately after quarters—immediately after Mr. Spencer was put in irons, as soon as the retreat was beaten.

Q. Had the commander then had Small aft?

A. No, sir; Small had had no conversation with the commander. . . . I do not recollect seeing Small aft, until after Sears left him; the commander called him aft at that time. . . .

Q. If Small had not been aft, when was it that he said the commander thought Spencer half crazy, or childish?

A. I don't know; I thought it strange at the time; I don't know that he had had any conversation with the commander. . . .

[115] [*Joseph Sears, age nearly 19,* EXAMINED BY COMMANDER MACKENZIE.] . . .

Q. Did you notice anything particular in the conduct of Cromwell and Small immediately after the arrest of Mr. Spencer?

A. Yes, sir; after Mr. Spencer was arrested and the retreat beaten, I went forward; Cromwell was leaning against the bitts, Small standing beside him; they were talking together. . . . I asked Small what Mr. Spencer was arrested for; I think it was Cromwell who answered me, I am not positive: he said it was for a supposed mutiny; I asked Small what "supposed mutiny" was; he said it was to murder one person or more; Small said that he supposed as the captain did, that there was to be no mutiny, that the young man was half crazy, half out of his head; Cromwell was leaning against the bitts, his hat over his eyes, apparently very mad, biting his lips and rolling his eyes about; he would look out from under his hat to see anybody, as if he did not want to let any one see his face. . . .

CROSS-EXAMINED BY JUDGE ADVOCATE.

Q. How long was it after retreat was beat that you had your conversation with Small?

A. Immediately.

Q. Had not Small been aft when he was talking with you? [116] . . . If Small had not been aft, how was it that he said he thought with the commander that Spencer was half crazy?

A. I can't tell you. . . .

Q. Was it Cromwell or Small who told you what a mutiny was? . . .

A. I told you before it was Small.

Q. Did you see Tyson by them?

A. I did. . . .

An anonymous letter to James Gordon Bennett, editor, the New
✓ ✓ ✓ York *Herald*, Wednesday morning, March 1, 1843.

You have taken upon yourself to vilify, abuse and slander the officers of the Somers, in a manner none but yourself are capable. . . . Beware, you are in danger. . . . Scoundrel and vagabond . . . , you shall no longer escape. . . . One more attack on McK., and you die!

✓ ✓ ✓ From the New York *Herald*, Wednesday morning, March 8, 1843.

On Monday morning, the Grand Jury of the United States Court heard an argument against taking up [the *Somers* case], from Ogden Hoffman, the U. S. District Attorney. The jury took a vote, and stood 12 to 11 against taking it up. Today we learn that another movement will be made—and the Somers boys will be brought up for examination. . . .

From *Proceedings of the Naval Court Martial . . .* (New York: Henry G. Langley, 1844), pp. 166-177.

✦ ✦ ✦

[MARCH 9, 1843.]

[166] Purser Heiskill recalled.

EXAMINED BY THE JUDGE ADVOCATE.

Q. Were any of the witnesses asked before the council of officers as to the carrying away of the mast, or as to the rush aft, as indicating an insubordination on board, or did any of them testify as to either of these matters?

A. I don't recollect that the question was asked.

BY COMMANDER MACKENZIE.

Q. What was the condition of the [167] officers of the Somers as to exhaustion, on the evening of the execution?

A. They were very much exhausted; indeed for myself I could scarcely stand, being obliged to walk continually during our watch. . . .

[169] [*Acting Midshipman Tillotson, age 16.* EXAMINED BY THE JUDGE ADVOCATE.] . . .

Q. Did you hear the conversation on the 26th, between the commander, Mr. Spencer, Small, and Wales, when Small was called aft.

A. Yes, sir; commander asked Small if Mr. Spencer ever said anything to him about mutiny. I think Small said that he had not. I don't recollect anything else that passed between the commander and Small. . . .

Q. Did the commander say anything about Mr. Spencer being half crazy or childish?

A. No, sir; not that I heard. . . .

Q. Can you remember the words of the commander to Small?

A. No, sir.

Q. Did Small say that he was in no mutiny, but had a foolish conversation with Mr. Spencer?

A. I think he did say something about a foolish conversation; I am not certain.

Q. He denied he was in a mutiny?

A. Yes, sir. . . .

[171] Oliver H. Perry was then called. . . .

BY THE JUDGE ADVOCATE. . . .

[172] *Q.* Do you know whether Mr. Spencer wrote home to his friends?

A. No, sir.

Q. Did you not say, in the presence of the secretary of the navy, and other gentlemen, that you were of the impression that Mr. Spencer did send a written message home?

A. At the time of the execution it was my impression he did send a message home; the captain was copying something. . . .

At this time, Captain Mackenzie came to the judge advocate, and asked him, "Why do you ask this question, about Mr. Spencer's not being able to write in irons? He declined to write." "Yes, sir;" the judge advocate replied, "but I am told he afterward dictated to you what to write." Captain Mackenzie then said, "He said he did not wish to write." "Yes, sir," was the reply of the judge advocate, "but I am told he afterward dictated to you what to write." "Yes, he did," was Captain Mackenzie's answer. The judge advocate then said, "Then he did dictate to you what to write." "Yes, he did," Captain Mackenzie answered, "the substance of it is in my report—my official report." The judge advocate then stated to the court, "There is no use of further examination on the point, as Captain Mackenzie admits that Mr. Spencer did dictate to him what to write." Captain Mackenzie then said "Yes, sir. . . ."

[MARCH 10, 1843.]

[173] Mr. O. H. Perry recalled.

BY THE JUDGE ADVOCATE.

Q. After the mast was carried away, were you sent for [by] the commander?

A. Yes, sir.

Q. Who came for you?

A. I don't recollect the person.

Q. Was it not M'Kee?

A. I don't recollect.

Q. What then occurred between you and the commander?

A. He asked me why I did not attend to my duties better, and said that I must do it better in future.

Q. What was the commander alluding to?

A. To my not attending to the brace at the time they were hauling on it.

Q. Did he say to you, "This is all your fault, sir," or words to that effect?

A. I don't recollect.

Q. What reply did you make the commander?

A. I did not make any; I said, I think, I understood the order to have been to haul on the brace?

CROSS-EXAMINED BY COMD'R MACKENZIE.

Q. . . . State what you observed and all that occurred.

A. . . . We were setting the fore-sky-sail; I was attending to it, the order, as I understood it was "a small pull of the weather-main-royal-brace." I passed that order; I then turned to attend the fore-sky-sail; I saw the commander jumping off the round house; he jumped off with some anxiety, as if he apprehended that the mast might be carried away. Small at this time was pulling on the brace, and I sung out belay; he gave it a pretty heavy jerk, and then belayed it. I went to do it, and I think I did [174] take the turns off, and by that time the mast went. . . . I was then called aft by the commander. . . .

[176] [*Daniel McKinley, age 21, landsman.* EXAMINED BY THE JUDGE ADVOCATE.] . . .

Q. Had you been spoken to by Mr. Spencer, as to mutiny?

A. No, sir.

Q. Did you know your name was on any paper of his?

A. Not till I got home, and got confined on board the North Carolina; I saw it in the Sun. I beg pardon, I should say I was in the ward-room, making up beds, the night Mr. Spencer was arrested; the paper was found in Mr. Spencer's locker; I then heard Mr. Rogers read the names off; I heard that my name was there, Green, M'Kee, and Wilson's, and then I came on deck, after I had the beds made, and told them boys what I heard; I told them I saw them read the names off a paper, and saw them take them down on another piece of paper.

Q. What boys did you speak to on the deck?

A. Green, Wilson, the sailmaker, and M'Kee; I think I told Van Velzor, I am not sure. . . .

Q. Do you know anything of Wilson's dirk?

A. I was ashore on the coast of Africa . . . , and saw one of the natives with a knife; I spoke to Mr. Heiskill about buying it for me. . . . [He] bought an African dirk instead of that, and gave it to me. I came on board with the knife, and wore it for two or three days. [177] Wilson saw the knife, and said he wanted to buy it as a curiosity to take to New York. . . . I let Wilson have it; he promised to give a dollar the first grog-money. . . .

Q. Have you seen Wilson use that knife afterward?

A. In cutting holes into hammocks, and shifting the numbers.

Q. Did you miss muster after the arrest of Mr. Spencer? and if so, state when and why?

A. It was after the arrest; I can not state the date and hour; me and M'Kee turned in and out with one another when the watch was called; we made a bargain in the first of the cruise to wake one another up, when the watches were called. I came up on deck; I asked M'Kee why he did not call me. He told me that the officers would not let him stir; that they were ordered to lie down on the deck, and when he lay down he fell asleep, and did not wake up—that was why I missed my muster being used to be awaked by one another. . . .

Part of a letter of Commodore W. B. Shubrick to James Fenimore Cooper, dated Navy Yard, Gosport, Va., March 10, 1843. Here reprinted by permission from *Correspondence of James Fenimore-Cooper,* edited by his grandson James Fenimore Cooper (New Haven: Yale University Press, 1922), II, 496-498.

This affair of the *Somers* is certainly the most extraordinary on record and one that has perplexed me beyond measure. When I first wrote to you on the subject I had not seen Mackenzie's narrative. The bad effect produced [497] on my mind by that singular production was in a measure effaced by the full and decisive opinion, in his favor, of the court of inquiry composed of men in whose judgment and intelligence I have great confidence. I have always held it to be a rule that a mutiny detected before an overt act has been committed is a mutiny suppressed, and Mack.'s crew must have been composed of very different materials from any that I have ever seen, if with the ring-leaders in irons, the officers, petty officers, and a part of the crew with him, he could not have taken care of the remainder. Large allowances must be made however in these cases for an officer thrown entirely on his own resources, with the responsibility of command for the first time on him, surrounded by very young officers and obliged to decide promptly for good or evil; he must certainly shew an imperious warranty for taking the law into his hands, or rather thrusting it aside, and administering "wild justice." We get the testimony given before the courts in detached portions, and it is hardly safe to make up a final opinion from it. I think however that the court martial will follow in the steps of the court of inquiry and acquit. What is to be done then? Can he be tried by a civil court? . . . Whatever may be the result of this business Mack. is ruined for the Navy and must fall back on his other vocation of [498] bookmaking. I do not think the Department is disposed to favor him *now;* the Spencer influence is too powerful— Mr. U. has not firmness enough to stand up against it. The appointment of the Judge Advocate was a bad one,—he is a young man and little known in his profession even in Baltimore.

✓ ✓ ✓ From the New York *Herald,* Friday morning, March 10, 1843.

[*Quoting from the* Courier and Inquirer:] . . . That John C. Spencer . . . has used and is still using his official influence and his most zealous personal efforts to procure the punishment of as good an officer as there is in the U. S. Navy, there is no room to doubt. . . .

[*Quoting from the New York* American:] In plain words, Mr. John C. Spencer . . . who imposed upon the nation a son, known to him to be unworthy when he obtained for him rank and station in an honorable service, is bending all the energies of his character, and all the influence of his station, to crush the man who . . . cut short the career of crime which this youth meditated. . . .

Item in *Niles' National Register* (Baltimore), LXIV (March 11, ✓ ✓ ✓ 1843), 20.

APPOINTMENTS BY THE PRESIDENT. *Confirmed by the senate.* John C. Spencer, of New York, to be secretary of the treasury, in the place of Walter Forward, resigned. . . .

✓ ✓ ✓ Items in *Niles' National Register* (Baltimore), LXIV (March 11, 1843), 32.

Serious efforts have been made to have commander Mackenzie indicted for murder before the United States district court for New York. Complaints were laid before the grand jury by Mr. [Henry] Morris, of the war department, also by Margaret E. Cromwell, the mother of one of the mutineers, charging him with murder on the high seas. Another also in behalf of Small was made by [Charles] Cleveland.

The New York Journal of Commerce says that the grand jury of the U. S. district court have not yet acted upon the subject of finding a bill against com. Mackenzie, for murder.

Judge Kent has delivered an elaborate opinion that the circuit court of the United States for New York cannot lawfully take cognizance of the case.

✓ ✓ ✓ From *Proceedings of the Naval Court Martial* . . . (New York: Henry G. Langley, 1844), pp. 179 ff.

[MARCH 11, 1843.]

[179] [EXAMINATION OF M'KINLEY, CONTINUED, BY THE JUDGE ADVOCATE.] . . .

Q. When was you arrested, and what occurred?

A. On the 30th of November, at morning quarters, I was arrested. The commander put Wilson in irons; when he was put in irons, the commander cried, "Send M'Kinley aft." I went aft; the commander and Mr. Gansevoort held pistols at my head, and told me to sit down; Mr. Gansevoort told King, the gunner, to stand by to knock out their brains, if they should make a false motion; I was put in irons then; he ordered Green and M'Kee aft; he put them in irons also. . . .

Q. Begin and give all that occurred on the day of execution.

A. . . . I should think it was about 2 o'clock; the commander came out of the cabin in full uniform; he went to Mr. Spencer and told him he had ten minutes to live; he went to Cromwell and Small—I did not hear what he said to them; I was six or eight feet from Mr. Spencer; I heard the commander after he had gone to Cromwell and Small, and had come back to Mr. Spencer, ask him if he had a prayer-book. . . . I heard the commander order three prayer-books. Mr. Spencer read a few prayers; I should think he was looking in the book; and then the commander asked him if he wished to write; Mr. Spencer said that he did; the commander ordered Dunn to fetch paper and camp-stool out of the cabin; Spencer took the pen in his hand—he said, "I can not write." The commander spoke to him in a low tone; I do not know what he then said; I saw the commander writing; whether Mr. Spencer asked him to write for him or not, I can't say. The commander told Mr. Thompson before he began to write, to tell him when the time was up; he did so . . . but the commander kept on writing. . . .

Q. Did Mr. Spencer say anything when the commander told him he was to die in ten minutes?

A. He told him he was not fit to die; that he wished to live longer to get ready. The commander said, "I know you are not, but I can not help it."

Q. Did you see Cromwell when the commander went to him?

A. I did. . . . He was reading; I don't know what the commander said to him, but he dropped the book, and fell down on his knees and [180] cried, "God of the Universe, look down on my poor wife; I am innocent." . . .

Q. While the writing was going on, what was the position of Mr. Spencer and the commander?

A. Mr. Spencer was sitting at the forward end of the arm-chest, and the commander in front of him on a camp stool. I could not say how long the writing continued; he sat there upward of twenty minutes, or half an hour. . . .

Q. Give the words of the commander when he asked Mr. Spencer if he wished to write. . . .

A. "Do you wish to write?" I believe that is all I recollect of hearing the commander say; whether Mr. Spencer said "yes" or "no," I do not know; the paper and camp stool came up after that. . . .

Q. Were you told you were not to be executed?

A. I was, while the men were hanging at the yard-arm—not before.

Q. Did you expect to be executed after hearing what was said to Mr. Spencer?

A. I did. . . .

[181] *Q.* Did the commander speak to you that day?

A. He did while the men were hanging . . . ; he came to me and said, "M'Kinley, did you hear what I said to those other young men?" I told him "No, sir;" "Well," he said, "it is the general opinion of the officers that you are a pretty good boy, but I shall have to take you home in irons, to see what the Secretary of the Navy can do for you. . . . I asked [Lt. Gansevoort] if he thought the commander thought I was guilty . . . ; he said, "No, I assure you if he did he would have strung you up."

Q. Before your arrest, had you any conversation at night with Wilson on a gun?

A. I think I did; I think it was the night before Mr. Spencer was arrested, Wilson asked me, "M'Kinley, what did Spencer say to you?" I told him that Mr. Spencer said he knowed what I was going to do when the brig got into St. Thomas . . . , [that] I was going to run from the brig. . . . I told him I was not—that I never had such an idea in my head. . . . That is all the conversation I had with Wilson. . . .

Q. Was any body by?

A. Not that I recollect.

Q. Did you see Tyson?

A. No, sir, I did not.

Q. Did you find Tyson asleep that night at all?

A. No, sir, I did not. . . .

Q. Did you talk with Tyson that night at all?

A. No, sir, I did not; if I did, I do not recollect it.

Q. Did you tell any one else but Wilson of this conversation of yours with Mr. Spencer?

A. Yes, sir; I told Browning, and Anderson, the captain of the fore-castle. . . . Browning told me if I had ever had any conversation with Mr. Spencer to go and tell it . . . to the officers. . . . I went to the mainmast to tell it. . . . Mr. Gansevoort came toward me, I touched my hat and said, "Mr. Gansevoort," intending to stop him, but he went forward and took no notice of me; they beat to quarters, and I went to my quarters; the captain came on deck; Wilson was standing aft at No. 5 gun starboard side, he spoke to Wilson . . . , he was put in irons, when he was ironed the captain ordered M'Kinley aft. . . .

[183] [CROSS-EXAMINED BY COMMANDER MACKENZIE.] . . .

Q. The night before Mr. Spencer was arrested did you have any conversation with Wilson between two guns on the quarter-deck?

A. I did; as I have stated to the court.

Q. Did you tell Wilson, "He has just told me we have spies, we had better be careful," or anything of that kind?

A. I do not recollect anything of the kind.

Q. Did Wilson say, "He need not fear me; he knows I have been in too many scrapes; I go straight ahead; I never look to what is to come after"; or anything of that kind?

A. I never heard Wilson make use of any such expressions or anything of that kind.

Q. Did you ever say to Wilson, "That is too much of the case with myself," or anything of that kind?

A. No, sir; I did not.

Q. Did you say to Wilson, "Will you join?" or words to that effect. . . ?

A. No, sir; I did not. . . .

Q. The night Mr. Spencer was arrested, or about that time, did you say to Peter Tyson, to Browning, or any one else, "I am sick—I expect to be in irons myself before a week," or words to that effect?

A. I said, after Mr. Spencer, Cromwell, and Small, were arrested, and I saw Mr. Gansevoort watching, chasing, and following me all round the vessel, to Browning and the rest of my messmates, that I expected to be put in irons before a week. . . .

[*On March 13, Lieut. Gansevoort and Midshipman Thompson were questioned by the Judge Advocate about Commander Mackenzie's writing for Mr. Spencer.*]

[MARCH 17, 1843.]

[191] [*Mr. O. H. Perry, questioned on the same point*]. . . .

Q. Allow me to ask you again if you did not admit, in the presence of the secretary of the navy and other gentlemen, that Mr. Spencer did send a written message to his friends?

A. I told the secretary of the navy that I was under the impression that Commander Mackenzie copied a letter from Mr. Spencer to his friends; what I mean, is, that Mr. Spencer dictated a letter, and the commander wrote: that was my impression.

CROSS-EXAMINED BY COMMANDER MACKENZIE.

Q. Was your impression derived from any other cause than seeing Commander Mackenzie sitting writing by Mr. Spencer?

A. That is all. . . .

[*Commander Mackenzie then submitted the following paper, swearing it to be* "the only memorandum or writing of any description made by him on that day, while in communication with Mr. Spencer."]

[193] "When asked if he had any message to send; none that they would wish to receive. Afterward, that you die wishing them every blessing and happiness; deserved death for this and other sins; that you felt sincerely penitent, and only fear of death was that your repentance might be too late. Many that he had wronged, but did not know how reparation could be made to them. Your parents most wronged . . . himself, by saying that he had entertained same idea in John Adams and Potomac, but had not ripened it into . . . Do you not think that a mania which should . . . Certainly. Objected to manner of death; requested to be shot. Could not make any distinction between him and those whom he had seduced. Justifiable desire at first to . . . The last words he had to say, and hoped they would be believed, that Cromwell was innocent . . . Cromwell. Admitted it was just that no distinction should be made. Asked that his face might be covered. Granted. When he found that his repentance might not be in season, I referred him to the story of the penitent thief. Tried to find it, could not. Read the Bible, the Prayer-book. Did not know what would have become of him if succeeded. Makes no objection to death, but objects to time. Reasons—God would understand of him offences. . . . Many crimes. Dies praying God to bless and preserve . . . I am afraid this will injure my father. God, who was all-merciful as well as all-wise, could not only extricate the difficulty growing out of shortness of time, and from the abundance of his mercy forgive. Be the death of my poor mother. Do you not think she would have felt worse, if, instead of dying, you had succeeded in your undertaking? Horrors

here. Others in course of piracy . . . Cut off by Cromwell, passing to gallows. Met at pump well. Asked for Mr. Wales. Mr. Wales, I beg you to forgive me for having tampered with your fidelity. Mr. Wales much affected. Are you not going too far? are you not going too fast? I think, sir, you . . . The best service he could render to his father, was to die. Small said, "Shipmates, give me a quick and easy death." Knot, toggle, ship-knot. Asked leave to give word. Granted. Took station on the trunk to see all parts. Waited, waited. Prayer. 'Shall I die?' Browning of opinion. . . . only then began to think . . . he really was going to die; he kept such good heart. Small up, suffocated. Told him, in scarcely audible voice, to tell the commander he must give the word himself. Preparations, live coal match, keep passing them up so as to be put on perpetually; then Cromwell and Spencer meeting. No notice of each other. Spencer as calm as at any moment of life. Wales, Small, asked forgiveness. No, by God, Mr. Spencer can't forgive you; consulted him Mr. Wales, so both together. Forgive me, Small, for leading you into this trouble; we shall soon be in the face of God Almighty, then see you must forgive me, Small. I told him to be more generous. He softened. I do forgive you Mr. Spencer; shook hands; may God Almighty forgive you also. Small on hammocks, asked leave to address the ship's company. Now boys, &c., now brother top-mates, give me a quick death; run me up smartly; do not let there be any interval between word and firing. Asked 1st lieut. if firing with lockmatch. Open a chest, and got wafers; ordered live coals to be passed up from galley. "Stand by, fire"; instantaneous shotted gun. Arrangements. Conversation about coffin. Beating to call. Gan't asked about covering face. No hangmen. You and nothing to do with respects of business and as done in secure and seamanlike manner. The rope-string shipped to the . . . of a . . . strain-hooks moved, tail-blocks well secured. Roll. S. Small stept up. Cromwell overboard, rose, dipping to yard-arm." *

From *Proceedings of the Naval Court Martial* . . . (New York: ✓ ✓ ✓ Henry G. Langley, 1844), pp. 214 ff.

[MARCH 18, 1843.]

[214] [*Alexander M'Kee, age nearly 18, 2nd class apprentice.* Examined by the Judge Advocate.] . . .

Q. When did you first hear of the mutiny?

---

* [The above paper of Commander Mackenzie is so illegible, as not to be correctly written—Ed.] †

† This was a footnote by the original editor of *Proceedings,* who used elision marks [*thus:* . . .] to indicate passages concerning which he was uncertain in his reading. All such marks occur in the book and none are inserted to indicate omissions by the present editor.

A. On the Monday after Mr. Spencer's arrest, I believe the commander addressed the crew and said there was such a plot on board.

Q. Had you ever spoken with Mr. Spencer or any other about taking the brig?

A. No, sir.

Q. When was you first arrested? state what passed.

Q. I was called aft the mainmast on the 30th of November; the commander said he did not think it worth while to put me in irons then; he told me to go to quarters; I think he then spoke to Mr. Gansevoort, I am not quite certain; he called me aft and then put me in irons: I was only put in double irons at first. . . .

[215] *Q*. After the execution, what passed between the commander and yourself?

A. He said he could find nothing against any of the four that were then in irons, if he had found any proof our fate would have been the same; and if he could find any excuse for not taking them home in irons he would do so; I understood him to mean he would release them from their irons. . . .

Q. Do you know anything of Mr. O. H. Perry being sent for when the mast went?

A. Yes, sir, I do; the commander sent me for him. . . .

[216] *Q*. Did you hear what passed between the commander and Mr. O. H. Perry?

A. I heard some part of it. The commander said, "Mr. Perry, this is all your fault"; Mr. Perry said he had obeyed orders—that is all. . . .

[*Benjamin F. Green, age 20, ordinary seaman*. EXAMINED BY THE JUDGE ADVOCATE] . . .

Q. When did you first hear of the mutiny?

A. On the evening of Mr. Spencer's arrest I first heard of the mutiny on the forecastle—I heard it from M'Kee; he said Mr. Spencer had been quarrelling with one of the other midshipmen; some one stood by, I don't recollect who, and said it was for something else. I asked what it was; they said for undertaking to take the brig. Mr. Gansevoort then came and asked me if I knew anything concerning Mr. Spencer. I told him I did not. He said, "You have been very thick with Mr. Spencer lately, and I know d——d well you do know something." I told him I knew nothing concerning him. That is all he said at that time.

Q. Did you have any conversation with Mr. Spencer, or any one else, about taking the brig?

A. No, sir.

Q. Did you miss muster after the arrest? . . . Why?

A. I did not hear the watch called at first, but when it was relieved, it waked me up. . . .

[217] *Q.* When were you arrested. . . ?
A. On the morning of the 30th. . . .

[MARCH 21, 1843.]

[223] . . . The judge advocate does not wish to protract this examination further, or he would call every unexamined member of the Somers, even, to prove that no plan of mutiny was known to any but Wales, before the arrest; and that no proposal of rescue was talked of afterward; if any witness can be named to prove the contrary, he offers to call him. . . .

[MARCH 22, 1843.]

[228] Mr. Griffin, the counsel of the accused, then read his defence as follows:— *

. . . In judging of the necessity of the execution, it is of vital importance to ascertain . . . whether a mutinous conspiracy in fact existed . . . , and whether the persons executed were parties to that conspiracy.

That such conspiracy existed; that it had for its object the conversion of the brig into a piratical cruiser; that such object was to be effected by the murder of the officers and faithful of the crew; and that Mr. Spencer and Small were not only parties but ringleaders in the conspiracy—appears from their own repeated and solemn declarations, and from the unequivocal documentary evidence. . . . [*Cites testimony of Wales; evidence of Spencer's list; and confessions of Spencer and Small at time of execution.*]

[229] The guilt of Cromwell is not less manifest. The badness of his general character and conduct; the sudden change of his demeanor toward the apprentices, ceasing to treat them with harshness . . . , and affecting toward them popular manners, as he found their adhesion to the conspiracy needed; his repeated and profane declarations of deep, desperate hostility against the commander and officers; his threat to the carpenter's mate a little before the discovery of the plot . . . that *his time* was short; his intimacy with Mr. Spencer, receiving gifts from him in money and other articles, and spending with him hour after hour almost daily in deep and secret consultation, an intimacy made more suspicious by the difference in rank of the parties; his being asked by Mr. Spencer, in private conversation, whether he could disguise the brig so that she would not be

---

* This defense, written by George Griffin, was at once printed as a pamphlet, which is often mistakenly attributed to Mackenzie himself: *Case of the Somers Mutiny. Defence of Alexander Slidell Mackenzie, Commander of the U. S. Brig Somers, before the Court-Martial Held at the Navy-Yard, Brooklyn.* (New York: Tribune Office, 1843.)

known, and his saying that he could easily do it; his advising Mr. Spencer, in another private conversation, to have the booms of the Somers cut away and her launch thrown overboard, with a view to render her more fit for piratical service, in singular coincidence with the subsequent declaration of Mr. Spencer to Mr. Wales, that he meant to have those things done; his being overheard to say to Small that they would soon be able to see the Isle of Pines (a noted rendezvous for pirates), also in strange coincidence with another statement by Mr. Spencer to Mr. Wales, that he intended to carry the brig thither; his withdrawing his money, just before the disclosure of the conspiracy, from the petty officer in whose [230] hands he had placed it for safe custody, with no possible motive but his wish to keep it out of harm's way when the work of destruction should ensue; his absence of mind for days before the arrest of Mr. Spencer, seeming to be brooding over desperate thought; his secret and repeated conversations with Small just after Mr. Spencer's arrest and before his own, betraying by his looks and manner deep emotion and revengeful feeling; his wilful disobedience of a standing order of the ship on the morning preceding his own arrest . . . ; Small's declaration the day before his execution, that if any one was leagued with Mr. Spencer, it was Cromwell; the cotemporaneous, united, and solemn opinion of all the officers that he was guilty, founded, at least in part, on their ocular view of many little incidents and appearances which, though collectively carrying home to their own minds a just and sure conviction, can not be adequately communicated to others in all their nice, and sometimes faint, though forceful import; are all circumstances in evidence before the court, and which leave no reasonable doubt of Cromwell's guilt. . . . [*Cites as further proof, testimony that Cromwell was shown the Greek paper by Spencer. Argues that absence of his name from the paper is of no significance: he was too wary to have it there, and doubtless E. Andrews was Cromwell's designation.*] [231] His persisting in the declaration of his innocence at the time of the execution only proves he was a more hardened offender than either Mr. Spencer or Small. . . . The declaration by Mr. Spencer that Cromwell was innocent, might have been owing to some deep pledge . . . , or it might have been owing to a hope . . . that Cromwell, if set at liberty by his means, would rouse his associates, and rescue him even at the last moment. . . . During the half hour preceding his death, when all hope of escape had vanished, Mr. Spencer ceased to say anything about Cromwell's innocence. . . . Of Small . . . , he pathetically implored pardon. . . . But to Cromwell, his bosom associate, who upon the supposition of his innocence, was the individual of all others most injured . . . , to him Mr. Spencer opened not his lips. He asked not forgiveness of Cromwell, though they calmly met face to face . . . , because he well knew that Cromwell, instead of being his victim, had been his prompter in guilt. . . .

It is then fully proved, not only that a mutinous conspiracy existed, but also that Mr. Spencer, Cromwell, and Small were the prime conspirators. It follows that they had forfeited their lives to the laws of their injured country. . . .

[232] But it does not follow . . . that . . . the commander of the Somers might therefore direct them to be executed. It is admitted, that under ordinary circumstances it would have been his duty to . . . bring them home to be tried. But the mutiny . . . created a case which the statute law did not contemplate and could not reach. It was believed, and for reasons of overwhelming force, that neither Mr. Spencer, nor Cromwell, nor Small, could have been brought into port, without the most imminent jeopardy to the brig and the lives of the faithful officers and crew. It was on this ground, the unyielding ground of imperative necessity, that the commander of the Somers found himself placed, when he reluctantly directed the execution. . . . And it is on this ground that he now appeals for his justification. . . .

[*Develops reasons supporting necessity of execution. The size and construction of the brig made safety impossible. The mutiny had reached "a formidable growth" when discovered.*]

[233] According to Mr. Spencer's statement, proved by the change in the conduct and demeanor of the crew not to have been exaggerated, he already numbered twenty determined associates, comprising, of course, the eldest and strongest. . . .

Still the mutinous spirit continued to gather strength [after arrest of Spencer, Cromwell, and Small]. Never was a crew where malcontents could have had a fairer chance of making proselytes. The crew of the Somers were . . . many of them men in physical strength, but all of them boys in mind. Their youthful feelings were peculiarly open to sympathetic appeals; their undisciplined imaginations liable to be easily beguiled by seductive pictures of the freedom and pleasure of the rover's course. The season of youth, especially of untutored youth, is proverbially exposed to temptations. . . . [234] The officers could no more check the progress of mutiny among the crew than they could the progress of contagious disease. . . . [Signs were:] the general disobedience of orders . . . ; the frequent gathering of the older and stronger of the crew in groups for secret consultation, and their stealing away at the approach of an officer . . . ; the carrying away of the main-top-gallantmast by the sudden and violent jerk of the weather-royal-brace by Small, who had just left the side of Cromwell, evidently by design, and with the intent to throw overboard the boy on the royal-yard, that confusion and a chance for the outbreak might thence ensue; the simultaneous mustering of the chief conspirators at the maintop-mast-head on that occasion, watching the moment for action, to which point was also directed the fixed and anxious gaze of Mr. Spencer; the refusal of the men to come aft at first, when ordered there to aid in sending up the new top-gallant-mast, and then the tumultuous rushing thither by nearly all the crew . . . ; the repeated missing of muster without excuse by those named in the Greek paper . . . ; the mysterious removal of the handspikes, heavers, and holystones . . . ; and the sharpening of [235] the African knife and battle-axe . . . ; . . . the declaration by one of the conspirators that he would like to get the African knife into the hands of Mr. Spencer, and that the knife would yet have to do a great deal of slaughter; . . . are among the numberless circumstances which collectively force on the intelligent and experienced observer the full conviction that the mutiny was rapidly maturing for its final outbreak. . . . The sullenness and moroseness, the violent and menacing demeanor, and the portentous looks of the crew between the arrest of Mr. Spencer and the execution, are not the creations of fancy. Every officer and many of the seamen have sworn to their existence. All these witnesses would not league together to deceive you; and they could not have been themselves deceived. They are nautical men, well acquainted with the usual manners, demeanor, and looks of seamen, and were eye-witnesses of what they state. . . . That one witness might be mistaken in such a case is not very unlikely; that a number of witnesses should be mistaken, is against all probability. . . .

[236] Under these circumstances, what was the commander of the Somers to do? He was alone on the ocean. He could not invoke a regular court-martial. He asked the best and only counsel within his reach. He made a written appeal to his officers for their advice. His officers, after examining the witnesses, with full deliberation, returned him their written, unanimous, and solemn judgment, that the execution of the three ringleaders of the mutiny was indispensably necessary. . . . With this judgment of the only court within his reach, his own opinion concurred. The high seas furnished no learned jurists with whom he might consult. But he had with him a volume of nature's laws, written by [237] the finger of God on the human heart. In that volume he read that necessity ordains its own controlling canons; that they who seek unlawfully to slay, may themselves be slain without formal process, when the self-preservation of the assailed renders the sacrifice inevitable. . . .

[239] The notion recently suggested that the council of officers on board the Somers should have proceeded more formally, and having first served written charges on the accused, should have conducted the examination in their presence, subject to their cross-examination, and regular defence, could not have been carried into effect. Each of the three persons executed, had, at the time of his arrest, been distinctly informed of the charge against him; and two of them had afterward repeatedly plead guilty to the charge. The certainty of the guilt of all three, had been placed beyond peradventure by the ocular view of the commander, and the summary inquest before the council of officers. A regular trial was utterly precluded by the exigency of that awful occasion. Necessity stood stern umpire, and allowed no time for the ceremonies or delays of the law. . . .

From an editorial attack on Wm. Norris, the Judge Advocate, in ✓ ✓ ✓ the New York *Courier and Enquirer,* Friday, March 25, 1843.

. . . The Circuit Court of the United States having determined on Monday, that the Civil Courts have no jurisdiction in the case of Mackenzie . . . , there no longer existed any object in procrastinating the sitting of the Court [Martial]; and accordingly at its first meeting after the decision was known, the Judge Advocate gave notice that the trial was at an end. . . . It was very apparent that the Judge Advocate intended to give the Grand Jury an opportunity to interfere. . . .

From the Boston *Courier* (edited by Joseph T. Buckingham), ✓ ✓ ✓ March 25, 1843.

The Naval Court Martial . . . is approaching its dissolution. . . . Commander Mackenzie declared to one of his victims, it would be impossible to convict of a crime any one who had money and friends. . . . The end of the trial proves that the Commander was a man of sagacity, and knew the power of gold and friendship to turn away the current of justice.

From *Proceedings of the Naval Court Martial* . . . (New York: ✓ ✓ ✓ Henry G. Langley, 1844), pp. 242 ff.

[242-243] [*The court was cleared, and on March 22, 23, 24, 25, 27 heard all the testimony read. On March 27, the judge advocate read a paper on the legal aspects of the case which should guide the finding of the court.*]

[246] [*From the judge advocate's paper:*]

It is not the duty of the judge advocate to sum up the facts. . . . In relation to the law I have, however, an official duty. . . . [*Expounds nature of the guilt of mutiny and an officer's duty to suppress it.*] [249] . . . Mutineers are supposed, in instances allowing of trial, to be discovered to be such by the judgment of a court-martial, and that, when the sentence shall be capital, the concurrence of two thirds of the members of the judicial tribunal shall be required, and the execution of the sentence shall be delayed until it receive the confirmation of the president of the United States; or, in case of the trial having been held out of the territory of the United States, until it receive the confirmation of the commander of the fleet or squadron. . . .

. . . The right to convene a court martial is exclusively confided to the president of the United States, the secretary of the navy, or the commander-in-chief of the fleet or squadron in foreign service. A commander of a single ship, therefore . . . , has no authority to order a court-martial. . . . He is thrown for his court and code on necessity, the last power which the law authorizes . . . ; he can not become a judge to try or execute an unallowed sentence, without taking on himself the risk of establishing the guilt of the criminal by legal [250] evidence, and of vindicating his usurpation of authority by the fact of a reasonable necessity. . . . The subordinates of a vessel of war, are not the serfs of an irresponsible power. They are shielded by guarantied [sic] privileges; guilt is not to be branded on them by imputation. The law of evidence, the forms of trial, the essential requisites for a lawful sentence—these have no flexible adaptation to rank; each and all are creatures of the Most High, and guarded in the equalizing moments of accusation and trial with indiscriminating equity. All this is in the law; and the frequent reading of the law in the hearing of every agent in the service, is enjoined. It tells of a legally constituted court, of the right of challenging the judges, of examination and confrontment of witnesses, of the vote of two thirds in capital cases, of the necessity of a death sentence being confirmed by the president or the commander of a fleet or squadron, when the trial is abroad, of liberty of pardon. . . . Such are the stipulated protective sanctions. . . . But to their formal recognition and enjoyment . . . a legal court must be present.

The next question is—are these superseded when attachment to a single ship precludes the possibility of judicial organization? Does the subordinate become outlawed? . . . Is he thus stripped of his privileges? Is the superior power furnished by that circumstance, with that unerring sagacity which dispenses with all the treasured securities of liberty, character, and life? The answer is obvious. . . . Crime is not to be licensed for want of a constitutional judicial tribunal. . . . The superior must execute his duty, by the law of necessity, with the caution and justice of a man possessed of ordinary [251] firmness, prudence, and sagacity. . . .

I shall now detail the specific propositions, under those general principles which I regard as applicable to the case.

First—as to the crime. Mutiny is treason at sea, and is the intent or act to supersede lawful authority, or resist it, or bring it into contempt, so that the power of command is likely or intended to be endangered.

Intent is the essence of every crime, where the law does not infer the intent from the act itself. A mutinous speech or expression once established, the duty of exculpation rests on him who made it. But this is assuming that it has been proved that it was made with a real and serious design. If it could be proved that a proposition in terms mutinous was a premeditated jest or amusement, no one would contend that the crime was established, though believed by its hearer. The attendant evidence, therefore, must ascertain the motive of the speaker. . . .

Second—as to the alleged criminals. This is their trial, their first and only trial. . . . You are not revising, as an appellate court, the trial and sentence of an inferior lawful judiciary. The judge was self-constituted under the law of necessity; he has no commission to secure him against the consequences of mistakes. The errors of a legal court are privileged; those of usurped authority are punishable. The jurisdiction of necessity is always exercised at the hazard of its administrator. . . .

[257] In estimating the necessity of any commander's position, all the attendant circumstances must be minutely analyzed and surveyed . . . , and the necessity must be found such as will justify a man of ordinary firmness and prudence in the taking of life. . . . The evidence *now* before you is the means you must employ. It is a question of fact, necessity, or no necessity; not whether or not it was deemed a necessity, when in truth it was not, for such a principle would excuse all bad judgment, want of firmness and discretion. Such considerations are applicable in assessing penalty, or prompting recommendation to mercy, but they can not vary the truth. . . . Whatever may have been the impressions and motives of the commander at the [258] time cannot affect the question of fact, as to whether the necessity did in truth or not exist. . . .

A letter from Theodore Sedgwick, Jr., to Charles Sumner, dated New York, March 26, 1843. Here reproduced from the original letter in the Sumner Papers, in the Houghton Library of Harvard University, by permission.

Can you not review [George] Griffin's Argument in the McKenzie case for the North American [Review]— It is very desirable to have all the Organs of "Public Opinion" sound the right tune—& you can do it better than any one I know of— You will confer a great benefit upon McK. & the theme is one worthy of your powers— Think of it & let me know—

Passage from a letter of Charles Sumner to Theodore Sedgwick, Jr., dated Boston, March 27, 1843. Here reproduced, by permission, from the original letter in the Houghton Library of Harvard University.

. . . I envy you your honorable connection with Mackenzie. I have no professional duty more agreeable, interesting, or distinguished than that in which you have been engaged. You have the good cause of a good man. I have always liked what I knew of Mackenzie through his writings, and common friends particularly Longfellow and Davis, and I most thoroughly approved of his conduct on board the Somers. . . .

From *Proceedings of the Naval Court Martial* . . . (New York:
↗ ↗ ↗ Henry G. Langley, 1844), pp. 243-244.

MARCH 28, 1843.

[243] *Finding of the Court Martial.* . . . The court . . . do acquit
Commander Alexander Slidell Mackenzie of the charges and specifications
preferred by secretary of the navy against him.

APRIL 1, 1843.

[244] . . . The judge advocate . . . read the following paper:—
"The judge advocate states to the court that, a long time back, he, in
pursuance of instructions from the navy department . . . requested . . .
the counsel of Captain Mackenzie to draw up charges against any of the
crew of the Somers against whom there was testimony of any participation in the alleged mutiny; . . . and that so far from hearing of any
intention to prefer charges, it is believed that Commander Mackenzie has
no such design. . . . Under these circumstances, the judge advocate can
see no objection to the final adjournment of the court. . . ."
The Court then adjourned. . . .

↗ ↗ ↗ From the New York *Herald,* Tuesday morning, March 31, 1843.

Although the case of Commander McKenzie may be criminally ad-
judicated, yet it must . . . come before the tribunal of far higher authority than a Court Martial, or even the Supreme Court of the United
States. It must come before the tribunal of public opinion—not only as
entertained and expressed by the American people, but by the civilized
world. By this tribunal, he may be forgiven, but never held guiltless. . . .

END

OF PART THREE

↗ ↗ ↗

Part Four

THE
COURT
OF
OPINION

April, 1843 to March, 1844

The court martial was now done with Mackenzie, and its final verdict was soon announced. In the civil courts there was some further harassment, prompted by John C. Spencer, which came to nothing. But the court of public opinion was not yet through with the case. For another year, strong voices reiterated praise and blame of Mackenzie, and then the affair was relegated to history and memory.

In this Part, three aspects of the case stand out.

Commander Mackenzie as a person emerges in a new light, in descriptions by Sumner, Lieber, Felton, and Dana. All of these men had approved his actions on principle, but now, after the court martial, they met him for the first time, and all were agreeably surprised by his manner and personality. Each of them saw and de-

scribed a Mackenzie who scarcely emerges from the court records
and newspaper accounts or from his own report. Their impression is
confirmed by Longfellow, from extended acquaintance, and corroborated by scattered reports we have already encountered. This
testimony amounts, in fact, to that of character witnesses. It requires
us to review the events of the cruise in the light of this image of the
man, and to reconsider our previous judgments, though not necessarily to change them.

Quite a conflicting image of Mackenzie emerges, however, from
three trenchant analyses of the case published at this time. One was by
William Sturgis, one by James Fenimore Cooper, and one by an
anonymous pamphleteer. All three interpret Mackenzie's conduct and
his mental processes—if not his character and motives—most unfavor-
ably. Only that of Cooper is extensively represented here. It deserves
careful study for its marshalling of the facts and its close reasoning
upon them. But too often it has been read out of the whole context, and
taken by later writers as a sufficient summary and judgment of the
case. Note especially what Cooper concedes to Mackenzie as well
as what he more conspicuously denies him, and what he makes of
Spencer's guilt.

Finally, in this phase of the case, the focus shifts from matters of
fact and personality to the spacious realm of legal principle. The general legal grounds of the case were examined, and several formula-
tions were offered: by Griffin in his defense and by Norris in his sum-
mation, at the court martial—already given in Part Three. Two more
were advanced, by Charles Sumner in his review article, and by James
Fenimore Cooper (the only non-lawyer in this group) along with his
analysis of the court-martial proceedings. For readers whose minds
move congenially in the realm of abstract legal principle, this may
prove the most fascinating aspect of the case; for those hitherto unaware of such a realm, its mere existence can be an important discovery. Less legalistic general principles also come into focus now.

Recall that this case occurred at the full flood of Jacksonian
democracy. Conservative Whigs confronted radical Democrats, in the
newly opened "era of the common man." A major ground of the
affair was the way in which the case seemed to array principles against
each other: aristocracy against democracy (perhaps Jeffersonian
against Jacksonian democracy); discipline against popular rights;

security of property against security of life; the safety of society against the right of individuals to due legal process. No one, of course, wanted either anarchy or arbitary government; everyone looked to the law for assurance of rights and saw "justice" on his side; but some saw the *Somers* case as a manifestation of law and order triumphant over mutiny and piracy, whereas others saw it as a display of privileged military arrogance overriding human rights.

These were some of the questions, and they remain significant: What *right* had a naval commander to hang his men, even if they were guilty? What *rights* had sailors as citizens? What *justification,* in short, was there for the hangings?

Item in *Niles' National Register* (Baltimore), LXIV (April 1, 1843),
✓ ✓ ✓ 80.

The court martial . . . have closed their proceedings, and transmitted their decision to the navy department at Washington. It was submitted to the cabinet at 11 o'clock on the 29th ult., at the president's house, the secretary of the treasury [Spencer] being present. The meeting held till 3 o'clock.

Passage from a letter of Charles Sumner to Theodore Sedgwick, Jr., dated Boston, April 1, 1843. Here reproduced, by permission, from the original letter in the Sumner Papers in the Houghton Library
✓ ✓ ✓ of Harvard University.

. . . You will see that I do not lack disposition to undertake what you propose for the N. American Review. But time is the impediment. I have promised for the next number a paper on Judge Story's judicial character. . . . If the Editor will excuse me from this, I shall be glad to take up the Mackenzie case, on which I have no misgivings of any kind. . . . I should write about Mackenzie as a labor of love. . . .

From the New York *Weekly Tribune,* Saturday, April 8, 1843,
✓ ✓ ✓ quoted from the *Madisonian* (Washington).

A most absurd and ridiculous report is going the rounds of the newspapers, that a personal conflict took place at a recent Cabinet meeting, between Secretaries Spencer and Upshur. We assure the public that there is not the slightest foundation for such a report. There was neither a fight nor even an angry or unpleasant word, between these Secretaries, on that or any other occasion. The whole story is a naked fabrication.

✓ ✓ ✓ From the New York *Weekly Tribune,* April 8, 1843.

Melancholy Suicide. We regret to learn that Passed Assistant Surgeon RICHARD W. LEACOCK, of the U. S. Brig Somers, committed suicide at 6 on Sunday evening [March 31] in the gun-room of his vessel lying at the Navy Yard, by shooting himself through the head just above the eye, with a pistol. . . . He has been attached to the Somers ever since she has been in commission. . . . He was 28 years of age and a native of Norfolk, Va. The sad occurrence by which he has closed his life is attributed to a settled melancholy and a partial derangement induced by a long and severe attack of the yellow fever, which he contracted on a former voyage to the Coast of Africa in the U. S. schooner Shark.

✓ ✓ ✓ From the Chicago *Express,* April 11, 1843.

The Boston Post contains the following extract of a letter from a British Naval officer, now on the West India station. After speaking of the Mutiny of the Somers, he says:

"The firmness and decision of Captain Mackenzie . . . has been much commented upon in our squadron, and we think the officer who dares to step beyond the letter of the law when circumstances require it deserves well of his country."

✓ ✓ ✓ From New York *Weekly Tribune,* April 15, 1843.

A subscription list has been opened at the Exchange, for the purpose of raising funds to present a sword to this gallant officer. In order that it may be a general matter the subscription price is limited to $1 each.
[Philadelphia Gazette.]

✓ ✓ ✓ From a letter of Richard H. Dana, Jr., to A. S. Mackenzie, dated Boston, April 16, 1843. Here reproduced, by permission, from the original letter in the Dana Papers in the library of the Massachusetts Historical Society.

Among the numerous congratulations which you have received and are receiving, I am unwilling to have no place. . . .

I need not say how earnestly I have watched the proceedings of the courts through whose tedious and wearing delays you have been carried; and how much I have sympathized with you in the contest there has been made to turn public opinion against you. I wish that, while subjected to the varying and unsatisfactory exhibitions in New York, you could have refreshed your spirit with a little of the more wholesome public breath of our peninsular city. Of course your matter engrossed attention here as elsewhere, and I had peculiar opportunities for learning the state of opinion and feeling among all classes. To say that it was all one way would hardly give a correct notion. There were doubters, and a few, very few and insignificant opponents of your course, but against them there was a current of strong *enthusiasm* in your favor. Among the educated people, in the professions, and in what we call in America the upper classes, you were (you must excuse me the indelicacy of a direct compliment to a stranger) a hero, and not a hero of the sword, but the hero of a moral conflict. Such, I assure you, is the feeling here. I have found no exception to this sentiment among those whose opinions are valuable.

The press, too, has been right; for here we are not influenced at all by an irresponsible and mercenary penny press, which has so great sway in New York. There is an element of *conservatism* and soundness in our city, of which, as a Bostonian, you must excuse me for boasting. Of this you have had the full benefit.

A few days since, our senator in Congress, Mr. Choate, in addressing a jury in defence of a person under indictment, likened the act of his client (a master of a merchant vessel) to your own in one particular, and tried to persuade the jury that the same reasoning and principles which "made us, *one and all,* sustain Captain Mackenzie &c" (these were his very words) should relieve his client. . . . I refer to this . . . as evidence of public opinion here. For Mr. Choate, a very wary advocate, would not dare to risk a prejudice of a single man in a jury of 12 men drawn by lot out of the middle classes of our community, unless he had felt certain that there was no probability of there being one who could doubt upon your course. . . .

. . . If I can in any way serve you in this or any other matter, and through you, the cause of sound principles in public service, the cause of law, order, religious principle, moral probity, and national honor, I shall be most happy to do so. . . .

↗ ↗ ↗ From the Boston *Courier,* April 17, 1843, quoting the Washington Correspondent of the New York *Herald.*

The rumors . . . about discussions in the cabinet, must be untrue, as no one can possibly be acquainted with them. . . . It is known that Mr. Spencer has absented himself from the last two . . . , and the cause is, of course, understood. But . . . it is very generally understood, that, with perhaps one exception, [the cabinet members'] sentiments are in unison with those of the great masses of the country, and any thing but favorable to Mackenzie's courage, discretion, humanity, or his sense of justice.

> From a letter of A. S. Mackenzie to Theodore Sedgwick, Jr., dated Tarrytown, N. Y., April 18, 1843. Here reproduced from the original letter in the Houghton Library of Harvard University, by permission.

The weather has prevented me from going to town today to consult as to what is best to be done with regard to the libel of the Journal of Commerce. If by bringing a suit against him the entire secret of the voting of the Court could be ascertained I should be glad. I do not believe that more than two at the most voted against me on any charge and I am inclined to think that there was only one, and he not of sound mind. . . .

From the Chicago *Express,* April 20, 1843.

The Baltimore Clipper states that several ladies and gentlemen of that city have it in contemplation to present Commander Mackenzie . . . with a pair of gold epaulettes, as a tribute of respect for his firmness and ability as an officer, and his character as a man. A considerable portion of the money necessary to defray the expense, has already been subscribed.

> From a letter, *"private and confidential,"* from Theodore Sedgwick, Jr., to Charles Sumner, New York, April 21, 1843. Here reproduced, by permission, from the original letter in the Sumner Papers of the Houghton Library of Harvard University.

. . . The papers have charged that the Acquittal is merely technical being 7 to 5 against him & that he only escapes by the ⅔ proviso— We are resolved to disprove this by examining some of the Officers of the Court. . . . We therefore institute a suit for Libel agst. the Editor of the J[ournal] of C[ommerce] & send a Commission to Boston to examine Comre. Downes & to Philada. to examine Captain Gwin &c. . . .

> An entry from the diary of R. H. Dana, Jr., dated April 25, 1843. Here reprinted from *Richard Henry Dana, A Biography,* by Charles Francis Adams (Boston: Houghton Mifflin, 1890, I, 58-63.

A gentleman by the name of Craney, late a lieutenant in the United States Navy, was introduced to me as wishing to study law in my office.

[59] After some conversation, in order to explain to me the fact of his leaving the service, he gave me the history of his unfortunate difficulty with the Department. It is a most sad story, if he has given it correctly, and I believe him to have done so. He entered the navy quite young, and toiled up to a lieutenancy, which gave him an honorable competency. While junior lieutenant of the North Carolina, receiving ship at New York, Captain Spencer of the navy, brother of the Secretary of War, came on board, bringing with him his nephew Philip Spencer, who had just received a midshipman's warrant. Mr. Craney happened to be officer of the deck, and being acquainted with Captain Spencer the latter introduced young Spencer to him, and asked him to assist the young beginner, by teaching him the ropes and looking after him in various ways. Mr. Craney was pleased with the opportunity of befriending the son of the Secretary of War and nephew of an officer of high rank, and thought it might be an advantage to himself if the young man turned out well. Soon, however, he saw that Spencer was a bad fellow and would make him trouble. He had invited him to use his state-room and his books whenever he wished to, and he found that Spencer had abused this liberty, by keeping lights in his state-room after the hour allowed, and by keeping bottles of liquor under his bureau, with which he got drunk while Craney was in the city. He spoke to Spencer several times about it, but it did no good. At length Craney was reported to the first lieutenant as having a light in his state-room after hours. Craney explained the matter to the first lieutenant, but nothing was done to the son of the secretary. [I, 60]

One night Craney was in his berth asleep, when he was waked up by a noise and saw Spencer in his state-room trying to draw a bottle from under some place where it seems he had hidden it. Craney ordered him out of the room. Spencer, who appeared to be a little intoxicated, said he would go when he chose. Craney ordered him out again, and then Spencer raised his arm and struck him a severe blow as he lay in his berth. Craney sprang out of his berth and pushed Spencer from the room. Spencer resisted, and the noise brought the officers down. Spencer was ordered below. The next morning the first lieutenant sent for Craney and asked him if he intended to report Spencer. Craney said he certainly thought it his duty to do so, as the offence of striking a superior officer was the worst that could occur on board ship. The lieutenant then told him that he would advise him as a friend to do no more about the matter. That it would do him no good at the Department; that Spencer's friends were powerful, and he had better let it drop. After some reflection, and thinking that Spencer was young and after an alarm might do better, he did nothing further.

Mr. Craney had an uncommonly good sextant, and had offered to the professor to explain the use of it to the midshipmen whom the professor was instructing daily in the steerage. One day the professor asked Craney to go down and explain the sextant to the young gentlemen, and having no duty on hand he did so. While there, in the presence of the professor, explaining the instrument to the midshipmen, he received a violent blow upon the side of the face, which pushed him backwards in his chair and threw him and the chair over upon the floor. [I, 61] This blow was struck by Spencer, who came up behind him while engaged looking upon the instrument. At the same time with the blow Spencer wrenched off Craney's epaulet, tearing off the button, and ripping down his coat. Craney sprang up, but was instantly seized by a number of those present and held back, while young Spencer was dragged out of the room.

Allowing himself time to cool, and a season for reflection, Craney reported this and the previous transaction to the Department. (I suppose from what followed that this report had to go through the hands of the commander of the ship.)

Either Captain Spencer or the commander of the ship, Commodore Perry, sent for the professor and several of the midshipmen present, and learned from them that Mr. Craney's report was rather understated than otherwise. Commodore Perry then sent for Craney and tried to persuade him not to report Spencer, telling him that he would do himself no good by it, etc. Craney said he could not pass over it. It was an offence which was punishable even by death if a court-martial so ordered, and being committed in the presence of the midshipmen, and known to the whole ship's company, his own honor as well as a duty he owed the service required him to do it. The Commodore then told him it would be of no use as Spencer had been ordered to join the John Adams at Boston; and offered him back his charges, which he had not sent to the Department. Mr. Craney says he instantly saw through this. Captain Spencer, finding Craney determined to report his nephew, had written to the lad's father and procured orders for him to join another vessel, and prevailed upon Commodore [I, 62] Perry to retain the charges until Spencer should be sent away.

Mr. Craney stated his opinion very freely, and demanded that Commodore Perry should retain the orders until the charges could be sent to Washington and Spencer arrested. This the Commodore refused to do, saying that he must obey his orders from the Department.

Mr. Craney then wrote a letter to the Secretary of the Navy, detailing the whole transaction. To this he received a reply slighting the whole matter, and treating Craney, as he thought, in a very insolent and contemptuous manner. To this, I think, but am not sure, Craney replied. At all events, it ended in Craney's being suspended, and Spencer sent upon a cruise in the John Adams. Craney remained suspended for weeks on board the North Carolina. He had been insulted and openly assaulted by an inferior officer; himself and the service in his person had been disgraced, and justice and satisfaction had been refused him; and all because of the influence of young Spencer's powerful friends. These reflections so wore upon Craney that he became ill. His pent-up indignation and his wounded feelings allowed him no rest. Under the influence of these feelings he sent in his resignation, which was accepted.

After twelve or fourteen years of the prime of his life spent in the service, and almost unfitted for anything else, he was thrown out upon the world.

Not long after his resignation the news of the execution of young Spencer by Mackenzie, on board the Somers, reached America. . . . [I, 63]

Whether he has exaggerated the story, or not, I have no certain means of knowing; but I never heard a story told in a more precise, methodical, and calm manner; subsequent events as to Spencer show its probability, and Craney impressed me very favorably for calmness, self-respect and candor.*

> From a letter from A. S. Mackenzie to Richard H. Dana, Jr., dated Tarrytown, N. Y., April 28, 1843. Here printed from the original letter in the Dana Papers of the Massachusetts Historical Society, ✓ ✓ ✓ by permission.

. . . Of the various articles that have appeared in the newspapers in defence of the course pursued on board the Somers, there was not one that I saw so well-suited [as Dana's] to convince the public mind and satisfy public opinion. In addition to the very able and convincing manner in which the subject was treated, the fact of its emanating from one who has so strenuously and ably exerted himself to reveal the iniquities that are practiced on the common seamen, and vindicate his claim to protection and justice, could not fail to give it weight and importance. I think

---

* [*Footnote by Charles Francis Adams*]: William Craney was appointed a midshipman 23 May, 1832; a passed midshipman 23 June, 1838; he was dismissed the service 31 May, 1839, by order of the Secretary of the Navy, J. K. Paulding, for reasons specified in a letter, a copy of which was filed in the Department; he was reinstated and appointed midshipman 3 September, 1841; and resigned 15 February, 1842. While the statements made by Craney to Dana, and which at the time impressed the latter so much, may be true so far as Philip Spencer was concerned, the letter of Secretary Paulding above referred to, though relating to other and earlier transactions, should be read in connection with them.

Editor's Note: The letter of Secretary Paulding, 31 May 1839, dismissed Craney for specified instances of intoxication, absence without leave, disorderly conduct, misrepresentation, and disrespect to his superior officer, all while attached to the *Consort* at Vera Cruz. Reinstated as passed midshipman in September, 1841, he was ordered to the receiving ship (*North Carolina*) at New York on October 15, 1841. His letter of resignation, dated from that ship, February 10, 1842, refers to his "having been suspended and confined to this ship for four weeks," and expresses the hope that "the department will order me released from my confinement." See Philip Spencer's letter of February 11, 1842, Appendix, Item 2. No further official records of the Spencer-Craney affair have been located. (Since passed midshipmen did duty as junior lieutenants, Craney, though misrepresenting his rank to Dana, was not necessarily misrepresenting his station and duty.)

indeed that the common sailor is quite as much interested in the maintenance of order on ship board, and in sustaining the course pursued on board the Somers as any other class. They are the most numerous class on the ocean, and the most concerned in its security.

↗ ↗ ↗   From *Niles' National Register* (Baltimore), LXIV (April 29, 1843), 133.

At a recent meeting of the friends of Commander Mackenzie, held at Tarrytown, (N. Y.) the following amongst other resolutions were adopted: That we cordially welcome back . . . our fellow-citizen. . . . That we regard with sincere pleasure his acquittal. . . .

↗ ↗ ↗   From *The Diary of Philip Hone 1828-1851,* edited by Bayard Tuckerman (New York: Dodd, Mead & Co., 1889), p. 183.

May 11.—A letter [dated April 18] is published, signed by three hundred merchants and others of our most respectable citizens, addressed to Commander Alexander S. McKenzie [*sic*], expressing their approval of his conduct in the unhappy affair of the mutiny on board the "Somers," and their congratulations on his honourable acquittal by the court of inquiry and court-martial. His answer [dated May 6] to this high compliment is much better written, and in better taste, than his unfortunate statement made to the government on his arrival. If he had said no more then, and said it as well, his case would have stood better before his fellow-citizens; particularly that portion of his friends who lament the necessity, while they justify the motives, of the dreadful act of discipline which he was called upon to perform. The merchants have raised a sum of money by subscription to pay the lawyers' fees and other charges attending the trials; but this fact is delicately kept out of view in the correspondence.

↗ ↗ ↗   From the New York *Herald,* May 11, 1843. "A poetic effusion in the old ballad style, which was sent to us. . . ."

The Somers

A BALLAD—By Horser Clenling, Esq., Quarter Master U. States Service.

> Come listen all ye sailors bold.
> Come listen unto me,—
> I'll sing you of a cruel deed;
> A bloody tragedy.

Come listen landsmen, one and all,
    Come listen unto me,
I'll make you bless your lucky stars
    You've never gone to sea.

It was the Somers, graceful, swift,
    As trim a little brig,
As ere was moddled by shipwright,
    Or sailor helped to rig—

That, right before the steady trades,
    Was she cleaving her swift way,
And dashing from her glancing bows
    The sparkling, snowy spray.

Like unto some live ocean bird,
    Swiftly and light she breasts
The up-curled, watery rolling hills,
    And skims along their crests.

Like unto some live ocean bird
    She spreads her wings of snow,
And piles the canvas, gleaming white,
    On spars aloft, alow.

On, on she fleetly rushes,
    Her wake, a track of foam,
Outstretching far, attests the speed
    With which she flies for home.

Home! home! ah! what a joyful word
    For every seaman's ear,
But, ah! vain word! vain word! to some
    Of that brig's crew I fear.

Stern sounds of import, dark and dread,
    Rise from her peopled deck;
They're not the thrilling battle cheers
    Or shrieking of the wreck;

They're not the friendly trumpet's hail
    Far o'er the waters cast;
Nor boom of cannon belching forth
    The fierce and deadly blast.

They're not the orders, loud and hoarse,
    High rising o'er the gale,
"Clew up! clew down! lay out and pass
    The gaskets round the sail!"

They're sounds of anguish and despair
    Low, mournful dread and drear,
Sighs, prayers, and inward curses
    The mutterings of fear.

They're sounds that ne'er were heard before
    Among a Yankee crew;
That ne'er before disgraced a ship
    O'er which our bright flag flew.

The grating's rigged—the hangman's whip
    Dangles from main yardarm,
The wond'ring crew gaze on the sight
    With terror and alarm.

In doubt and fear they whisper low,
    Scarcely above their breath,
"What mean these novel sights and signs,
    These signs of crime and death?"

Alas! the meaning's soon too clear;
    The noose is round the neck
Of three poor men, but men as brave
    As walk the Somer's deck.

But what's the cause, and what's the crime,
    That thus, in manhood's bloom,
And without form of law, three men,
    To such a death, can doom?

Alas! suspicion, hate, and fear,
    And vanity, are rife;
And a poor pride, that will not count
    The worth of human life.

A lubber's heard a wild boy's yarn,
    That makes his cheek grow pale,
And straightway to the quarterdeck,
    He tells the wond'rous tale.

'Tis taken up, and for this cause
    These men are doomed to die;
A tale, which most men would have called,
    A weak and silly lie.

On one side, Small and Cromwell stand,
    Bold men and sailors true,
They quail not, though the boldest might,
    With such a death in view.

The meanest Yankee tar that lives,
    Will dare the ghastly foe,
Where bullets fly; where cutlass, pike,
    Gives fiercely, blow for blow.

Amid the flashing cannon's roar,
    When hand to hand we board,
But, ah! 'tis different far to face
    The hangman's cruel cord.

Starboard, young, foolish Spencer stands;
    The tears are in his eye;
What feelings of deep agony
    Must through his bosom fly!

He thinks of home, his father, friends,
    His mother's fond caress;
He thinks of all the hopes and fears
    That promised life to bless.

He thinks, too, of his comrades bold
    Doomed by his idle tales,
And their dread fate more than his own
    He bitterly bewails.

The whips are manned with pistol raised
    The first Luff bravely stands
To guard that on the murd'rous ropes
    Are laid unwilling hands.

Now, doomed men, look your last on life
    Look on the gathered crew;
Look on the bounding joyous brig;
    Look o'er the waters blue.

Look on the fleecy floating clouds;
    Look on the sun's calm light;
Look on that banner waving free,
    Emblem of law and right.

Look! look your last! for hark! a gun
    Sends forth its smoky breath,
"Whip!"—instantly upon the word
    Their eyes are sealed in death.

The deed is done! that cruel deed—
    "Three cheers" the captain cries,
"Three cheers" for that dark blood striped flag
    That o'er us mocking flies.

"Pipe down! Pipe down!" the Captain cries,
    " 'Tis dinner time o'day,
That over, in their ocean tombs
    These corpses we will lay."

And sad and slow our messmates dead
    We launched into the waves,
And watched them sink, mid ocean's moans,
    Deep in their watery graves.

O'er them the winds a requiem sing;
    Deep, mournful sounds the blast;
And shriller hiss the curling waves
    As homeward we speed fast.

Our brig flies like some guilty thing
    Faster, more fast she flies,
From where the blood of murdered men
    From the deep ocean cries.

In vain! In vain! Thus can'st escape,
    Fatal, perfidious bark!
The stains of blood are on thy deck,
    Thy freight is curses dark!

And other hands than flesh and blood
    Thou numberest 'mongst thy crew;
And a ghostly "mess" thou'lt always hear
    Across the ocean blue.

And not alone by mortal hands,
    Will be, when howls night's blast,
Thy reef points knotted, earrings hauled,
    Or mainyard gaskets passed.

No! often on that gallows spar
    The yardsmen brave will quail,
In the midnight watch at figures three
    Unearthly—fleshless—pale.

Strange sounds will float upon the air,
    And in the blast will speak;
And round the main-yard arms three ghosts
    Will play, and dance, and shriek!

And ill luck, and misfortune dire
    Will follow in thy wake,
Till the ghastly three, where lie their bones,
    Thy last dark haven make.

Oh! better far to yield her then
    At once unto the dead,
Than keep the bloody, cursed craft,
    An honest seaman's dread!

Take—take her far away from land,
    Her rudder lash midship;
From every yard-arm, fore and main,
    Let hang the murderous whip.

Sheet home on every cursed spar,
    Set every rag of sail,
And leave her to the ocean ghouls,
    And demons of the gale!

Excerpt from the "Preface" to James Fenimore Cooper's pamphlet, *The Battle of Lake Erie; or Answers to Messrs. Burges, Duer, and Mackenzie* (Cooperstown, N. Y.: H. & E. Phinney, 1843). The Preface is dated May 16, 1843. The pamphlet was published in July or August, 1843.

[*iii*] The writer has not sought this discussion. It has been forced on him by his assailants, who must now face the consequences. For years the writer has submitted in comparative silence to a gross injustice, in connection with the matter . . . , because he "bided his time," knowing, when that should arrive, he had the truth to fall back upon. He [*iv*] has seen his own work condemned, and, so far as the public authorities were concerned, excluded from the District School Libraries, and all on account of its supposed frauds in relation to the Battle of Lake Erie, while, on the other hand, he has heard Capt. Mackenzie's Biography of Perry lauded from one end of the Union to the other, and preferred to that place in the libraries mentioned, from which his own work has been excluded. The day of reckoning has come at length, and the judgment of men will infallibly follow. . . .

[11] [*The first review-attack on Cooper's* History of the Navy *was written by William A. Duer, president of Columbia College, in the New York* Commercial Advertiser, *June 8, 9, 1839.*] As it contained gross personal imputations, I prosecuted the editor for libel. . . . [Duer] was nearly a stranger to me. His article was written with a peculiar malignancy. . . . Some persons may think it pertinent [that] Mr. Duer is Mr. Mackenzie's uncle by marriage. . . . [31] . . . His beautiful article may be taken as part of the family picture. . . . I sued the editor. . . . The case was referred to arbitrators, and the result was a decision in my favor; a *moral* as well as a legal decision. [11: *Another review-attack was made on the* History of the Navy *by Captain Alexander Slidell Mackenzie in an unsigned article in the* North American Review, *October, 1839.*] [12] The agency of Captain Mackenzie in this affair is probably to be imputed to his connection with the family of Perry, the present Com. M. C. Perry having married his sister. . . .

[49] No man has had a larger share in injuring both Com. [Jesse D.] Elliott and myself than Capt. Mackenzie, and I now propose to prove how loosely and falsely he has endeavored to rob us of our characters. . . .

[58] I think Captain Mackenzie's mind to be very singularly constituted. . . . [He] can see only one side of a question. He is a man of prejudice and denunciation, and he accuses, less under evidence, than under convictions. . . .

Passage from a letter from Miss Catharine M. Sedgwick to Mrs. K. S. Minot, New York, June 6, 1843. Here reprinted from *Life and Letters of Catharine M. Sedgwick,* edited by Mary E. Dewey (New York: Harper & Brothers, 1871), p. 285.

Anne. A. and I went a few evenings since to take a sociable dish of tea with Mrs. Banyer, and Fenimore Cooper dropped in. I rather think the light by which we see the world emanates from ourselves. He moves in a belligerent spirit, waging war with classes and masses, boarding and broadsiding his fellow-creatures. He maintained that his own country was below France, Italy, and even England in civilization, intellectual development, *morals,* and manners; that we were going in everything backward; that in common honesty we were below any other nation. Being in the presence of Mrs. Banyer and Miss Jay, who sanctify the very names of Christian and saint, he attacked the whole class with man-of-the-world slang, and wound up with promising me a pamphlet of his, just coming out, which is to grind M'Kenzie [*sic*] to powder. With all this, he was good-humored, and talked strongly and amusingly. . . .

From the journal of R. H. Dana, Jr., Boston, June 19, 20, 1843. Here reproduced, by permission, from the original manuscript journal in the Dana Papers of the Massachusetts Historical Society.

June 19. . . . Called upon Miss Catharine Sedgwick at Mrs. Minot's [her sister]. Speaking of McKenzie, she says Cooper told her he was about publishing a pamphlet in which he should not leave enough of Mackenzie to put between his thumb and finger.

June 20. . . . Mr. Sam. A. Elliott called to invite me to take the letter from the Boston subscribers to Mackenzie. I declined on acc. of engagements. The letter is written on parchment with the names of 500 subscribers, & enclosed in a beautiful silver book of a large 8vo. size, which is again enclosed in a neat morocco case. . . .

From *Niles' National Register* (Baltimore), LXIV (July 1, 1843), 275-276.

The Journal of Commerce, after publishing the atrocious falsehood, that Mr. Mackenzie's acquittal by the court martial, was by a minority— gives place today to the annexed conclusive refutation, without one word of apology to its readers. . . . The charge, it may be remembered, was that seven of the twelve members thought the accusation proved, a charge for which there was no shadow of foundation.

[*N. Y. American.*]

From the Journal of Commerce.

In our paper of the 15th April we stated that "we had learned from an undoubted source, that although the decision of the court martial . . . was technically in favor of acquittal, a majority of the members, viz. seven out of twelve were of opinion that the charges or some of them, had been proved."

Captain Mackenzie, considering this publication not only injurious, but believing it incorrect in point of fact, commenced a prosecution against us for libel; his counsel stated that they had no vindictive feeling to gratify, and no wish for pecuniary satisfaction. . . .

We publish below the result of the examination of Captain McKeever, one of the members of the court; it proves that our information was erroneous—the vote of the court being nine in Captain Mackenzie's favor, to three against him; and on the first charge the three last voting with a very material qualification.

Com. Downes's testimony has also been taken. It agrees substantially with that of Capt. McKeever, upon the three charges.

. . . The suit is now discontinued.

From "The Mutiny of the Somers," an unsigned review article [by Charles Sumner] in the *North American Review*, LVII (July, 1843), 195-242.

✓ ✓ ✓

[228] . . . We assume the existence of a mutiny, or mutinous conspiracy, on board the *Somers,* as established by evidence beyond a doubt. Laying aside, for the present, all question as to who were the partakers in this guilt, or as to the necessity of their execution, we begin by inquiring, What were the duties imposed upon the commander by this event? Of course, to suppress the mutiny, protect the lives of his officers and crew, and save the ship which had been committed to his charge. But the law does not impose extraordinary duties, without conferring at the same time, co-extensive powers, or means for the performance of the duties. It does not enjoin upon its servants arduous exertions, without, from its ample armory, intrusting them with weapons adequate to the difficult purpose. These will differ much from the powers to be exercised on ordinary occasions. We will not undertake to decide the question, whether a national ship, on the high seas, in time of peace, and in the absence of mutiny or disturbance, is under the rule of the municipal law or of the martial law. But, however this may be in ordinary circumstances, we cannot doubt that, by the mutiny on board the *Somers,* this ship was placed, for the time being, in a state of war. It was as if the enemy were at the gates, or rather already within the walls, of the city. . . . [229] Amid the sound of arms the ordinary municipal law, which might before have controlled the duties and responsibilities of officers, became silent.

Martial law prevailed. By the course of events, the commander was invested with a duty not unlike that of the dictator, *to see that the ship received no detriment.* The law, that laid on his shoulders the burden of these transcendent powers, required in his case . . . only their honest and conscientious exercise to the best of his abilities. In the flagrant proof of the existence of the mutiny, and the melancholy circumstances by which he was surrounded, he might read legibly, as in a warrant of the law, the customary *formula* of that instrument—"for which these shall be your warrant"—and proceed, without fear of the future, to the execution of a citizen.

It is a principle of the common law,—and probably a principle of universal law, for it has its foundations in natural equity,—that a person having judicial authority will be protected by the law in all cases where he has exercised it honestly and conscientiously, even though grievous error may have occurred. This principle is to be found in the earliest records of our jurisprudence, and is upheld by an unbroken series of decisions. The reason of it has been succinctly stated by a distinguished judge of our country [James Kent]. "Judicial exercise of power," he said, "is imposed upon the courts. They *must decide and act according to their judgment;* and, [230] therefore, the law will protect them." The rule was expressed another time in more technical language. "Therefore, by the law of England," said Lord Mansfield, "if an action be brought against a judge of record for an act done by him in his judicial capacity, he may plead that he did it as a judge of record, and that will be a complete justification."

Analogous to this in principle, is the justification of the commander of the *Somers.* The character cast upon him was at once *judicial* and *executive.* He was to judge and execute. The judicial authority does not depend on the ermine or robe. It may be muffled even under a military cloak. . . . [231] We are prepared to assert, that the legality of the means employed by Commander Mackenzie in suppressing the mutiny may be judged by the answer to the simple question, whether, under the circumstances of the case, he acted honestly, to the best of his judgment, and without any corrupt motive, or wilful thought. But, in giving this effect to the motives of the commander, we assume that the mutiny had acquired such foothold as to cause reasonable and well-grounded apprehensions for the safety of the ship. In other words, there must have been an *apparent necessity* for a resort to *extraordinary* means to arrest the mutiny. There must have appeared to be no other alternative, equally consistent with the safety of all. In characterizing this necessity as *apparent,* rather than real, we adopt the distinction which lies at the foundation of the right of self-defence. The consideration of this distinction will throw additional light on the rule by which the responsibility of Commander Mackenzie is to be judged.

But what is the right of *self-defence?* It is a right founded in the law of nature. It springs from the character of man. It is one of the essential elements bound up in his being. It had its origin in the instincts of humanity, and is ratified by the calm judgments of reason. It is older than books, for it was born when the pulsations of the heart began. It is broader than civilization or law, for it is [232] common to the whole human family. . . .

A right so important, which, in its exercise, may override the ordinary municipal law, can only be employed under circumstances of a peculiar character. It is like the sword suspended in the temple in ancient times, which could only be taken down on a great emergency. The law, which sanctions this right, limits and guards its exercise. It is not on every occasion of anxiety, or fear of imagined danger, or impending harm, that a person will be justified in taking the life of a citizen. But the law, while careful to restrain the right within its natural limits, recognizes its force on every just and proper occasion. What, then, is a just and proper occasion for its exercise? We answer, Whenever a person of ordinary firmness and courage, has *reasonable grounds* to believe his life in danger; or, according to another form of expression, whenever it *appears* that he can save his own life only by the sacrifice of that of another. It is not necessary that the danger should in *reality* be imminent; it is sufficient, if there are reasonable grounds to believe that there is a design to destroy life, although it should afterwards appear that no such design existed. [*Footnote citations.*]

[233] This is the rule of municipal law, derived from numerous authorities, and applied to cases between citizens on the land. It was recognized in our country as long ago as the trial of the soldiers for what has been called the Boston Massacre; and was accurately defined by the court, after learned and acute discussion at the bar, in the trial of Selfridge for the killing of Austin. There are many reasons, why the rule might receive a more enlarged and vigorous application in the case of a soldier, than in that of the citizen. We will, however, only allude to one. As the soldier is bound to maintain his *post* and his *arms,* it would seem that in the defence of these, he would be justified in resorting to the same extreme measures by which he might protect his life.

Applying this rule to the circumstances of the *Somers,* it will be needful to the legal justification of the Commander only to establish the existence, at the time of the execution, of an *apparent* danger to the ship, or to the lives of his officers and crew. It should be such a danger as seemed to him, in the exercise of his best judgment, to threaten fatal results, unless arrested by instant and extraordinary exertions. We repeat, that, in strictness of law, it is not requisite for him to go further than this. And we present this view of the case, not because we believe that the necessity, under which he acted, was not at once real and *apparent,* but because we are anxious to define what seem to be the proper legal grounds of defence. In this view, the question to be asked is not, whether, looking at the circumstances of the case from the vantage-ground of the present time, it was in reality possible [234] to carry the prisoners to St. Thomas, or to the United States; but, whether, *at the time of the execution,* it did not *appear* impossible to do it, without imminent danger to the ship and all on board.

And this leads us to an important consideration. In determining the existence of this *apparent* necessity, we are to banish from our minds all knowledge or impressions derived from recent results or evidence; we are to carry ourselves back to the morning of December 1st, 1842, and to the actual point of time when the execution took place; we are to put ourselves in the position of the commander; to scan the countenances of the crew; to note the signs of disaffection; to breathe the atmosphere of distrust. We are, with him, to examine the narrow accommodations afforded by the brig, and to consider the difficulty of preventing communication between the prisoners and the crew; and, finally, with him we are to listen to the unanimous recommendation of his officers, that Spencer, Cromwell, and Small should be put to death.

As it is not in our power to place ourselves actually in this situation, it is important that we should employ the means, which, after personal observation, are best calculated to give us an accurate impression of the appearance of things at the time of the execution. In the first place, we are to consider the size of the *Somers;* and here the opinion of Mr. R. H. Dana, Jr., who so happily unites in his own person the apparently incompatible experience of the seaman and the lawyer, is entitled to the highest consideration. . . . [*Here Sumner quotes a passage from Dana.*]

[235] Having the appearance of the *Somers* in our mind, we are prepared to listen to the evidence with regard to the mutiny of which she was the scene. The persons on whom we naturally rely for testimony as to the condition of things on board a ship, are the officers. There can be no reason why those of the *Somers* should be disqualified from being witnesses. Examine them; they all concur in expressing their belief, entertained not only at the time of the execution, but down to this day, in the actual existence of a formidable mutiny, in the guilt of Spencer, Cromwell, and Small, and in the necessity of their execution as a means of securing the command of the ship to the lawful authorities. They describe the appearance of the crew; they repeatedly speak of the "indescribable something," the disobedience to orders, the sullenness, which were tokens of the mutinous disposition. It is trifling with human testimony to say, that the ship was not at least in *apparent* danger, when all the officers join in testifying to its existence. On the testimony of these men, we leave this part of the subject. . . .

[236] Looking, then, at the circumstances of this case, by the best lights within our reach, we cannot hesitate to express our conviction of the necessity, at once real and apparent, under which the commander acted. And this brings us to the distinct question, whether it is incumbent

on him to proceed further in his justification in any point of view; certainly it is not requisite to his legal justification. The utmost that can be required of him is to establish the *apparent* guilt of these persons. But even this is not imperative. And here we conclude, as we began, this portion of the argument, by saying that it is sufficient, if it be shown that the Commander, in taking the steps that he did towards the suppression of the mutiny, acted in good faith, even supposing a subsequent knowledge may have made it evident that he erred in judgment. In this respect, his situation differs materially from that of the citizen, who takes the life of another in self-defence. He is summoned by necessity to take extraordinary steps for the safety of the ship. The law that has invested him with such sudden and indefinite powers to meet a peculiar emergency, considers properly all the circumstances of the occasion. It does not expect from him on the deck of a man-of-war, and in the midst of the ocean, the protracted deliberations of a court of justice, nor a nice balancing of suspicions and evidence. It further considers wisely the infirmity of human nature, and its liability to error. But over all errors of judgment, under such circumstances of necessity, it throws it ample shield. "Whatever the commander does, we repeat again, *in such an emergency, in good faith, and in the conscientious discharge of his duty,* [237] *believing it to be necessary to the safety of his ship, or of the lives of those on board, receives the protection of the law.*

It is on this ground, that the many instances, in the history of the world, of extraordinary military punishment, under peculiar circumstances, may be justified; as by the suspicions under which parties have fallen, or by the impossibility of discovering the real offender, and the necessity of making an example. Thus, it has not unfrequently happened, that the leader of a forlorn hope, or other officer in the heady current of battle, has, with his own arm, struck down the soldier who seemed to shrink from his post. In all these cases, the justification is found in the conscientious discharge of duty, under the apparent necessities of the occasion.

In our examination of this matter thus far, we have, for the most part, followed a course of argument different from that so ably occupied by the counsel of Commander Mackenzie. We have forborne all inquiry into the guilt of Spencer, Cromwell, and Small, believing that it is irrelevant to the determination of the merits of the defence. If we are right in this view, it may be justly regretted, that in the protracted proceedings of the Court-martial, so much time was consumed on this question. The effect of this was, to widen the field of inquiry beyond the requirements of law.

We should do wrong, however, to close our remarks without one glance at a matter, which has been deemed by many so important. It is with regard to the *actual* participation of Cromwell in the mutiny, that the chief question has been raised. The concurring opinion of the officers at the time, marking him as one of the leaders, indeed as the *dux facti,* establishes at least *apparent* guilt, though it may not be manifested by facts susceptible of narration or evidence. In a matter like this, we are bound to adopt the convictions of those who were on the spot, and saw with their own eyes, and heard with their own ears, all that passed. It would be impossible to add to the admirable [238] force, with which all the circumstances in the various testimony bearing on this point have been presented by the counsel of the Commander. And it must be difficult for any one, after reading their argument, to entertain a doubt of the actual guilt of Cromwell. There is no opportunity for hesitation with regard to the guilt of the other two, as both confessed it previous to their execution. . . .

The judgment of the Court-martial, by which Commander Mackenzie was honorably acquitted of the charges and specifications against him, stands on the immovable foundations of law. But we should not convey our strong convictions of its justice, if we did not add our opinion, that it cannot fail to be ratified by every unprejudiced mind. Through the confusion and obscurity, which prejudice and ardent discussion have thrown over this subject, this judgment will appear, like the country's flag revealed in the smoke of battle. . . .

From a letter of Theodore Sedgwick, Jr., to Charles Sumner, dated New York, July 6, 1843. Here reproduced from the original letter in the Sumner Papers, in the Houghton Library of Harvard University, by permission.

On returning to town I find yours with the Review. We are all under obligations to you—I have read it currente *oculo* [*sic*]— But not carefully enough to talk of it as yet— Abundantly however to see that you have said nothing more of the Report [Mackenzie's Narrative] than was proper— It was a diabolical Document & I hope yr. Paragraphs will help to winnow McKenzie's brain of the notion that he is a Lawyer as well as a Sailor & Historian.

I did not for one desire you to write a quacksalvering advertisement of Mr. Griffin's speech nor a Puff of McKenzie— I think you have done quite right. . . .

From a review of the *North American Review* for July, in the Boston *Courier,* July 6, 1843.

. . . The whole paper [on the *Somers* mutiny] is written in a spirit of justice and independence. The writer . . . indulges in no undue partialities for Mr. Mackenzie. . . . Whether the reader is convinced by the reasonings of the article, he cannot fail to applaud the temper and ability of the writer. . . .

✓ ✓ ✓   From the Boston *Courier,* July 7, 1843, by the editor, Joseph T. Buckingham.

The analytical notice . . . in the *Courier* of yesterday was . . . from a friend. . . . We cannot suffer his approving remarks . . . to pass off without expressing our entire dissent. . . . We differ not only from the writer [Sumner] in the North American Review, but from the great majority of our fellow-citizens, whose opinions we have been permitted to know. This is a misfortune; —and a grievous misfortune it certainly is, to differ from all the gentlemen of Boston, who have requested Commander Mackenzie to sit for his portrait. . . .

✓ ✓ ✓   A passage from a letter from Henry W. Longfellow to A. S. Mackenzie [July, 1843]. Here reproduced from the original letter in the Houghton Library of Harvard University, by permission.*

. . . The voice of all upright men—the common consent of all the good—is with you. Of course you have seen Sumner's Article in the North American. I have not yet seen it, but hear it spoken of by all as very able, and as putting your defence upon stronger and more unassailable grounds than even your own legal advisers did. —You will see more and more, my dear Mackenzie, how strongly you are supported in this quarter for maintaining the right at any sacrifice. . . .

✓ ✓ ✓   From *Niles' National Register* (Baltimore), LXIV (July 8, 1843), 295-296.

[295] The committee appointed at a meeting of the citizens of Boston . . . to communicate to this gallant officer [Mackenzie] their approval of his noble and heroic conduct . . . have addressed to him a letter [May 25] and received from him a reply [June 24]. The letter . . . is signed . . . by nearly four hundred of the most eminent citizens of Boston. It is handsomely written on parchment, and was transmitted to Commander Mackenzie in an elegant silver case, with an envelope of morocco. . . .

---

* Longfellow had met and travelled with Alexander Slidell (who had not yet changed his name to Mackenzie) in Spain, in 1827; had occasionally seen and corresponded with him in the meantime; and later, in 1846, entertained him as an overnight guest, remarking in his journal: "A very good fellow, with sound sense and a great love of literature." See *Life of Henry Wadsworth Longfellow,* edited by Samuel Longfellow (Boston: Houghton Mifflin, 1893). The quotation is from II, 67.

From a letter from Charles Sumner to Dr. Francis Lieber, Boston, July 17, 1843. Here reprinted from Edward L. Pierce, *Memoir and Letters of Charles Sumner* (London: Lowe, Marston, Searle, and Rivington, 1878), II, 264.

. . . I am happy that you and I agree about Mackenzie. It is an encouragement to believe that one is right, when another at a distance, revolving in his mind the same thing, arrives at the same result. I sent you my article in the "North American Review," on the mutiny of the "Somers." You will see that I take a different line of argument from that adopted (injudiciously, I think) by Mackenzie's counsel. Mr. Jeremiah Mason and Judge Story tell me that mine is the only tenable one. . . .*

From a letter from Dr. Francis Lieber to his wife, dated "Near Tarrytown, Capt. Mackenzie's Farm, August 3, 1843." Here printed, by permission, from the original letter in the Huntington Library.

Here I sit, Cpt. and Mrs. Mackenzie in the room, at a window which looks upon the noble Hudson, down nearly to N. York. . . . At 3 o'clock [July 31] Mackenzie and I started in one of those smaller steamboats for short routes, to Tarrytown. Mrs. Mackenzie could not go with us, because her boys were not quite well. In Tarrytown we found Mackenzie's plain, country wagon; stopped at the p. office where I got a friendly letter from Fanny Lgf. [Longfellow] telling me where I might find them and promising to write to you soon, and in the evening arrived at Mackenzie's plain, simple, comfortable, neat farm-house, where we made ourselves very comfortable according to a very detailed memorandum of his wife's, what to give me, what to do, what to look after. Mackenzie is one of the simplest, unfashionablest, kindest, plainest men I know, speaking to me very freely and frankly about his whole affair. . . . On Tuesday we [visited] Commodore Perry's. He commands at present the squadron on the African coast; his wife, an exceedingly good-looking grandmother, I believe of not more than 40 at the utmost, resides here, where they have

---

* Lieber wrote Sumner a long letter presenting an analysis of his own legal grounds for believing Mackenzie was fully justified in the execution. His opinion, he wrote, was formed before reading Sumner's article. It was "the settled result of repeated reflexion . . . neither warped nor biased by any personal or other attachment. My opinion was formed in a country place in the South, where not one individual knew Cpt. Mackenzie, the Spencer family, or any person directly or indirectly connected with the Somers Tragedy or the ensuing trial. . . . I am conscious of as great a degree of impartiality as any one can have in the consideration of the case; and, may I add, that my personal bias and general bent of mind, must be supposed to have originally inclined me toward those who suffered death and not those who inflicted it!" (Here quoted from the undated holograph letter to Sumner, now in the Huntington Library.)

built a beautiful cottage on the bank of the river, near Mackenzie's. Here we took tea with some women and girls, and then walked home—smoked, saw a fine moonlight view of the river from a hill and turned in. The next morning I wrote my view of Cpt. Mackenzie's Case, until two, dined, wrote again, and while he went to meet his wife at Tarrytown . . . I went to swim, then smoked, went to the Perry's, and on my return at last made Mrs. Mackenzie's acquaintance. She was formerly a great belle, but is wholly free of all coquetry, a fine, a good woman who stood by her husband in his late trials with advice and love. . . . One of her children is very good looking. With them had come a Mr. Dexter . . . sent by the Bostonians to take Mackenzie's bust for Boston. I saw the original letter in a fine silver box, which the Boston people sent him. This morning I read a good many papers of Mackenzie's. (The letters of young Spencer, found with him, I read on Monday evening. A greater villain and deeper dyed scamp probably never lived. He robbed his father repeatedly, as a brother of his forged the father's name and was actually already to be put on trial. The letters of the mother are shocking to read—full of the deepest distress. The father begins one [of] his letters: "Philip" and signs it "Spencer." It is a shocking breed, and Mackenzie abstains from publishing certain things, although the father has been outrageous enough to put an article in the Washington papers speaking in the highest strains of his sons, at least every one ascribes the article to him.) —At this moment Mackenzie is sitting for the sculptor, Mrs. Mackenzie reading my views of the Somers' Mutiny. . . . I shall probably leave this place tomorrow. . . . *Boston,* August 6 (?) Sunday. . . . I left Mackenzie's on Friday afternoon, feeling when I separated that I cherish him. He is neither lively, nor bright in conversation; very quiet, yet so kind and mild, so true and unaffected, that one cannot help liking, nay cherishing him, especially, when with all this one remembers his unswerving will. I am very much gratified with my visit. . . . I intended to have passed a day at Stockbridge [Mass.], at the Sedgwick's, but Theod. Sedgwick with whom I have become very intimate, and who had promised me letters, left N. Y. without leaving any letters. . . . [*Goes on to tell of his visit in Boston, warm reception by Mr. and Mrs. Longfellow, Sumner, C. C. Felton, and others, and of plans to appoint him to a Harvard professorship.*]

✓ ✓ ✓   The Boston *Courier,* August 4, 5, September 13, 1843.

[*Three long letters by William Sturgis * on "The Somers Mutiny" argue strongly against Mackenzie's course of action.*]

---

* William Sturgis (1782-1863) had started as a sailor before the mast, had become a ship-captain, made his fortune in the China trade, and was at this time one of the wealthiest and most influential merchants of Boston.

From a letter from A. S. Mackenzie to Charles Sumner, dated Tarrytown, N. Y., August 9, 1843. Here reproduced from the original letter in the Sumner Papers in the Houghton Library of ✓ ✓ ✓ *Harvard University, by permission.*

Since the appearance of your very able article . . . I have had a strong desire to write to you to express the great gratification I had derived from your flattering view of my efforts to do my whole duty to my country on that trying and momentous occasion. . . . In a recent letter from Commander S. F. Dupont . . . he remarks in speaking of your article, "The legal argument struck me as very superior to Mr. Griffin's." You have certainly placed my defence on very high grounds. . . .

✓ ✓ ✓ *From a letter to the editor, Boston Courier, August 15, 1843.*

. . . I cannot refrain from thanking Wm. Sturgis for having spoken. . . . I believe he has expressed the sentiments of experienced shipmasters, and the general sentiment of those uninfluenced by considerations such as we fear influence some of "you city folks". . . .

We "country folks" read with unprejudiced views, and . . . we find few among us who can acquit him. SOUTH SHORE.

From a letter from Richard H. Dana, Jr., to the editor, Boston Courier, August 18, 1843, under the heading "MR. STURGIS' LET- ✓ ✓ ✓ *TERS."*

. . . Mr. Sturgis is willing to believe that Mr. Mackenzie acted in good faith and without ill intentions, therefore he thinks it best that on a criminal trial he was acquitted. . . . Mr. Sturgis . . . proposes to the public another question, as a matter of opinion between man and man. . . . His conclusion may be stated . . . : *Judging from the circumstances as they now appear to us, we have a right to say that the execution could not have appeared necessary to men of sound judgment, courage, and resources. . . .*

In considering this proposition, it behooves every reader to remember one fact which has been but little noticed. *Every man on board the Somers of known fidelity and superior experience and intelligence, thought that the execution was necessary. . . .* Against this weight of opinion, Mr. Sturgis says the execution was not necessary, and could not have been thought so by men of proper judgment and courage.

Upon what grounds does he say this? Upon the grounds of inferences and arguments drawn from the facts as they come to him through newspaper reports and pamphlets; sources the uncertainty of which he himself alludes to. Let the reader remember that the men on board the *Somers* had superior means of judging to any that we can have now. They saw with their own eyes, things present, and as they occurred. We see things in a mass, from a distance, darkly, indirectly, and through various media. . . .

. . . I shall not attempt to follow him in his argument upon the facts. It is easy to take the sticks from a bundle, one by one, and ask,— What strength is there in this, and what in that, And Mr. Sturgis will excuse the writer for saying that he seems like a person doing this, and refusing to believe that the whole bundle could have been strong, though a score of able-bodied men solemnly assure him that their strength could not break it. . . .

⚊ ⚊ ⚊ From a letter to the editor, Boston *Courier,* August 18, 1843.

The Mackenzie papers are very particular in giving an account of the *hilt* of the sword to be presented to the commander of the Somers [*in Philadelphia*], its "diamond eyes," &c., procured by *one dollar* subscriptions;—but they say nothing about the *blade.* . . . Whether *this* weapon has a blade of steel, or of tin, or of lath, or, none at all, is left in painful doubt. Since some of our navy officers have acquired so much glory in conquering with *halters* . . . , the blade might, with propriety . . . be made of *hemp.* . . .

From a letter of Charles Sumner to Dr. Samuel G. Howe, Boston, September 14, 1843. Here reprinted from Edward L. Pierce, *Memoir and Letters of Charles Sumner* (London: Lowe, Marston, ⚊ ⚊ ⚊ Searle, and Rivington, 1878), II, 270.

. . . Mackenzie is here. I like him very much. He is a modest and unassuming man, with a countenance expressive of firmness and courage. Any one who sees him must believe in his complete justification. I took him to Longfellow's yesterday; they were old companions in Spain. . . .

From a letter of Cornelius Conway Felton, professor of Greek at Harvard, to Dr. Francis Lieber, dated Cambridge, September 17, 1843. Here printed, by permission, from the original letter in the ⚊ ⚊ ⚊ Huntington Library.

. . . Since you were here, we have been much interested and gratified by Mackenzie's visit. His calmness, self-possession, gentleness and refinement of manner, are the admiration of everybody that has met him.

I am sure his reception must have gratified his feelings, and convinced him that some of the best of his countrymen can appreciate and sympathize with his own heroic spirit. He stands in such a position as no man ever stood in before; and his bearing and demeanour are faultless. In my opinion, Mackenzie is one of the greatest men now living among us; and if ever the country should be placed in a situation of imminent peril, his genius and moral courage will shine with distinguished lustre; but he can never again be called upon to perform an act requiring so much resoluteness of soul, so high and daring an obedience to duty and conscience, as the saving of the Somers. A Secretary of the Navy, who should reward Mackenzie as he deserves, shall have my vote for any and every office he aspires after, be his political bias what it may. If Henshaw [*David Henshaw, Secretary of the Navy in 1843*] gives him a command within a year I shall admire the man, whom in times past I have not excessively admired, and pardon all his radicalism—past, present, and to come. . . . Friday we dined at Longfellow's—i.e. Charles [Sumner] and I, with Mackenzie and his brother [John] Slidell. I never spoke with the latter before; and the little I saw of him I was much pleased with. I shall try to see more of him. . . . By the bye, Mackenzie shall be the Lord High Admiral, or anything he pleases, when our government comes in. [i.e., *after the 1844 national election places the Whig party in power.*]

From a letter of James Fenimore Cooper to his wife, dated September 17, 1843. Here reprinted from *Correspondence of James Fenimore-Cooper,* edited by his grandson, James Fenimore Cooper (New Haven: Yale University Press, 1922), II, 508-509.

Poor Mackenzie is losing ground [509] daily. An old seaman, of the name of Sturgis, is writing against him, under his own name. Three letters have appeared; the two first are good, as far as they go, but do not go far enough, but the third is unanswerable. It is much the best thing—the only good thing, indeed—that has appeared on the subject. In a word, it is as good as it can be, on the point it treats, and makes Mackenzie thoroughly contemptible, as well as the government. I fancy the plan is to be silent on the subject of my pamphlet.

From a letter of James Fenimore Cooper to William Sturgis, Philadelphia, September 17, 1843. Here reprinted from *Correspondence of James Fenimore-Cooper,* edited by his grandson James Fenimore Cooper (New Haven, Yale University Press, 1922), II, 510-514.

[510] I have read your letters in *The Courier* with great interest. . . . Your third letter, I hold to be one of the simplest and best arguments on

the point it treats of [*failure to prosecute the sailors arrested by Mackenzie*], that can be imagined.

I regard the affair of the *Somers* as one of the darkest spots on the national escutcheon. . . . [*Cooper's letter outlines much the same analysis that later appeared in his* REVIEW.]

[514] . . . I wish it were in my power to send you a pamphlet of mine on the Battle of Lake Erie. That will show you the real character of Capt. Mackenzie. He has hanged Cromwell exactly as he has pressed facts into his own service, in making his accusations against Com. Elliott. Public opinion in this country is more apt to go wrong than right, in the outset. The press is venal, corrupt, ignorant, and impervious to principle. It seizes the common mind, in the outset, but the intelligence and honesty of the community are brought to bear in the end, and then public opinion gets in the right quarter. . . . But for the peculiar political position of Mr. John C. Spencer, the public mind would, long since, have been disabused on the facts and principles of this dreadful case. I hope we shall hear farther from you. . . .

> Entry from the journal of Richard Henry Dana, Jr., Boston, September 19, 1843. Here reprinted from Charles Francis Adams, *Richard Henry Dana* (Boston: Houghton Mifflin, 1890), I, 103.

. . . Commander A. Slidell Mackenzie called with Lieutenant Davis. His appearance and manners are very prepossessing. He is quiet, unassuming, free from all military display in manner, self-possessed, and with every mark of a humane, conscientious man, with sound judgment and moral courage. He is unusually interesting, and creates a feeling of personal affection towards him in those whom he meets. Such was the impression he produced upon me, and I find he made a similar impression upon all who fell in with him during his stay here.

> Passage from a letter of James Fenimore Cooper to his wife, dated September 22, 1843. Here reprinted from *Correspondence of James Fenimore-Cooper,* edited by his grandson, James Fenimore Cooper, (New Haven: Yale University Press, 1922), II, 517-518.

My pamphlet [on the Battle of Lake Erie] tells, wherever it is read. The circulation [518] is not large, but it goes into the right hands. Capt. [Robert F.] Stockton is here. He tells me he was ordered on Mackenzie's court, but frankly told the secretary his mind is made up, and *that he should vote for hanging the accused,* if he sat. On this hint, he was excused. I am told several others got off, on the same ground. *He* feels confident Capt. [Benjamin] Page was against him.

Passage from a letter of James Fenimore Cooper to his son Paul, dated November 9, 1843. Here reprinted from *Correspondence of James Fenimore-Cooper,* edited by his grandson, James Fenimore ✓ ✓ ✓ Cooper (New Haven: Yale University Press, 1922), II, 519-520.

I . . . am now at work on a review on the *Somers* mutiny case. This . . . would be soon finished had the record of the Court Martial arrived. I expect it soon, [520] however. I find Mackenzie's case grows weaker and weaker, as I look into it.

Excerpt from "Appendix to the Fifth Edition" of A. S. Mackenzie's *Life of Commodore Oliver Hazard Perry* (New York: Harper and Brothers, 1844), II, 271-328. The Appendix is dated Tarrytown, ✓ ✓ ✓ November, 1843.

[271] Soon after the original publication of the present work in 1840, Mr. J. Fennimore [*sic*] Cooper, author of the Naval History of the United States, took occasion [*in a letter in the New York* Evening Post, *March 26, 1841*] to put the public on its guard against what he alleged to be the inaccuracy of that part of my work which related to the battle of Lake Erie . . . until he could more fully exhibit this inaccuracy in a pamphlet. . . . [*Mackenzie had replied to Cooper's letter, in the* Evening Post, *April 7, 1841.*]

After brooding during this long interval over the fancied injustice done to his Naval History . . . , Mr. Cooper has at length come forth with more than a hundred pages of special pleading, sophistry, and venomous abuse. . . .

[272] I alleged, both in the article in the North American Review, in 1839, to which a portion of Mr. Cooper's pamphlet refers, and in the Life of Perry, that Mr. Cooper had disparaged the victory of Lake Erie generally, and the extraordinary heroism of Perry . . . , while, on the contrary, he had exaggerated the services and suppressed the delinquency of Captain Elliott. . . .

[289] It may be remarked . . . of [Cooper's] seamanship, that it is quite effective when it is exercising its appropriate functions, and assisting him in his character of a novelist. . . . But when Mr. Cooper attempts to exhibit himself as a nice nautical critic, it is not strange that he should be betrayed into gross blunders of seamanship, which the writer feels some compunction in exposing. . . . To make manifest Mr. Cooper's want of fairness, of justice, of good taste, or of decency, might be forgiven; but to detect his ignorance of seamanship is to touch him to the quick. . . .

[326] In the pamphlet he has contrived . . . to enrich his pages with abundant allusions to the case of the Somers. . . . It remains to be seen

what will be the result [*by way of political reward*] of the "experiment to obtain capital" from the Somers case. If some worthy associates may have found this path a ready one to preferment, why should not Mr. Cooper bring his higher priced wares to as sure a market? He has "bided his time!" Let any one consider the coincidence of circumstances under which the first insolent announcement of his pamphlet was made, and observe how completely it calls up the image of the assassin lurking in ambush, and watching to take his enemy unawares. . . .

✓ ✓ ✓ Extracts from James Fenimore Cooper's "Review" in *Proceedings of the Naval Court Martial in the Case of Alexander Slidell Mackenzie* . . . (New York: Langley, 1844), 263-344.

[274] . . . In forming our estimate of the conduct of Captain Mackenzie and his officers, it is indispensable, first to ascertain on what points it turns. Many varying positions have been laid down in the premises. Some have contended that Captain Mackenzie was bound to show first, that a mutiny actually existed; second, that the parties executed were connected with it; third, that the executions were indispensable to the safety of the brig; and, in the last place, that every opportunity *that was necessary, and which the safety of the vessel would allow,* was given to the men hanged to vindicate themselves from the charges on which they were executed. This, as we understand him, was substantially the ground taken by the judge advocate.

We do not conceive this to have been the true issue, though we subscribe in part to the last condition.

Others maintained it was sufficient for the vindication of Captain Mackenzie, that he conscientiously *thought* the first three facts just named, existed. These persons were silent on the subject of the last condition; probably under a secret consciousness it never was fulfilled. A variety of modified positions have been given, varying between these two. We conceive the true issue, both in law and in morals, to have been this. Captain Mackenzie was bound to show that such a case was presented to him, as JUSTIFIED him in BELIEVING in all the facts mentioned in the first of the two cases given, and then to show that he allowed the accused every opportunity of defence, that he was *justified* in *believing* could be granted to them, with safety to his vessel.

The reader will see our issue does not turn on the literal facts of the case, but on the manner in which these facts, real or supposed, were presented to Captain Mackenzie. . . .

[276] Having thus laid down our premises . . . , we will attempt to settle one or two other principles of a very different character, before we enter on the investigation of facts. It has been said that Captain Mac-

kenzie's literary pursuits had given him the support of many literary men. Among others of that class, has appeared a gentleman who has high claims to be heard, and who lays down the position, that the *size* of the Somers, was greatly against the officers in the event of a conflict with the crew! We conceive that nothing can be more erroneous. . . .

The size of the Somers was, perhaps, as near as possible to that which was the most desirable for her officers, in the event of such a conflict. Had she been much smaller, all her officers and petty officers might not have been able to act together, and thus have lessened their efficiency; while, had she been much larger, there might have been too much to defend or to avoid, for so small a party. . . . It is merely the old fact that a small body can defend a defile against an enemy that would overwhelm it in a plain. . . . We see nothing to have prevented Captain Mackenzie from sending all but his officers below, of securing the gratings, and of carrying the brig across the ocean, if needed, with the gentlemen of the quarter-deck alone. . . . To say that ten men and boys could not handle a vessel like the Somers in the tradewinds, is to say that they were unusually inefficient. But Captain Mackenzie was not reduced so low. All the [277] best of his crew, the petty officers, and a seaman or two, to the number of nine, had so much of his confidence as to be armed at the crisis of the execution. . . . Grave pictures have been drawn of the risks run at night; of the danger of a rush aft, whenever an order was given to do any duty on the quarter deck, and of the general hazards of the darkness. . . . There was no necessity for darkness, every man-of-war possessing means of lighting her decks; in the next place, there was no necessity for a single individual of the crew coming on the quarter-deck at all. . . . A rope might have been stretched across the deck, and an order given for no man to pass it, unless called by name, on the pain of death. This would have prevented everything like a surprise of the quarter-deck; did that fail, Mr. Spencer's own alleged expedient, that of two of the quarter-deck guns pointed forward, loaded with canister, would have rendered the quarter-deck of so *small* a craft, as inviolable as a sanctuary. . . .

To come to the facts; the testimony [278] of Wales is first in order. . . . The first thing that strikes us . . . is the abruptness with which Mr. Spencer opens his plot. . . . What is the just inference? Clearly, that he who could proceed thus, was not very formidable as a conspirator, unless indeed he thoroughly knew his man. . . . Among other things, Wales is told that *about twenty* of the crew . . . were engaged in the conspiracy. Spencer had all the details of the plot in writing. . . . A paper was subsequently discovered in a razor-case. . . . Here then we get an insight, at once, into the probabilities of the extent of this conspiracy. The paper contains in all, thirty-two names. Of these, *four* are down as *certain, ten* are down as *doubtful; eighteen* are down as to be retained *nolens volens*. The four *certain,* were Spencer, himself, Andrews,

M'Kinley, and Wales. Among the *doubtful* it will be seen that four names are marked, as being likely to be *induced* to join the plot, previously to its execution. The remainder of the doubtful, it is stated in the paper, would be likely to join when the vessel had been taken; if not, they were *to be forced*. Of the eighteen down as the *nolens volens* men it is hardly necessary to speak. The paper itself acquits them of anything but being such persons as Mr. Spencer *wished* to *coerce*. . . .

Here then we get the details of the conspiracy, as made out by its leader, down to the last moment of his liberty. The interview with Wales took place at night, just before the lights are out on board a man-of-war. His own name was probably put on the next day . . . , though the supposition has been hazarded . . . that Wales's name *may* have been set down *before* the plot was revealed to him. . . . What is the document worth at all, if names were set down as *certain,* before the parties had been consulted? If this *may* be true of Wales, it *may* also be true of Andrews and M'Kinley, and yet no one on that side has thought of applying this violent probability to *them!*

Taking the paper as a guide, this conspiracy is reduced, as to any serious danger, to three individuals, Spencer, Andrews, and M'Kinley. Admitting the most, or that the four who it was thought would be *induced . . . had* been so induced, the serious danger was then confined to [279] seven! This, even admitting it to be true, does not strike us as a conspiracy to derange the propriety of a man-of-war's quarter-deck, with the ringleaders in irons and all the details in the captain's own hands! But we do not think the four doubtful ought to be placed anywhere but where they are placed on the paper. The quick insertion of Wales's name proves that Spencer had a boyish anxiety to make his scheme look as formidable on paper as possible, and there can be little doubt his muster-roll was corrected at every plausible occasion. . . . The circumstance that Mr. Spencer showed this paper to some of his brother midshipmen who could not read Greek, proves the sort of feeling that reigned in his mind, as respects this document, which he evidently regarded as boys are apt to regard things which first seem to connect them with active life. . . .

. . . Captain Mackenzie . . . says, "I believed then in the existence of a plot in which, by the declaration of Mr. Spencer, *at least* twenty of the crew were concerned."

Were the same proposition submitted to a million men, it would be difficult to find one, that would not have substituted at *most* for Captain Mackenzie's "at *least*." Who, before, ever heard of a conspirator's giving the *minimum* instead of the *maximum* of his force to one whom he wished to enlist in his enterprise? We deem this instance of the reasoning powers of Captain Mackenzie important to the issue, inasmuch as we think . . . that such is the habit of his mind. . . . We ascribe the great calamity that has befallen us . . . to be owing to a disposition in Captain Mackenzie to regard things as he has at first conceived them to be, and to act under his *convictions,* rather than under *the authority of evidence.*

. . . In arresting this young officer Captain Mackenzie did no more than his duty, though the *manner* of the arrest was a little too melo-dramatic. . . . We think it was unwise to arrest Mr. Spencer in so public a manner, and then to place him on the quarter-deck, in full view of the crew. We entertain no doubt that much the greater portion of the ominous conversations, groupings, shakings of the head, and strange looks, which seem to have awakened so much distrust aft, had their origin in the natural wonder of the crew, at seeing an officer in this novel situation; and he, too, not only a favorite forward, but one who was known to be the son of a minister of state. In our opinion, Captain Mackenzie would [280] have shown more judgment, had he sent for the young man into his cabin, and . . . endeavored to get the facts from him. He might have been ironed there, were it thought necessary, but what judge of human nature can suppose that a man of forty, possessed of authority, could not have got complete control of the feelings of a lad of nineteen by means of kindness and judicious representations. . . .

After the arrest of Mr. Spencer, nearly twenty-four hours passed with-out the occurrence of any event to awaken new distrusts. The men collected in knots, it is said, and conversed together, separating as the officers ap-proached, and would look aft at the prisoner. . . . The Somers had one hundred and twenty souls on board her,—at least thirty more than she should have had—and it is scarcely possible that, with her boats stowed, and one third of the deck reserved for officers, one hundred men could be on her remaining deck, without being in what is called knots.

[281] The turning point of the danger, according to Captain Mac-kenzie's account . . . was the carrying away of the main-royal-mast. Previously to this accident, however, the men were inspected at quarters, it being Sunday, November 27. . . . In his report Captain Mackenzie gives this extraordinary specimen of his own reasoning powers, as con-nected with the appearance of Cromwell and Small at this Sunday in-spection. . . . [*See his narrative.*] Here . . . were two men who mani-fested guilt, according to Captain Mackenzie, by directly contrary deportment. In order to escape his distrust, a man must be neither firm nor irresolute; look frightened, nor look determined; hold his battle-axe quiet, nor pass it from hand to hand; stand erect with his muscles im-movable, nor shift his weight from leg to leg; look steadily, but indiffer-ently, across the deck, nor let his eyes wander, without looking, however, at mine! Evidence like this, of the judgment that was brought to bear on this important case, awakens reflections of the most painful character. . . .

Next comes the affair of the mast. . . . [282] Now Captain Mackenzie attributes the loss of his main-royal-mast to the fact that Small gave the brace a sudden jerk, the brace leading forward, and pulling in the direc-tion of the wind. . . . Captain Mackenzie says . . . "To my astonishment . . . all those *who were most conspicuously named in the pro-gramme of Mr. Spencer* . . . , no matter in what part of the vessel they might be stationed, mustered at the main-top-mast-head. . . . THE CO-INCIDENCE CONFIRMED THE EXISTENCE OF A DANGEROUS CONSPIRACY. . . ."

. . . The inference is very remarkable for the premises. Cromwell was acting boatswain, and there is nothing surprising that he should go aloft, on an occasion like this, in a vessel with the peculiar crew of the Somers. Had he remained below, no doubt it would have been deemed a *con-firmation* that he stayed on deck to profit by circumstances in the way of seizing the vessel. . . . As for Small, he was a captain of the main-top, and if any one was to go aloft, *he* clearly ought to have been there. . . . Cromwell, Small, Wilson, and Golderman, are the names most promi-nently given. Now the name of neither Cromwell nor Golderman appears on Mr. Spencer's programme at all! We know it is contended that the name of Andrews . . . was an alias for Cromwell; but it might just as reasonably be affirmed that it was an alias for any one of the officers, as to assert this without proof. . . .

. . . Anderson . . . was one of those aloft. Now this man so far possessed the confidence of Captain Mackenzie, that he was armed at the execution. . . . So long as [283] one individual was among them who was not in their secret, how could men *conspire* . . . ! Unless *they went aloft* with purpose attributed, the whole conjecture fails. And *would* men be apt to go to a place where the chances were as twenty to one they could not be alone . . . ? There were others: Gedney was there, and no one seems to suspect him; the boy Gagely must have been there, too, and he is spoken of in favorable terms. . . .

Captain Mackenzie adds . . . as a matter of moment: "The eye of Mr. Spencer travelled perpetually to the mast-head, and cast thither many of those *strange* and *stealthy* glances which I had heretofore noticed." . . . Can anything be more violent than the inference as to Mr. Spencer's motive? He was at sea, seated on an arm-chest, in irons, with nothing to do, and nothing but the vacant ocean to gaze at outward. . . . A mast is carried away in full view of him, and it is thought extraordinary that he sought the very natural relief of gazing at what was going on . . . !

. . . The points attempted to be established are as follows:—[284] Cromwell instigated Small to jerk the brace; an order existed never to jerk or pull upon the light braces which lead forward; Small belonged aft, and was never known to do duty forward before; the moment would have been favorable for the purpose of the mutineers.

Now we deny the reasoning as connected with every one of these propositions. As for the first, it is a fact, and was only to be established by direct affirmative evidence. . . . As for the second, it is proved that Mr. O. H. Perry said he told Capt. Mackenzie he understood the order was to "*haul* on the brace," though, when cross-examined by the commander himself, he says he understood it was an order for *"a small pull,"* . . . and that Captain Mackenzie publicly reproved him for his conduct. The third comes more within the category of a mental effort. As Small belonged aft, it was extraordinary he should pull upon a main-royal-brace. . . . Small was seated on the bitts forward, probably within five feet. . . . Nine men in ten, on board of any ship . . . would have sprung to the brace. . . . The braces which led aft *were* hauled upon, and he may very well have acted under a habit. Then Small is described as the shortest man in the brig, and small men are apt to throw their weight upon light work. . . . As for the order itself, it is disputed. . . . Next, the moment would not have been favorable, nor . . . could it have been seized by the mutineers. The order emanated from the mind of an officer, and could not have been anticipated. . . . [285] It appears to us, that there is nothing connected with this affair of the mast, to justify any part of Captain Mackenzie's reasoning. . . .

[286] It will probably be said, it is a strong circumstance in favor of Captain Mackenzie, that *all* his officers coincided in opinion on the subject of the necessity for the executions. Under ordinary circumstances, there would be great force in this argument; there is . . . much less under those which actually existed. . . . She was sent to sea with too much of the character of a family yacht. . . . The purser and surgeon . . . would be men of unusually decided characters to venture opinions opposed to those of the sea-officers. . . . Of the five sea-officers who signed the opinion . . . , four were just of an age to render them active assistants in quelling a physical attempt to seize a vessel, but to render them questionable counsellors. . . .

[287] . . . It is in proof that three members of this council were of opinion of the necessity of the execution as early as the 28th; it is scarcely probable these early consultations were confined to these three, and did that council meet, its members holding preconceived opinions, they must have been more than human, if their inquiries were not quite as much directed to obtaining confirmation of what they already believed, as to obtaining the truth. When this bias was left to act on a tribunal before which *the accused had not even a hearing,* it is easy to imagine its effect. . . .

[289] We come next to the proofs of the necessity. These proofs have all the same general tendency. . . . All . . . were founded on the presumed danger of a rescue. . . . [290] As for the collecting in knots, looking at the prisoners, and apparently conversing about them, and changing the discourse as an officer approached, it strikes us as the most extraordinary reason for apprehending danger, that has been given. Had *not* the men done what was so very natural, it might have justly created suspicion. . . .

The next point is the circumstance that the crew did not obey the orders, as promptly as before the arrest of Mr. Spencer. . . . The accounts of the state of the crew are not uniform. Mr. Gansevoort tells us that Captain Mackenzie remarked that the ship's company was in a state of good discipline, when the existence of the plot was first revealed to him. . . . The discrepancies in these opinions go unanswerably to show that the change could not have been very marked, and they leave the probability that many if not most of these opinions were formed *after* the revelation of Wales. A distinction must be drawn, moreover, between disaffection and ordinary offenses. . . .

[291] [M. C. Perry] and others speak of the exhaustion of the officers, as a reason for the necessity of the execution. . . . What was there to cause all this exhaustion? These gentlemen were in watch and watch; so are thousands of others daily. We have ourselves, at a tender age too, been watch and watch for weeks and weeks, and had our rest broken night after night. . . . [292] We have a better opinion of the physical powers of these gentlemen than they seem to have themselves. . . .

A reason given by Mr. Perry, for supposing that a rescue would be attempted, was, that Mr. Spencer, Cromwell, and Small looked *unconcerned,* as if they *expected a rescue.* If required to distinguish between this species of unconcern and that which belonged to innocence, we apprehend the witness would have been embarrassed. . . .

[293-296: *Disposes of other reasons advanced as supporting necessity —Wilson's knife and his sharpening his battle-axe; the position of the brig; the rushes aft.*]

[296] We think the case of the mast-rope, and of the tramping aft, might justify Mr. Gansevoort in believing a crisis had come, *under his previous impressions,* though we think the impressions themselves to have been insufficiently sustained. The conduct of Mr. Gansevoort, *always allowing for his impressions,* was spirited and good. It gives us sincere pleasure to be able to say this, for he bears an honorable name, and the reputation of his gallant old grandfather was a pledge that the heart of this young officer would be right, whatever might be his mistakes of judgment. . . . But Mr. Gansevoort admits himself it was all a mistake, and is rejoiced he did not fire. . . .

[299 ff. *Considers question of the guilt of the prisoners.*] [299] As there can be little question that Mr. Spencer and Small, were, to say the least, extremely indiscreet, sufficiently so to bring them within the provisions of the statute, we shall not waste our time on their cases . . . ; that these two were engaged in a *seeming* plot, resembling the one described, we hold to be proved; though we greatly question if an attempt would ever have been made to carry it into serious execution. . . .

[299-313. *Disposes of evidence advanced to support Cromwell's guilt: the name E. Andrews on Greek paper; his bad conduct and language; his intimacy with Spencer and accepting gifts from him; the remarks attributed to him over several months, out of context; the opinions others had of him; his being shown a paper by Spencer; and other points.*]

[312] Captain Mackenzie has one of his remarkable reasoning processes for getting rid of the dying assertion of Mr. Spencer. He went to the latter and told him what the petty officers had said, and he assures us a demoniacal expression took possession of the young man's countenance. After this Mr. Spencer said no more of Cromwell's innocence! The two even passed so close to each other as to touch, and yet neither spoke to the other. Mr. Spencer asked Wales and Small to forgive him, but he did not ask Cromwell. The last made no appeals to the first to come to his succor! This disposes of the matter.

Now, it is not probable that such arguments were ever before offered in defence of such a point. In the first place, Small and Wales had something to forgive to Mr. Spencer, according to the theory of the mutiny, while Cromwell, if innocent, had *not*. Captain Mackenzie was the man for him to forgive, were he not guilty. Then why should Cromwell appeal to Mr. Spencer? This unfortunate young man had already asserted his innocence, openly, and in a way to [313] stagger Captain Mackenzie, and he was powerless. *He could not save his own life;* much less that of another. Cromwell kept asserting his innocence to the last, TO THOSE WHO ALONE COULD RELIEVE HIM: and, alas! he asserted it in vain. THEY HANGED HIM WITHOUT ANY OTHER HEARING THAN THESE DYING PROTESTATIONS!

. . . It is no answer to say, Captain Mackenzie could not tell the facts, as he was situated; he was bound to forbear, so long as the absolute certainty of all the points stated in our issue was covered with any doubts. *Fiat justitia ruat coelum,* meant in his case, you are to sacrifice the Somers before you do an unjust thing. The preservation of that brig was far from being the first object in morals. . . .

. . . Against Green and M'Kee we find nothing like evidence at all. . . . As respects Wilson and M'Kinley we find nothing to criminate them, but the testimony of Tyson. . . . Even this does not prove that the last ought to be down as *certain,* BUT THE CONTRARY. If M'Kinley preferred a slaver to any other scheme, it shows he had *not* enlisted in the alleged conspiracy. . . .

[314-317: *Points out examples of contradictions in the testimony.*]

[318] . . . We will now proceed to a brief analysis of Captain Mackenzie's report. . . . It is to Captain Mackenzie's mind and motives that the world is to look for solution of this unusual and sad occurrence, and the best clues we have to [319] both of these, are to be found in his own account of the events. . . .

The first feature that strikes us in this report, is its positiveness on points about which grave doubts exist, after every opportunity has been given for inquiry. To this may be added the habit of giving to mere *assumptions* the force of proof. [319-324: *Points out numerous examples of this.*] [321] . . . Captain Mackenzie alludes to the missing of their musters by two or three of the men, in the following words, and as a strong evidence of an intention to rise: *"That they should have been asleep at all, that night, was not likely,"* he says. Here he *assumes* guilt to *prove* guilt! "That they should have missed their muster on that particular occasion, never having done so before, otherwise than intentionally, *was impossible."* This is valuable, as giving us an insight into Captain Mackenzie's views of the *possibilities.* . . . [M'Kinley] says he and M'Kee turned in and out together, and that they relied on each other for calls; that M'Kee did not call him that morning in consequence of being obliged by the officers to lie down on the deck, where he fell asleep. This is not only *possible,* but it is highly *probable.* . . . But, Captain Mackenzie's reasoning on the subject is the most extraordinary of all. "There was probably an agreement to meet, around the officer of the deck, and commit some violence," he says. . . . As nothing of the sort *was* attempted, it is reasonable to suppose nothing was meditated. . . .

[323] The exaggeration of feeling and morality that prevailed in the brig, is apparent throughout the report and the evidence. . . . Of this character is the story told by Collins to the boys, at Captain Mackenzie's instigation, after the execution . . . , of [his] having been in a ship, in which there was a box of doubloons, and of his not letting the fact be known until the vessel got in. Upon this Cromwell laughed, and said "had the case been his he would have run away with the box." . . . We are of opinion had Collins told his story . . . to one hundred sailors, quite fifty would have made some such idle remark as this attributed to Cromwell. . . .

We have limits for only one more of Captain Mackenzie's decided assumptions. Speaking of Cromwell . . . he says: "HE ONLY could answer to the description of the individual alluded to by Mr. Spencer, as having been *already in the business!"* Those who have not had as much occasion to analyze the accuracy of Captain Mackenzie's references and quotations as have fallen to our share, may be surprised at the boldness of this statement, when they come to look into the fact. . . . [Wales's] statement, of course, is all Captain Mackenzie's authority for what he says. Wales says: "The brig was to *proceed to Cape St. Antonio, or the Isle of Pines, one of* these place, *and* THERE TAKE ON BOARD, one who *was familiar with their* INTENDED BUSINESS. . . ." Now Cromwell COULD NOT BE the man, for he could *not* BY POSSIBILITY, "answer to the description." And yet Captain Mackenzie, with *Wales's deposition on the subject at his command,* DOES NOT HESITATE TO ASSERT THE CONTRARY, in order to make out his case. . . .

We conceive that the world will never know the literal merits of this extraordinary transaction. The testimony comes to us through such channels as to cause a doubt of its accuracy, if not of its motive; and there is, and probably [324] ever will be, something of mystery connected with many of its details. . . .

[324: *Cooper's theory of the state of the crew.* 325-328: *Examines,*

without deciding, question whether evidence indicates that Captain Mac-
kenzie wrote more at Spencer's dictation than he has revealed.]

[328] We know of persons, good judges of evidence too, experienced members of the bar, who doubt of there having been any serious design of a mutiny on the part of even Mr. Spencer. They think the whole the idle mystification of a youth practising on Wales, and possibly on Small, and the accessories to have been either invented, or imagined by the different witnesses. . . . The improbability of the story is urged against its truth. . . . We confess, however, that the reasoning does not strike us as satisfactory. . . . We believe . . . a plot existed in the mind of this young man, quite likely with as much of imagination in it, as of reality, but still a plot. We greatly doubt if an attempt would ever have been made to carry it into execution. The very fact that he is said to have entertained a similar plan on board a ship like the Potomac, throws a shade of distrust over the seriousness of the design; for the idea of converting a frigate of the largest class [329] into a pirate . . . is so preposterous as almost to defy credulity. . . .

We incline to the opinion that Mr. Spencer told the truth, when he said this scheming on such projects, was a mania with him . . . of which he found it difficult to get rid. It really seems to us that a youth making these admissions, expressing penitence, under nineteen years of age, and who admitted the ties of family, might have been managed for four or five days without hanging him!   •

[330-331: *Points out evils that will result from the transaction and the way it has been handled.* 332-334: *Points out instances throughout of Mackenzie's lack of good judgment.* 335-344: *Further considerations.*]

[343] Most persons who condemn the course of Captain Mackenzie and his officers attribute it to fear. This solution of the difficulty is so natural, as to be the first to suggest itself. Such, however, is not our opinion. . . . We distinguish between the exaggeration of danger, and the unmanly dread of meeting it. We suppose the tendency of the commander to regard one side of a question, suddenly took the direction of magnifying this mutiny. We think it evident Mr. Gansevoort had a strong disposition that way from the first. We believe the opinions of the two to have influenced all the rest of the quarter-deck. Under these opinions occurred the *"scenes"* of which we have spoken, when the previous impressions gathered intensity from the necessity of the case, and the executions followed.

Many may imagine that Captain Mackenzie's report betrays the evidence of a disposition to glean personal renown, from the manner in which it is pretended he saved his own life and those of his associates. The feebleness of this extraordinary document renders its writer obnoxious to very injurious suspicions certainly, [343] and this among the number; but the mental obliquity, so very obvious throughout the whole affair, renders any ordinary analysis of human motives exceedingly precarious. God alone can say how far any selfish feeling was mixed up with the mistakes of this terrible transaction. The act was, unquestionably, one of high moral courage, one of the basest cowardice, one of deep guilt, or one of lamentable deficiency of judgment.

> From the Preface, dated March, 1844, to an anonymous pamphlet: *The Cruise of the Somers: Illustrative of the Despotism of the Quarter Deck; and of the Unmanly Conduct of Commander Mackenzie* (New York: J. Winchester, 1844).

✓ ✓ ✓

There is a singular fact connected with the sad affair of the United States brig Somers which has prompted the writer of the following pages to his present work. The fact is this: that while the great majority of private opinion, both among landsmen & seamen, is decidedly against the course pursued by Commander Mackenzie on the occasion of the supposed conspiracy; the public expression, with some few exceptions, has been in his favor. This *should* not be so. . . .*

---

* The anonymous author goes on to a close day-by-day examination of the events of the cruise, particularly those from November 26 to December 1, exposing the actions of Mackenzie as "disgraceful," "outrageous," and "unmanly." For some reason the pamphlet has regularly been attributed to James Fenimore Cooper, but the attribution is quite doubtful. It has been questioned by James Grossman in his *James Fenimore Cooper* (New York: Sloane Associates, 1949), pp. 190-191*n*. The second edition added an appendix with the three anti-Mackenzie letters by the Hon. William Sturgis, from the Boston *Courier;* by July, 1844, a third edition was issued.

END

OF PART FOUR

..

✓ ✓ ✓

Part Five

INTO
MEMORY

1845 to 1924

The *Somers* affair soon dropped out of the public mind, to be replaced by other nine-day wonders. Individual minds preserved memories of its men and events, and as the century wore on reminiscences were now and again recorded. Here there is space only for the few that give valuable biographical information about Philip Spencer and Commander Mackenzie, and for the only one—Thurlow Weed's—which even purports to "reveal" anything new. Even these display to some extent the curious workings of memory.

Other reminiscences (cited in the Bibliography), although clearly having some basis in fact, show vitiating admixtures of hearsay, confusions of detail, distortions of perspective, and egoistic reconstructions—to say nothing of hindsight. More valuable than any new information they reveal is their illustration of the ways in which the mind shapes "remembered" matters.

On the whole, the materials from memory reprinted here lie toward the factual end of a spectrum along which other materials (those relegated to the bibliography) range toward and into the realm of legend and fiction. At this extreme of the spectrum of transformation lies Herman Melville's short novel, *Billy Budd*. In the composition of this story, not memory alone and unconscious mental processes were at work, but also conscious invention and deliberate artistic purpose.

One of the most interesting ramifications of the *Somers* case is its connection with Herman Melville (1819-1891), the third, along with Cooper and Dana, of America's great sea writers. Melville is best known, of course, as the author of *Moby-Dick* (1851). Unlike his first-cousin Guert Gansevoort, he had served as a common sailor—on a merchant ship to Liverpool (1839), on three whalers in the South Seas (1841-1842), and finally for a year as an ordinary seaman in the U. S. Navy (1843-1844). In *White-Jacket* (1850), his fifth book, he described the whole routine of life on a man-of-war, giving the best picture we have of naval life in the days of the *Somers* affair. Here he vigorously championed the common sailor and attacked the cruel and undemocratic usages of the officers, alluding twice (Ch. 70, 72) to the *Somers* case as an example of the enforcement of the "murderous" and "bloodthirsty" Articles of War. "Three men," he wrote, "in a time of peace, were then hung at the yardarm, merely because, in the Captain's judgment, it became necessary to hang them. To this day the question of their complete guilt is socially discussed."

Between the writing of *White-Jacket* and that of *Billy Budd* Melville's attitude may or may not have changed. Several times he alluded very favorably to his cousin Guert Gansevoort. (See Leyda's *Melville Log, passim.*) At his death in 1891, he left the manuscript of *Billy Budd,* written in the last few years of his life. Certain clear resemblances to the *Somers* case were first pointed out in the story by Charles R. Anderson in his article, "The Genesis of *Billy Budd,*" *American Literature,* XII (November, 1940), 329-346. The story is too long to be represented here. But it is fascinating to study the similarities and differences of various sorts between the situations, persons, and issues involved in the two cases. *Billy Budd* has been often reprinted since its first publication in 1924, and is easily available. Books about Melville contain relevant discussions.

Most critics have interpreted the story as revealing Melville's final "acceptance" of, or "reconciliation" to, the universe as it is, after a lifelong rebellion against it. These interpreters feel that Melville accepts Captain Vere's practical solution to the conflict expressed in the story—as in many of Melville's earlier works—between ideal or heavenly justice and the "justice" found practical or necessary for worldly purposes. Such a conflict was evident in the *Somers* case, where we have seen the different attitudes that were taken toward it. More recently, since about 1950, a number of critics have argued strongly that on the contrary Melville in *Billy Budd* still holds strongly to the same rebellious attitudes toward the injustices of naval discipline and of the world and universe in general that he expressed so eloquently in *White-Jacket*. Some readers may wish to compare the two books, in the light of the *Somers* affair.

From a biographical sketch of Commander A. S. Mackenzie written by his wife between 1850 and 1856, at the request of Evert A. Duyckinck, for his use in preparing the article on Mackenzie in his *Cyclopedia of American Literature* (New York: Scribner, 1856), II, 360-365. Reproduced here from the original manuscript in the Duyckinck Collection of the New York Public Library, by permission. The accompanying vignette, with Mackenzie's facsimile signature, is from the *Cyclopedia*, II, 361.

Commander Mackenzie was born in New York on the 6th of April 1803; his father was Mr. John Slidell, of New York; his mother, Margery or, as she was called, May, Mackenzie, was a native of the Highlands of Scotland but came to America when quite a child. Mr. Slidell was a man of great intelligence and of a very high moral and religious character; he had a great love of reading and most of his evenings were passed in reading aloud to his family. . . . Of my husband's early life I can find but little. . . . I have heard him say, that as a child he was no student and not at all precocious. He was sent to a boarding school at the age of eight and I believe remained at school until his entrance into the Navy, January 1st 1815. Entering the Navy at this early age, being not yet twelve, his education was necessarily very incomplete and as the Midshipmen did not then enjoy the advantages which they now have he had but little opportunity afterwards of receiving any regular or systematic instruction. He had, however, the most untiring industry, an unbounded thirst for knowledge, and powers of observation rarely equalled; these enabled him to overcome the difficulties and disadvantages of his position and to make himself what he became. . . . [In] 1818-1819 . . . he was on duty on board the *Macedonian* in the Pacific. . . . [Following this]

he commanded a merchant vessel for some time that he might inform himself professionally. I believe he was about 19 when he took command. In 1824 he was on duty in the Brig *Terrier* on the West India Station occupied in seeking for Pirates. He had been ill when on board the *Macedonian* (in a second cruise in her in the West Indies) of the yellow fever and on a second attack of illness in the *Terrier* his health became so much impaired that he returned home and in the autumn of . . . 1825 obtained leave of absence that he might go to Europe for . . . his health. He accordingly sailed for France and after spending a year there much of which was devoted to study he commenced the tour in Spain the incidents of which have since been given to the public. I send you some notices of the *Year in Spain* sent to Mr. Slidell's family by Mr. Washington Irving with whom Mr. Mackenzie had lived on terms of intimacy while in Spain and who took much interest in the success of his book. . . . The first edition of the *Year in Spain* was published in 1829 by Hilliard Grey and Co. of Boston. . . . It was translated in the Swedish language and I believe that a copy of it in that tongue, sent to my husband by Mr. [Henry W.] Longfellow, is now in the Library of the New York Historical Society. . . . You will doubtless remember its great success.

In the years 1830, 31, 32, he was on duty in the Mediterranean in the *Brandywine,* Commodore Biddle, and during that cruise he was called upon to mourn the loss of [his] Father. . . . After remaining a few months in America after his return in the *Brandywine* in the summer of 1833, he sailed early in the autumn for England that he might spend a couple of years in travelling through Great Britain. After spending some months in England he made a short visit to Spain and then returned to finish his tour in England and Ireland, but in February, hearing rumors of an impending war between the United States and France, he hastened home that he might be ready to take his part in the active duties of his profession. . . . On the 30th of September 1835 we were married and very soon after the *American in England . . .* was published by Harper and Brothers. *Spain Revisited* followed very soon after, I think early in 1836, and in June 1836 a carefully revised edition of the *Year in Spain.* . . . In January 1837 he was ordered to the *Independence* as 1st Lieutenant and Executive Officer, Commodore Nicholson taking with him no commander. The *Independence* was destined to the Brazil Station but was ordered first to convey our Minister to Russia, Mr. Dallas, to St. Petersburgh. The *Independence* sailed from Boston and Mr. Mackenzie passed three months there while she was fitting out. He prepared an account of their arrival at Cronstadt with the visit of the Emperor to the *Independence* to be published in one of our papers but it was afterwards determined not to publish it. . . . From Cronstadt the *Independence* proceeded to Brazil where he was placed in command of the *Dolphin.* His cruise was one of much interest; he was at Bahia during the siege of that place and at its surrender and witnessed many scenes of interest. . . . He was in the Rio de la Plata when the French blockading squadron was there and I send a letter from Mr. Hamilton our consul there at Montevideo showing the views my husband then entertained and referring to a pamphlet written by him. . . . Whilst in Boston previous to the sailing of the *Independence* he was requested by Mr. [Jared] Sparks . . . to furnish a *Life of Paul Jones . . . ;* his professional duties while on the Brazil Station prevented him from carrying out his plan of writing it while at sea but he commenced it soon after his return and it was published . . . in 1840 or 1841.

Although he had from his literary reputation, ever been a welcome and courted guest in the best circles in the cities of his own country and . . . had access to the highest in England he retained the native simplicity of his character and greatly preferred the seclusion of a country life. Consequently in April 1840 he removed to a farm on the Hudson about midway between the towns of Sing Sing and Tarrytown; he there passed his days in reading, writing and superintending his farm (an occupation in which he took great delight); his evenings in reading aloud to his family, which mode of life he ever pursued when the duties of his profession did not call him away. In the summer of 1840 at the request of Dr. Grant Perry, son of the late Commodore Oliver Perry, he commenced a Life of the Commodore which was published by the Harpers in 1841. I find that I have omitted to mention the date of his promotion to a Lieutenancy which was January 15th 1825. In the Autumn of 1841 he received the rank of a Commander and in December of that year was ordered to the *Missouri* Steamer. He was in her in the disastrous voyage to Washington when through the carelessness or ignorance of her Pilot she was run aground in the Potomac. . . . He remained in the *Missouri* until May 1842 when he was ordered to the command of the Brig *Somers* to be used as a School ship and manned by apprentices. Although he took great pleasure in literary occupations and had obtained much celebrity as a writer his professional reputation was far dearer to him; he was thoroughly devoted to the Navy and ever had her best interests at heart. It had long been a cherished hope that he might do something to improve the character of the sailors and to make them if possible a better and happier class of men. After long observation and experience he had become convinced that there was little hope of effecting much with the old sailors and he greatly desired to try what could be done with the apprentices; his wish was that some of the smaller vessels might be used as school ships and worked only by boys. He thought that in our smaller towns and villages and in the adjacent country a class of boys might be found of a higher moral tone than those about our larger cities; if these could be collected and the best professional and religious instruction given them he had the hope that a class of sailors might be formed far superior to any that have yet been found in our Navy. When he took command of the *Somers* he hoped to carry out his views successfully although he was not able to procure such a class of boys as he wished. The *Somers* was fitted out in New York and in order to further his plans for the welfare of the boys he prevailed on a young student of divinity to accompany him on his first cruise, to hold the services of our Church (a practice which he never failed to observe in every vessel that he commanded) and to instruct the boys. The first cruise of the *Somers* was made in June or July 1842 to the Island of Porto Rico; she was absent about a month and in one of my husband's letters at the close of the cruise he says that all has gone on well and the boys have done very well. I now approach the most important event of his life, the cruise of the *Somers* to the coast of Africa, the mutiny on board, and the punishment of the ringleaders. I have great pain in bringing again before the public, occurrences which cannot fail to cause much sorrow to the relatives of the sufferers on that occasion but justice to my husband's memory requires that his character (so cruelly assailed) should be placed in a proper light before the country. I therefore earnestly entreat and in this request I am joined by my brother-in-law Mr. Slidell, that you will find room for the Report of the Court of Enquiry convened to examine all the circumstances of the Case— This Court was formed of three of the highest officers in the Navy in rank and character, Commodore Stewart, Jacob Jones, and Dallas, all of whom became afterwards his warm personal friends. The action of this Court was fully sustained by the Court Martial afterwards held. . . . As the motive for this Court Martial was somewhat misunderstood at the time it having been supposed that Mr. Upshur had ordered it (for his own satisfaction or that of the public mind) in spite of the full and honorable acquittal of the Court of Inquiry I am glad to have an opportunity here to state that it was ordered at the request of Commander Mackenzie himself. His reasons for this were first, that he desired that his vindication should not rest on the verdict of three officers only although so honorable and able as those above mentioned and secondly because the daily repeated efforts to bring his case into the civil courts showed that the public mind was not yet entirely satisfied. He thought a Court Martial the only tribunal having a just power of jurisdiction in his case and a jury of officers the only one capable of understanding fully and impartially judging its merits. . . .

At the termination of the Court Martial my husband was allowed to return to his home after nearly four months spent in New York in scenes of daily trial such as few have known but cheered and sustained by daily testimonials of approbation of all classes, from all quarters, by the warm sympathy of friends, and above all by the consciousness that he had performed without shrinking the most painful and stern duty to his country and his fellow creatures that man was ever called upon to perform. This he had done at the price of a personal suffering such as few could know because few have the capacity so keenly to feel; fully aware that his country would justly hold him responsible to her for the act and ever mindful that what he was doing was done in the presence of Him "to whom all hearts are open, all desires known, and from whom no secrets are hid. . . ."

He remained at home until the summer of 1846. During this time he occupied himself in writing the Life of Commodore Decatur which was published late in the summer of that year and was well received. In May 1846 he was sent by the President on a private mission to Cuba and he accordingly sailed in the *Truxton* to Cuba and thence in the same vessel to the seat of war in Mexico. . . . He returned in August of 1847 and was then put on Ordnance duty. He went out about the 1st of March 1847 as Ordnance officer in the *Mississippi,* Commodore Perry, to the Gulf of Mexico and arrived at Vera Cruz just before that place was taken. In the attack on Vera Cruz the Navy played a prominent part, their battery making the first breach in the walls. As Ordnance officer Mr. Mackenzie was charged with the duty of landing and placing the guns . . . and he also had charge of firing one of the guns for some hours. . . . He returned home in August 1847. In October he was ordered to take command of the *Mississippi* and went out to join her, remaining in her until her return . . . in April 1848. He returned with his health much impaired and his disease slowly gained ground until the fatal termination, Sept. 13th 1848. . . .

A woodcut vignette of Philip Spencer in R. M. Devens, *Our First Century . . . One Hundred Great and Memorable Events of Perpetual Interest in the History of Our Country* (Springfield, Mass.: C. A. Nichols, 1879), p. 419.

    This is the earliest known representation of Philip Spencer, and all later pictures are based on it. A steel engraving adapted from it was published in the Chi Psi Fraternity journal, *Purple and Gold*, IX, 1892, frontispiece, and pp. 40-41, 134. A painting was subsequently made from the steel engraving. [See The *Chi Psi Story,* edited by H. Seger Slifer and Hiram Kennicott (Ann Arbor, Michigan: Chi Psi Fraternity, 1951), p. 73.] The steel engraving embodied one or two corrections suggested in 1891 by two college mates and fraternity brothers of Spencer, particularly in the shape of the nose, which was said by both to have been faulty in Devens' woodcut.

        An account from memory, from *Autobiography of Thurlow Weed,* edited by his daughter, Harriet A. Weed (Boston: Houghton, Mifflin & Co., 1883), I, 515-519.

[I, 515] . . . The Somers arrived in New York about the 20th of December. I reached New York on my way to Washington on Sunday morning, the Somers having arrived on Saturday. There was a midshipman on board who was a sort of protégé of mine. Immediately after breakfast I went to the navy yard to see him. Commodore Perry informed me that Captain Mackenzie had gone with his officers to church, but that as soon as they returned he would ask Captain Mackenzie to give Midshipman Tillotson leave to come to the Astor House. As I was leaving the hotel on my way to dinner with my friend Moses H. Grinnell, the young man joined us, and I took him with me to dinner. He was instructed by Captain Mackenzie not to converse on the subject of the mutiny until after the captain's official report had been made. He remarked, however, before he left me, that it required all the officers of the vessel except Captain Mackenzie and himself, the junior midshipman, to constitute a court. He, therefore, was officer of the deck, where Captain Mackenzie remained during the trial. Lieutenant Gansevoort, who presided, came on deck twice during the trial and conferred with Captain Mackenzie. He also stated that the arrest of the accused parties took them all by surprise. Midshipman Spencer was very unpopular with the officers, while Small, one of the sailors who was executed, was greatly liked [I, 516] by officers and crew. After the arrest everything was quiet on board, and there were no signs of insubordination among the crew when their comrades were run up to the yard arm.

On Sunday evening I left New York for Washington, stopping over night at Philadelphia, where I met Passed Midshipman [Hunn] Gansevoort, a cousin of Lieutenant Gansevoort, who was first officer on board the Somers. Both of these officers were from Albany, where I had known them in their boyhood. Of course the Somers affair formed the staple of our conversation. He informed me that his cousin, on his way to Washington with the official dispatch, passed the previous evening with him at that hotel, and at a late hour, and after much hesitation, he had made a revelation to him which he thought proper to make to me as a friend of them and their families. That revelation, as literally as I can remember it, was as follows:—

After the witnesses had all been examined, "I," said Lieutenant Gansevoort to Midshipman Gansevoort, "went on deck and informed Captain Mackenzie that the testimony was not as strong as had been represented to him, and that I thought from the indications the court did not attach much importance to it. Captain Mackenzie replied that the witnesses had not been thoroughly examined, and directed me to recall them, and put certain interrogations to them, a copy of which he handed to me. I returned and complied with this request, but elicited nothing more specific than the first examination had brought out. Some general conversation after the conclusion of the testimony satisfied me that the court was not prepared to convict the accused. I again repaired to the deck, and expressed my opinion to Captain Mackenzie, who replied that it was evident these young men had wholly misapprehended the nature of the evidence, if they had not also misapprehended the aggravated character of the offense, and that there would be no security for the lives of officers or protection to commerce if an example was not made in a case so flagrant as this. It was my duty, he urged, to impress these views upon the court. I returned and did, by impressing these considerations, obtain a reluctant conviction of the accused." Passed Midshipman Gansevoort, who gave me this startling narrative, sailed the next day in a United States brig, which, with all on board, was engulfed at sea.*

[I, 517] I was greatly disturbed as to the course I ought to pursue in reference to this painful revelation. The father of Midshipman Spencer, Hon. J. C. Spencer, was then Secretary of War. We had been for several years intimately associated in public life, and were warm personal friends. I was to meet him in Washington, and the question with me was whether the above statement ought or ought not to be laid before him. I called at his house, undetermined how to act. The servant, who took my card, returned, saying that Mr. Spencer was engaged. . . . [*Here Weed explains Spencer's refusal to see him, in terms of a recent political break between them.*] [I, 518] . . . Mr. Spencer declined to see me, thus depriving himself of the opportunity of proving at the court of inquiry, subsequently held on Captain Mackenzie, that his son had been unjustly executed.

While the court was holding its sittings at the Brooklyn Navy Yard, a sense of justice involuntarily drew me thither, intending either to offer myself as a witness to Mr. [Henry] Morris, the son-in-law of Mr. Spencer, who was managing the prosecution, or to suggest questions to be put to other witnesses. But Mr. Morris, whom I had known intimately, understanding, if not sharing in Mr. Spencer's feelings of hostility, declined to recognize me, and I returned again disappointed. In the following summer, at Boston, in visiting the United States seventy-gun-ship Ohio, I encountered Lieutenant Gansevoort, and invited him to dine with me at the Tremont House. At dinner the sad fate of his kinsman was spoken of, when I remarked that I had passed the evening with him previous to his sailing from Philadelphia, adding that we sat gossiping over our hot whiskey punch into the small hours. The lieutenant, with evident surprise, asked, with emphasis, "Did he tell you that I passed the previous night with him?" I answered in the affirmative. He said, "What else did he tell you?" I replied, with equal emphasis, "He told me all that you said to him about the trial of Spencer." Whereupon he looked thoughtfully a moment, then drank off his champagne, seized or raised the bottle, again [I, 519] filled his glass and emptied it, and, without further remark, left the table.

I did not see him again for seven years,—seven years which had told fearfully upon his health and habits. In the last years of his life he was stationed at the Brooklyn Navy Yard, then a sad wreck of his former self, he came frequently to see me, but was always moody, taciturn, and

---

* Hunn Gansevoort (1818?-1843) was midshipman, 1832; passed midshipman, 1838; lieutenant, February, 1842; detached from court survey duty, and waiting orders, November, 1842; ordered to the *Grampus,* January, 16, 1843; lost in the *Grampus,* March, 1843. According to items in *Niles' Register,* LXIV (1843), 195, 232, the *Grampus* sailed from the Chesapeake about February 20, 1843, and Charleston, S. C., on March 11; she was lost shortly thereafter with all hands.

restless.* In my conversations with him I never again referred to this affair, nor do I know that he ever spoke of it to others. But I do know that a bright, intelligent, high principled, and sensitive gentleman, and a most promising officer of the navy spent the best part of his life a prey to unavailing remorse for an act the responsibility of which belonged to a superior officer.

Public opinion was at the time, and has always remained, much perplexed with regard to the motives which prompted Captain Mackenzie to this unusual act of severity, and, although acquitted by a naval court of inquiry, that lenient judgment was never quite in accordance with popular feeling. It is obvious, from the narrative which I have now given, that there was no necessity for or justice in the execution of the alleged mutineers, one of whom, Small, a great favorite of the crew, exclaimed, "God bless the flag!" at the moment he was run up to the yard-arm. I never coincided in the opinion which attributed the execution to cowardice on the part of Captain Mackenzie. I could not then and cannot now resist the belief that he was influenced by ambition for the *éclat* which would follow the hanging of a son of the Secretary of War as a pirate. Captain Mackenzie was Alexander Slidell, a brother of John Slidell, United States senator from Louisiana [*from 1853-1861*]. He appended the surname Mackenzie to his own for the purpose of availing himself of a legacy bequeathed on that consideration by a relative.

Memorials of Philip Spencer, collected and published by William W. Gay in *The Purple and Gold*, April, 1885. Here reprinted, by permission, from an article by W. Jackson Chaille, "Philip Spencer," *The Chi Psi Story,* edited by H. Seger Slifer and Hiram L. Kennicott (Ann Arbor, Michigan: Chi Psi Fraternity, 1951), pp. 74-79.

[74] [*Philip Spencer, born in 1823, youngest of three sons of John C. Spencer; grandson of Ambrose Spencer (1765-1848), Chief Justice of New York State; attended Canandaigua Academy where (a classmate remembers) he was* "a sprightly, delicate lad who was quite a favorite with many of his schoolmates, though his queer stories and sharp tricks made him unpopular with others," *and where he compiled both a Latin and a Greek catalogue of teachers and students; entered Geneva College, Geneva, N. Y., in 1838.*]

[*A classmate, I. H. McCollum wrote of him:*] Philip Spencer, for a part of two years, was a classmate of mine at Geneva College (now Hobart). My class—of '42—dwindled from about twenty freshmen to seven seniors at commencement. Spencer was one of those who dropped out by the way. He was a talented young man, very quick to learn, pleasant and companionable, and to those whose kindness justified it, confiding. He seldom

---

* Weed's account jumps over Guert Gansevoort's later distinguished naval service and his promotions.

mingled with the students in their sports and games on the campus, and I
do not now remember if he was a member of either of the literary societies.
The ease with which he mastered the Greek and Latin was remarkable.
Frequently he would be applied to for assistance by other members of the
class, some, in fact whose standing was higher than his. This remarkable
talent proved a source of weakness to him, for it led him to neglect the
proper preparation of his lessons, giving them only a few minutes' attention before time for recitation, the time which should have been given to
his lessons being devoted to light reading. I do not remember Spencer as
a vicious or reckless or mischief-making young man. Whilst his habits
were inclined to indolence he had great self-will and firmness when occasion called it out. While at Geneva he was operated upon for strabismus
and refused to be bound or held during the operation. He had an ear for
music and played fairly well on the violin and cornopaean.

[*Another classmate at Geneva, Mr. Paul F. Cooper, remembered:*] His
manner was remarkably good, quiet, courteous, and self-possessed. His
voice was very low and pleasant. My recollection is that he had a decided
cast in his eyes and that otherwise he would have been thought good-
looking, if not handsome. He seemed to live very much by himself and
to mingle little with the other students. If he had any intimates I do not
know who they were, and my belief is that he had none. His class standing
for scholarship and attendance was very low, but it was generally thought
that he had ability enough had he chosen to exert it in the direction of his
studies. Though this is often said of young fellows in college merely because they neglect their studies, I am inclined to think it was true in his
case. In one thing he excelled the whole college. He was by far the best
declaimer I have ever heard with the exception of one or two men whose
reputation is national. His speaking of one piece in particular keeps its
place in my memory vividly even to this day. I think Spencer's manner
must have been [75] really remarkable or it would not have made the
lasting impression that it has upon my memory. I recall it as more like
that of a high bred man of the world than a boy's just growing into man-
hood.

[*Prof. Charles D. Vail, of Hobart College, contributed the following
from the college records, in 1884:*] February 21, 1840: Philip Spencer
for negligence and going to Canandaigua without permission was formally
sent to Greene to remain for a time under the care of Rev. I. V. Van Iryen.
. . . On November 23, 1840, Philip Spencer was a participant in the
cider disturbance so-called, but does not appear to have been regarded
as a leading spirit. . . . On April 21, 1841: Philip Spencer, at the request of his father received a dismission from the college. The request
was made in consequence of his continued neglect of college exercises and
this neglect stated in the letter of dismission; but inasmuch as a change of
association might prove favorable, it was also stated that the faculty of
this college would make no objection on account of his deficient standing
here, to his immediate reception at any other college. He was subject to

college censure on no other account but neglect of exercises. . . . [*Prof. Vail adds:*] Mr. E. J. Burrall of this place tells the story that on the occasion of a commencement procession of the college, Spencer brought up the rear wearing a lofty conical hat elaborately decorated with a streamer showing the legend, "Patriarch of the Freshman Class!" The President and Faculty were walking at the head quite unaware of this characteristic demonstration in their rear. I understand that Spencer was a great reader of sea stories, particularly those about pirates.

[*James Lafayette Witherspoon, who with Spencer was, in May, 1841, one of the founders of Chi Psi fraternity, wrote:*] In the year 1841, Robert H. McFaddin of Greensboro, Ala., and myself went on to Schenectady, N. Y., and entered Union College . . . occupying a room together in West College. Soon after entering college, we became acquainted with Philip Spencer, Wm. F. Terhune, Samuel T. Taber and four or five other students whose names have become familiar to Chi Psi. Phil Spencer, who did not like the kind of men who composed the other secret societies then in college, conferred with us and the others above mentioned, about forming a new society, to be composed of kindred spirits. We readily agreed to the proposition. After canvassing the matter we decided to organize a new society and call it Chi Psi. William F. Terhune was our poet and writer, and he wrote out the ceremony of initiation. Spencer, who gave most of his time to the business of organization, devised the signs, grips, and pass words, and made arrangements for the badge of Chi Psi to be worn by the members. . . . I recall Philip Spencer as a tall man of dark complexion, with black hair and eyes, and noble-hearted and generous to a fault. He always took great delight in the initiations, grips, signs and pass words, and studied how to make them more mysterious and impressive. I attribute the success of the Society in Union College, and its spread to other colleges in the United States, to the principle on which its founders acted in receiving new members. This was, "that we would receive no man as a member, unless we were fully satisfied that he was a gentleman"; and as long as this principle is adhered to, the Society will continue to flourish.

From "Oh, Here's to Philip Spencer," written by W. H. Ross in 1871 and published in a Chi Psi song book in 1878. Here reprinted, by permission, from *The Chi Psi Story*, edited by H. Seger Slifer and Hiram L. Kennicott (Ann Arbor, Michigan: Chi Psi Fraternity, 151), p. 78.

Oh, here's to Philip Spencer,
  Who when about to die,
When sinking down beneath the wave,
  Loud shouted out Chi Psi!

So fill your glasses to the brim
  And drink with manly pride;
Humanity received a blow
  When Philip Spencer died!

A cartoon illustrating the article, "The Murder of Philip Spencer," by Gail Hamilton [Mary A. Dodge], *Cosmopolitan Magazine,* VII (June, July, August, 1889), 134-140, 248-255, 345-354. From *⁄ ⁄ ⁄* p. 139.

"I LEARN, MR. SPENCER, THAT YOU ASPIRE TO THE COMMAND OF THE SOMERS."

From "Some Reminiscences of Philip Spencer and the Brig 'Somners'," *United Service,* N.S. IV (July 1890), 23-36. This article, *⁄ ⁄ ⁄* signed R. C. R., was written by Robert C. Rogers.*

* Robert C. Rogers was midshipman, 1839; passed midshipman, 1845; acting master, 1852; resigned, 1854. In 1846 he was on the *Somers,* blockading the coast of Mexico, but was not aboard when she sank, having been captured on a shore raid a few days before. He relates in this article (pp. 34-36) that "many of the crew believed the vessel haunted" and that on several occasions he himself had imagined he saw ghostly forms suspended at the yardarms.

[23] My first cruise was to the coast of Brazil, on board the frigate Potomac [in 1841-1842]. . . . Forty years ago she . . . [was] properly esteemed as among the most efficient ships afloat. . . .

[24] One more than ordinarily sultry mid-day [in Rio de Janeiro] . . . I heard hot words in the street below, a clashing and outpour of English and Portuguese expletives by no means decent or peaceful. There were passionate, menacing outreaches of fists, promising the catastrophe of blows. One of the disputants was an American naval officer, and the other a brawny boatman; the riot, a question of [25] fare. The contest was unequal, in so far as he who wore the buttons was tipsy, and the other was being reinforced by some chuffs who approached from the Mole. I hastily descended . . . and led the unsteady middy into the hotel. That was my introduction to Philip Spencer. . . .

During Spencer's service on that station, I held a certain intimacy with him. . . . As a rule he appeared to eschew an intimacy with officers of his own grade. Mine was an unaccustomed face and he found me unprejudiced by the generally unfavorable criticisms I had heard of him. He saw that I preferred to take my own measure of him rather than to accept that of others. . . .

He was a person in his rare normal moods not without congruous and intelligent activity and observation. He had derived advantages from the generous educational opportunities a fond and accomplished father had offered him. He had a fair acquaintance with the humanities, spoke Spanish with fluency, even if it were, in some phrases, marred by grammatical blunders; had retained somewhat of his hold on Latin and Greek, and was a tolerably experienced draughtsman. These attainments, while they made him, when he pleased, a pleasant and plausible companion, infrequently restrained a nature which appeared to be absolutely bereft of all conservative principle. He always impressed me as having an inbred, if not an inborn, inclination, I will not say to crime, but to the vicious at least. It was not, by any means, an eccentricity in the sense of whimsical, but a vagation so listless, indifferent, as to lead one to plunder a hen-roost or a house. He had had, as he told me, religious example and culture enough during his early years; but it was all a mere matter of memory without any potency to shape, control, and exalt his maturer life. Indeed, it is only true when I say that a more unbalanced, vacillating, and easily-corrupted nature I have never encountered. Besides, he had not that quality of mind which forelooks, which measures responsibilities, and calculates consequences. . . .

[26] He was of that irresolute and arbitrary temperament which frets and rebels under the restraints and limitations society imposes for its own conservation. . . . I observed in him on several occasions acts which led me to carry to his account qualities beyond mere moral infirmities, rather to a lack of conscientiousness, or, as Shakespeare has it, "a most inherent baseness." I said to him one day when he was normal,—I mean

not warped by numerous nobblers,—"Spencer, it seems to me that you are a mutinous, insubordinate sort of a fellow, constantly kicking against discipline, always in hot water. What in the devil's name induced you to enter the service?"

"I hardly know," he drawlingly muttered. And then, after a little waiting, he continued: "The fact is, I wasn't a model boy by any means,— pretty bad, lawless, if you like that better; and my father, perhaps to get rid of me,—perhaps to reform me,—put me in the navy. I am disposed to think it has done me harm."

"And you do not like it, then?" queried I.

"Like it! Like it!" he exclaimed. "Hell, no; I hate it!"

"What would you like, then?" I asked.

"That's hard to say," he answered lazily. "But I think I would like to own a vessel outsailing anything afloat, with a crew who would go to hell for me; going where I pleased, doing what I pleased."

"I would call that," I said, "the life of a freebooter."

"Well, I can't say I'd dislike that," replied he. "Would you, old fellow?"

"Decidedly, yes."

And in testimony of the fact that he was obsessed by just such vicious motives, he was wont to spend many leisure moments in sketching [27] fanciful portraits of the notorious villains of buccaneering, from Drake to Lafitte, or of sinister-looking crafts of the rover trim; and retreats lying in remote waters where plunder could be safely hoarded, and idle days spent in dalliance with captive beauties. . . . All that may have been the innocuous whim of an errant, fanciful mind . . . ; but, taken in connection with my own youthful, but fairly accurate judgment of him, the fruit of an intimate intercourse, together with the facts which were brought out by the court-martial, I have no hesitation in expressing my conviction of the justice of the conclusions of that court. I do not believe that anyone of his messmates of the period when I knew him was surprised at the catastrophe. . . . One of the most intelligent of the petty-officers . . . who was on board the "Somers" at the time of the mutiny and execution, and served with me several years later on the same vessel, I think, has, in relations running through hours, communicated to me circumstances and facts which exclude all doubt of the justice of Spencer's execution. I will frankly confess, though, that to this day survive the indeterminables,— the "doubts insoluble" as to the necessity of an immediate execution. I am disposed to believe that I would, at least, have essayed to bring them home, manacled "neck and feet together." As to the condignity of the punishment, that I do not question, but there was scarce need of an immolation of three mutineers,—Spencer's alone would have been expiation enough. . . . Let me say in this connection that Spencer had good impressible material to practice his deviltry upon. . . . He was a dipsomaniac, brutalized by the love of liquor, and too frequently intoxicated in places and under circumstance which showed how small was his self-respect and how indifferent to public judgment. That vice, together with sometimes churlish and irritable ways, and many other personal and unfortunate repellings, made him the most unpopular of the junior officers of the squadron, and he was generally shunned. That punishment by Coventry affected him so far as to lead him to an indulgence of his love of liquor as often as he had an opportunity. When he went on shore he rarely sought persons of his own class, was indifferent to places of note. . . . He wandered into places where gathered the odds and ends of society, in and out of *cabarets borgnes;* the reeky bagnios of the Rue Sabôa, and with people who would not have paused to cut his throat, except that there was no need of it, for his maudlin and promiscuous hospitality impoverished him quicker than a sheath-knife could have done. . . .

[29] One day Spencer was upon the Mole, the crowded point of embarcation . . . , abusively, incoherently fuddled. He was unsteadily but resolutely questing an English officer, against whom he had a real or fancied grudge, and whom he vehemently threatened to shoot on sight. He was in uniform, and he was too obstreperous to escape observation. He was seen by the late Admiral Wyman, who sent him to his own ship, and the facts were duly reported. Commodore Morris was the very last person in the navy to condone so gross an indecorum. The "Potomac" was on the eve of her departure for home, and Spencer was ordered to her in disgrace. Just before she sailed—the evening before (she was to go to sea at daylight)—I went on board to say good-by to many warm hearts. . . . When I was leaving Spencer followed me on deck, talking to me while the boat was being "called away." I remember well his valedictory, so passionately uttered under the glowing Cross of that clime. He damned fleet and flag, the commodore and Wyman, rounding off with oaths and the threat to be "even with them." . . .

"Billy in the Darbies," the poem with which *Billy Budd* ends. Written by Herman Melville, c. 1890; first printed, 1924. Here reprinted by permission of the publishers from Melville's *Billy Budd,* edited by Frederic Barron Freeman and corrected by Elizabeth Treeman (Cambridge, Mass.: Harvard University Press, Copyright, 1948, 1956, by the President and Fellows of Harvard College), pp. 280-281.

    [In this poem, represented as written by one of Billy's shipmates, ✓ ✓ ✓ Billy is speaking, on the night before his execution.]

Billy in the Darbies

Good of the Chaplain to enter Lone Bay
And down on his marrow-bones here and pray
For the likes just o' me, Billy Budd.—But look:
Through the port comes the moon-shine astray!
It tips the guard's cutlas and silvers this nook;
But 'twill die in the dawning of Billy's last day.
A jewel-block they'll make of me tomorrow,
Pendant pearl from the yard-arm-end
Like the ear-drop I gave to Bristol Molly—
O, 'tis me, not the sentence they'll suspend.
Ay, Ay, all is up; and I must up too
Early in the morning, aloft from alow.
On an empty stomach, now, never it would do.
They'll give me a nibble—bit o' biscuit ere I go.
Sure, a messmate will reach me the last parting cup;
But, turning heads away from the hoist and the belay,
Heaven knows who will have the running of me up!
A blur's in my eyes; it is dreaming that I am.
No pipe to those halyards.—But aren't it all sham?
A hatchet to my hawser? all adrift to go?
The drum roll to grog, and Billy never know?
But Donald he has promised to stand by the plank;
So I'll shake a friendly hand ere I sink.
But—no! It is dead then I'll be, come to think.—
I remember Taff the Welshman when he sank.
And his cheek it was like the budding pink.
But me they'll lash me in hammock, drop me deep.
Fathoms down, fathoms down, how I'll dream fast asleep.
I feel it stealing now. Sentry, are you there?
Just ease these darbies at the wrist,
And roll me over fair.
I am sleepy, and the oozy weeds about me twist.

W. B. Scott, Jr.

END

OF PART FIVE

❡ ❡ ❡

Appendix

(*DOCUMENTS PERTAINING TO THE NAVAL SERVICE OF PHILIP SPENCER, IN THE NATIONAL ARCHIVES, NAVY BRANCH.*)

1. Letter from Secretary A. P. Upshur to Philip Spencer ("Care of Hon. J. C. Spencer, Washington"), Washington, November 20, 1841.

You are hereby appointed an Acting Midn. . . , and if your Commanding Officer shall after six months of actual service at sea, report favourably of your character, talents and qualifications, a warrant will be given to you bearing the date of this letter. . . .

2. Letter from Acting Midshipman Philip Spencer to Commodore M. C. Perry, Commanding U. S. Naval Station, New York, dated New York, February 11, 1842.

You have informed me that Passed Midshipman Craney has made an official report of the transaction which occurred between us on Thursday the 10th inst. I would respectfully represent that the aggravation which induced the assault, was of such a character, that my feelings were highly excited, and laboring under the imputation of being a liar, I was led to an act of insubordination and breach of discipline, which reflection has taught me was highly improper. May I respectfully request that this letter may accompany the report of Commander Moorhead, and Midshipman Craney, to the Hon. Secretary of the Navy.

3. Letter from Acting Midshipman Philip Spencer to Commodore Charles Morris, Commanding U. S. Naval Station, Coast of Brazil, May 25, 1842, aboard U. S. Ship *John Adams*.

I have taken the liberty of addressing you, for the purpose of giving you an exact account of my conduct on the 21st inst. Knowing that many false and erroneous reports of it have gone abroad, which though utterly groundless themselves, may nevertheless have a tendency to injure me in the opinion of others.

On the morning of the 21st, I had been on shore in the Market boat; when there I had drank considerably, when I came off I also drank with several persons, and when I went on shore for the day, by permission of the first Lieut. I was overcome by the liquors I had drank. I am very certain that I drank nothing while on shore on liberty. I am perfectly sensible sir, that I behaved in a manner highly disgraceful to myself and the service, but if the following can be given as an excuse, I would offer it in extenuation of my offence. It is well known that Midshipmen have gone ashore from the John Adams, and behaved in a manner full as disgraceful as I did on the 21st, still a chance of retrieving themselves by another trial has been given them. But this may be considered as a principal reason for my punishment. The thing has been done before, and should be stopped by the punishment of some one. True, but there is one more reason I would offer to your consideration. My previous good conduct. This is my first offence, and I know my last. If martial law and discipline could be satisfied without my punishment and disgrace, I would ask you to pardon the offence.

But if not I would ask if you would receive my resignation and save my name from that disgrace that would accrue to it by sentence of a court martial.

My Father's station is such that my disgrace would be widely spread and he would deeply feel it. But perhaps I am asking too much; but if it could be that the offence could be overlooked, I would solemnly pledge myself that the offence should never be repeated.

4. Letter from Commodore Charles Morris to Acting Midshipman Philip Spencer, May 27, 1842.

After careful consideration . . . , and with a desire to adopt the mildest course . . . consistent with . . . the interest of the service . . . , I have concluded to withdraw the charge . . . upon receipt of your resignation and to forward your resignation to the secretary of the Navy with the facts in the case and to direct your return to the United States there to receive his decision upon your conduct.

5. Letter from Philip Spencer to Commodore Morris, May 28, 1842.

I . . . enclose my appointment as Acting Midshipman. . . .

6. Letter from R. Harris Wyman, U. S. Ship *Delaware,* to Philip Spencer, U. S. Ship *John Adams,* Rio Janeiro, May 29, 1842.

In reply to your letter of the 29th I have to state that the report I made to Comr. Morris was simply that such report had been circulated, leaving it entirely to him to investigate and ascertain the truth of such reports, and I would have you to understand that I did it considering it my duty to have any reports derogatory to my grade investigated by the commander in Chief—of anything further I am not to be the Judge.

7. Letter from Commodore Morris to Philip Spencer, May 30, 1842.

Your letter of the 28th instant resigning your appointment as acting Midshipman has been received— I have no authority to accept the resignation of an officer. . . . I hereby withdraw the charge which was preferred against you on the 23rd instant and shall direct your relief from arrest.

You will report yourself on the first day of June next to the Commanding Officer of the U. S. Frigate Potomac to return to the U. States in that Ship—there to receive the decision of the Secretary of the Navy. . . .

8. Letter from Philip Spencer to his brother John C. Spencer, Jr., dated from U. S. Frigate *Potomac,* Boston Navy Yard, July 31, 1842.

You will be surprised to hear that I have returned to the U. States. But it is so. I had a difficulty while at Rio de Janeiro and the Commodore ordered me from the John Adams to the Potomac which was about to return home. So here I am. While I was at Brazil I visited but two places[:] Rio de Janeiro & San Salvadore. I staid more than a month in Rio but was only a few days [at] Bahia (San Salvadore). I was so short a time in the country that I had not time to collect curiosities but employd myself in visiting the country and eating fruit, the most delicious in the world.

I shall probably be in Albany in a few days as soon as I can get detachd from the ship. But shall not stop more than a day as I shall apply for sea service immediately— I should be extremely obliged to you if you could conveniently lend me forty or fifty dollars as I am at this time in great want of money. I assure you it shall be punctually paid on the first of October.

Remember me to all friends & believe me Your Affectionate Brother. I shall expect a line from you immediately.

9. Letter from Secretary A. P. Upshur, to Philip Spencer, Washington, August 6, 1842.

I have perused with pain the correspondence transmitted to me by Comdr. Morris. . . . I am mortified to learn that one more young officer of the Navy and one brought up as you must have been has been guilty of the degrading and disqualifying vice of drunkenness. . . .

Your frank and manly acknowledgment of your offence, your penitence for it, the fact of its being the first known to your Commander & his interposition in your behalf have upon the whole induced me to overlook the Transgression reported to me—and to put you upon trial by your future conduct— If that is such as the country has a right to expect from one who wears her uniform—what has passed will be forgotten but if otherwise it will be remembered against you.

Your appointment and resignation are returned to you not being accepted by me and you will soon receive orders.

> 10. Orders from Secretary Upshur to Philip Spencer, August 13, 1842.

Report to Capt. M. C. Perry for duty on board the U. S. Brig Somers.
[*Certificate attached:* "I certify that the above is a true copy of the orders received by me and in obedience to which I left my domicile on the 18th of August 1842. Philip Spencer."]

> 11. Letter from E. K. Stoddard to Philip Spencer, dated from Geneva College, August 16, 1842.

I received your letter some days since, and I suppose you will think me very negligent in not answering it before, but you may be sure that it was not because I did not think of you. I have been expecting you here for a long time, and would like so to see you again very much. I am very sorry to learn by your letter, that you are sent back to the United States, and am very anxious to know the reason of it and to hear the account of your various adventures from your own mouth. We were all very much gratified to learn Luther was so much better. I hope this voyage will entirely cure him. I suppose you know that it is now our six weeks vacation and that I have the honour to be elevated to the rank of Junior. When I rec'd your letter Dan. McCarty was staying in the village, but he has now gone back again to Oswego, where he is studying law. The students have almost all of them gone home. We have had some tall scrapes this last term, and of course, a good many suspensions. One of the Freshmen tripped up "big Teddy," and held him down, and another broke little Pizzletintums spectacles, while the whole scene was enlivened by packs of fire crackers, squibs &c. But I have written all I can think of at present and it is time for me to stop, so good bye.

P. S. I hope you have not been carrying on very tall at Rio, but do come and tell me all about it as soon as you can.

Bibliography

A. WORKS QUOTED IN THIS BOOK

Adams, Charles Francis. *Richard Henry Dana.* 2 vols. Boston: Houghton Mifflin, 1890.

Callahan, Edward W. (ed.). *A List of Officers of the Navy of the United States and of the Marine Corps from 1775 to 1900.* New York: L. R. Hamersly, 1901.

Cooper, James Fenimore. *The Battle of Lake Erie: or Answers to Messrs. Burges, Duer, and Mackenzie.* Cooperstown: H. & E. Phinney, 1843.

Dewey, Mary E. (ed.). *The Life and Letters of Catharine M. Sedgwick.* New York: Harper, 1871.

Freeman, F. Barron (ed.). *Melville's* Billy Budd. Cambridge: Harvard University Press, 1948.

Hone, Philip. *The Diary of Philip Hone,* ed. Bayard Tuckerman. 2 vols. New York: Dodd, Mead, 1889.

Leyda, Jay. *The Melville Log: A Documentary Life of Herman Melville.* 2 vols. New York: Harcourt Brace, 1951.

Mackenzie, Alexander Slidell. *Life of Commodore Oliver Hazard Perry* (5th edition). 2 vols. New York: Harper, 1844.

Melville, Herman. *White-Jacket: or, The World in a Man-of-War.* New York: Harper, 1850.

Pierce, Edward L. *Memoir and Letters of Charles Sumner.* 2 vols. London: Lowe, Marston, Searle, and Rivington, 1878.

Proceedings of the Court of Inquiry Appointed to Inquire into the Intended Mutiny on Board the United States Brig of War Somers . . . , Reported for "The New-York Tribune." New York: Greeley & McElrath, 1843.

Proceedings of the Naval Court Martial in the Case of Alexander Slidell Mackenzie . . . , To Which is Annexed an Elaborate Review, by James Fennimore [sic] Cooper. New York: Henry G. Langley, 1844.

R., R. C. [Robert C. Rogers]. "Reminiscences of Philip Spencer and the Brig *Somers," United Service,* Series 2, IV (July 1890), 23-36.

Seward, Frederick W. (ed.). *William H. Seward: An Autobiography from 1801-1834. With a Memoir of His Life, and Selections from His Letters 1831-1846.* . . . New York: Appleton, 1877.

Slifer, H. Seger, and Hiram L. Kennicott (eds.). *The Chi Psi Story.* Ann Arbor: Chi Psi Fraternity, 1951.

[Sumner, Charles.] "The Mutiny on the Somers," *North American Review,* LVII (July, 1843), 195-242.

The Cruise of the Somers: Illustrative of the Despotism of the Quarter Deck; And of the Unmanly Conduct of Commander Mackenzie (3rd edition). *With an Appendix Containing Three Letters by Hon. William Sturgis.* New York: J. Winchester, 1844. [Partially reprinted in *Mutiny!* edited by Edmund Fuller. New York: Crown, 1953. Pp. 118-150.]

Weed, Harriet (ed.). *Autobiography of Thurlow Weed.* 2 vols. Boston: Houghton Mifflin, 1883.

B. *FURTHER WORKS*

(*Starred items contain "memories" of the affair.*)

Anderson, Charles R. "The Genesis of *Billy Budd," American Literature,* XII (November, 1940), 329-346. [Shows in detail the relation of *Billy Budd* to *Somers* case.]

Armstrong, Warren. "Nightmare Ship [The *Somers*]," *Mutiny Afloat: A Dramatized Record of Some Famous Sea Mutinies.* London: Frederick Muller Ltd., 1956. Pp. 109-122. [Recreates the mutiny. Fantastically inaccurate.]

Arvin, Newton. "A Note on the Background of *Billy Budd," American Literature,* XX (March, 1948), 51-55. [Points to passage in Weed's *Autobiography.*]

Arvin, Newton. *Herman Melville.* New York: Sloan, 1950. Pp. 293ff. [Discussion of *Billy Budd* in relation to *Somers* case.]

Baldwin, Hanson W. "Mutiny on the Brig *Somers," Esquire,* August, 1935. [Reprinted: (1) Baldwin, *Admiral Death: Twelve Adventures of Men Against the Sea.* New York: Simon & Schuster, 1939. Pp. 225-254, 274-277. (2) *World's Great Tales of the Sea,* edited by William McFee. Cleveland: World, 1944. Pp. 158-173. (3) Baldwin, *Sea Fights and Shipwrecks.* Garden City: Hanover House, 1956. Pp. 183-200, 200-206 (valuable revised notes). The best retelling of the events of the cruise.]

Barrows, Edward W. *The Great Commodore: The Exploits of Matthew Calbraith Perry.* Indianapolis & New York: Bobbs-Merrill, 1935. [Summary of case (somewhat inaccurate), presented in naval and political context.]

Benjamin, Park. *The United States Naval Academy.* New York: Putnam's, 1900. [Account of affair, in context of need for naval training school.]

* Benton, Thomas Hart. *Thirty Years' View*. 2 vols. New York: Appleton, 1856. II, 561-562. [Senator Benton devotes a chapter to a hostile analysis of the case, but it is mostly based on Cooper's *Review*. Gives questionable anecdote of Mackenzie's diplomatic mission to Cuba, 1846, of which see criticism by Van de Water, *The Captain Called It Mutiny*, pp. 214 ff.]

* Davis, George. *Recollections of a Sea Wanderer's Life*. New York: Kellogg, 1887. P. 306. [Inaccurate "memory."]

Devens, R. M. *Our First Century. . . . One Hundred Great and Memorable Events of Perpetual Interest in the History of Our Country*. Springfield: C. A. Nichols, 1879. [Pro-Mackenzie account. Woodcuts of Mackenzie and Spencer.]

Duyckinck, Evert A. and George L. (eds.). "Alexander Slidell Mackenzie," *Cyclopedia of American Literature*. New York: Scribner, 1856. II, 360-365.

G., A. M. "Stern Justice," *Blackwood's Magazine*, CCLXXIX (June, 1956), 495-504. [A retelling.]

Glick, Wendell, "Expediency and Absolute Morality in *Billy Budd*," *PMLA*, LXVIII (March, 1953), 103-110. [Discusses the story in terms relevant to issues of *Somers* case.]

[Griffin, George.] *Defense of Alexander Slidell Mackenzie . . . Before the Court Martial. . . .* New York: Tribune Office, 1843.

Griffis, William Elliott. *Matthew Calbraith Perry*. Boston: Cupples & Hurd, 1887. [Valuable for contextual material, especially "The Naval Apprenticeship System," pp. 435-439.]

* Gouverneur, Marian. *As I Remember*. New York: Appleton, 1911. P. 93.

Grossman, James. *James Fenimore Cooper*. New York: William Sloane Associates, 1949. [For Cooper's quarrels with editors and Mackenzie.]

Hamilton, Gail [Mary Abigail Dodge]. "The Murder of Philip Spencer," *Cosmopolitan Magazine*, VII (June, 1889), 134-140; (July, 1889), 248-255; (August, 1889), 345-354. [Hostile to Mackenzie.]

* "Hanged at Sea," *Frank Leslie's Budget*, October, 1889. Pp. 78-79. [Purported reminiscences by John W. Davis, said to have been a crew member of *Somers*.]

Howard, Leon. *Herman Melville*. Berkeley and Los Angeles: University of California Press, 1951. Pp. 324-328. [Brief account of Melville's use of *Somers* case in writing *Billy Budd*.]

Hunt, Rear Admiral Livingston. "Attempted Mutiny on the U. S. Brig *Somers*," *United States Naval Institute Proceedings*. November, 1925.

Lawson, John D. (ed.). *American State Trials*. St. Louis: Thomas, 1914. I, 531-613. [Summary, and digested report of Court of Inquiry, based on *Tribune* pamphlet.]

Liebling, A. J. "The Navy's Only Mutiny," *New Yorker,* February 18, 1939. Pp. 35-38. [Journalistic retelling, hostile to Mackenzie.]

Manwaring, G. E., and Bonamy Dobrée. *The Floating Republic: An Account of the Mutinies at Spithead and the Nore in 1797.* London: G. Bles, 1935. [The *Somers* mutiny was associated with these mutinies, during the court martial; by Sumner in his review; and later by Melville in *Billy Budd.*]

McFee, William. *The Law of the Sea.* Philadelphia: Lippincott, 1950. [Contains account of *Somers* case.]

Outland, Ethel R. *The "Effingham" Libels on Cooper.* University of Wisconsin Studies in Language and Literature, No. 28: Madison, 1929. [Cooper's suits against Whig editors, 1837-1845.]

* Parker, William Harwar. *Recollections of a Naval Officer 1841-1865.* New York: Scribner's, 1883. Pp. 1-5, 17. [Remembers Philip Spencer.]

Paullin, Charles O. "Alexander Slidell Mackenzie," *Dictionary of American Biography.* New York: Scribner's, 1933. XIII, 90-91.

Ioseph Schiffman, "Melville's Final Stage, Irony: A Re-examination of *Billy Budd* Criticism," *American Literature,* XXII, (May, 1959), 128-136. [Interpretation of *Billy Budd,* and discusion of other interpretations.]

* Sears, Louis Martin. *John Slidell.* Durham: Duke University Press, 1925. [Biography of Mackenzie's brother. Inaccurate reminiscence by a descendant, pp. 20-22.]

Smith, Lt. H. D. "The Mutiny on the Somers," *American Magazine,* VIII (June, 1888), 109-114. [Favorable to Mackenzie.]

* Stanton, Henry B. *Random Recollections.* New York: Harper, 1887. Pp. 145-146. [Recalls meeting Philip Spencer and his brother in 1841.]

Van de Water, Frederic F. *The Captain Called It Mutiny.* New York: Ives Washburn, 1954. [The only book-length account of the affair.]

Vincent, Howard P. (ed.). *Collected Poems of Herman Melville.* Chicago: Hendricks House, 1947. Pp. 169, 174-175. [See Melville's poem, "Bridegroom Dick," which contains passages on his cousin Guert Gansevoort.]

Waples, Dorothy. *The Whig Myth of James Fenimore Cooper.* New Haven: Yale University Press, 1938. [Gives context of Cooper's quarrels with Whig editors and with Mackenzie.]

* White, Andrew Dickson. *Autobiography.* 2 vols. London: Macmillan, 1905. I, 17-18. [Describes Philip Spencer's room at Hobart, in 1849, and his copy of *The Pirates Own Book, or Authentic Narratives of the Lives, Exploits, and Executions of the Most Celebrated Sea Robbers,* presented by him to the Hermean Society.]

Whitton, Lieut. Col. F. E. "A Mutinous Midshipman," *Blackwood's Magazine,* CCXXXIII (March, 1933), 378-389. [A retelling, pro-Mackenzie.]

Willson, Beckles. *John Slidell.* New York: Minton Balch, 1932. [Incidental material on Mackenzie in this biography of his brother. Undocumented.]